THE FREACH AND KEEN MURDERS

THE FREACH AND KEEN MURDERS

The True Story of the Crime That Shocked and Changed a Community Forever

Kathleen P. Munley and Paul R. Mazzoni

ROWMAN & LITTLEFIELD
Lanham • Boulder • New York • London

Published by Rowman & Littlefield
A wholly owned subsidiary of The Rowman & Littlefield Publishing Group, Inc.
4501 Forbes Boulevard, Suite 200, Lanham, Maryland 20706
www.rowman.com

Unit A, Whitacre Mews, 26-34 Stannary Street, London SE11 4AB

Copyright © 2015 by Rowman & Littlefield

All rights reserved. No part of this book may be reproduced in any form or by any electronic or mechanical means, including information storage and retrieval systems, without written permission from the publisher, except by a reviewer who may quote passages in a review.

British Library Cataloguing in Publication Information Available

Library of Congress Cataloging-in-Publication Data

Munley, Kathleen Purcell.
The Freach and Keen murders : the true story of the crime that shocked and changed a community forever / Kathleen P. Munley and Paul R. Mazzoni.
pages cm
Includes bibliographical references and index.
ISBN 978-1-4422-4579-2 (cloth) — ISBN 978-1-4422-4580-8 (electronic) — ISBN 978-0-8108-9608-6 (pbk)
1. Murder—Pennsylvania—Scranton—History—20th century. 2. Murder victims—Pennsylvania—Scranton—History—20th century. 3. Trials (Murder) —Pennsylvania—Scranton—History—20th century. 4. Murder—Pennsylvania—Scranton—History—20th century. 5. Rape—Pennsylvania—Scranton—History—20th century. 6. Middle school students—Pennsylvania—Scranton—History—20th century. I. Mazzoni, Paul R., 1935– II. Title.
HV6534.S39M86 2015
364.152'3092—dc23
2014045593

The authors dedicate this book to the memory of Paul "P. J." Freach and Edmund "Buddy" Keen.

This book is also dedicated to Captain Frank Karam, who led the investigation and worked relentlessly to bring William Wright to justice.

This book was written for the sole purpose of informing those who remember the tragic event of November 1, 1973, of the truth—the "whole truth," so to speak—of this sad, horrific event. Although many people of northeastern Pennsylvania remember the murders, few have awareness of the details and of some of the parties that were so instrumental in moving the case forward. Two in particular should be mentioned: the camper and the hitchhiker. Both persons were key to the arrest and successful prosecution of the murderer, William Wright. Thomas Nasser, the hitchhiker, had come so close to being a victim of Wright and lived to describe the circumstances of this encounter and identify Wright as his assailant. Joseph McNamara, the camper, accidentally discovered the boys' schoolbooks at the dumping site in Wyoming County and reported his findings to the police. The information provided by the camper led police to the bodies of Freach and Keen and changed the nature of the case from missing persons to murder. The actions of both men made it possible for law enforcement to connect William Wright to the commission of the murder of the two boys from Minooka.

CONTENTS

Acknowledgments ix
Introduction xi
Prologue: The Hitchhiker's Tale xiii

1 Missing Boys 1
2 Investigation and a Camper's Discovery 9
3 Who Murdered Paul Freach and Edmund Keen? 23
4 The Murderer 45
5 Who Is William J. Wright? 61
6 The Investigation Concludes 91
7 Preliminary Hearing 107
8 Preparing for the Trial 135
9 The Trial—September 12, 1974 145
10 Trial—October 16, 1974 181
11 Trial—December 12, 1974 211
12 The Aftermath 251

Notes 257
Bibliography 293
Index 299
About the Authors 303

ACKNOWLEDGMENTS

The authors thank the following for their assistance in the completion of this book:

The people who consented to be interviewed and shared their memories of this event.

The *Times-Tribune* and Brian Fulton, librarian manager, for his help in gathering articles and pictures.

Mary Ann Moran Savakinus of the Lackawanna Historical Society, Kay Stephenson of the Wayne County Historical Society, and Joseph Pearce of the Centre County Library and Historical Museum for researching their archives for pictures.

Karen Boland for her technology assistance in editing and formatting the manuscript and gathering the photos and files.

Marywood University students and former students Stanley Kania, Gia Reviello, Paige Costanzi, Yeslene Dijol, and Kenny Luck for their able assistance with the research.

Marywood University for the internal research grant they provided.

INTRODUCTION

This book is about the brutal murder of two boys in Scranton, Pennsylvania, in 1973. It is written not to sensationalize or minimize the circumstances of this dark segment of a community's history but to tell a story about a crime—a crime that had wide-reaching impacts on the lives of many in this region. Scranton is perhaps best known for the illustrious role it played in the economic history of the United States as a center for coal mining and other major industries and businesses—a region that by the 1970s was no longer an economic giant but supported a declining economy and unemployment. This was a crime that never should have happened, committed by a cold-blooded killer who had murdered at least twice before and who should have never been released back into the public. As the truth of this dark tragedy that befell these two young boys unfolded, their loving families, friends, neighbors, and people of the region in general were joined as one in feelings of total unbelief, anger, and fear.

While a story of deep pain, this is also a story of courage and fortitude—in particular of the families who lost so much and all whose lives changed as a result of this unspeakable crime. It is a story of quiet dedication and firm determination of multiple law enforcement personnel, men and women hardened by the nature of their work but who, nonetheless, reacted in horror at the brutality and senselessness of this crime and devoted long hours to finding the killer and prosecuting him to the fullest extent of the law.

The Freach and Keen murders forever changed the people of the region in and around Scranton, Pennsylvania. In many ways it was a defining time for the people of this area, a time that marked a change in the way the community thought of this region and the safe neighborhoods they had come to take for granted. The murders of the two young schoolboys forever cast a shadow on the lives of so many—a shadow that persists to the present, in the knowledge that, even in the pleasant light of day, evil can and does exist, and one must be on guard always.

PROLOGUE
The Hitchhiker's Tale

On October 26, 1973, Thomas Nasser, from Montrose, Pennsylvania, was nineteen years old and a sophomore at Lock Haven State College (now Lock Haven University of Pennsylvania), located in Lock Haven, Pennsylvania. As he did most Fridays, he was planning on returning home to Montrose for the weekend, a trip of some 125 miles. Usually he traveled home in the company of two friends, but on this Friday, his friends had decided to go to Penn State, about a half hour drive from Lock Haven. Tom did not normally hitchhike, but this day, owing to the fact that his brother was playing in an important soccer game later that afternoon and he wanted to be there, he decided to make his way to the highway to pick up a ride northward. Tom would later recall that it was a beautiful, warm October day with a temperature of about seventy-two degrees. He got a ride quickly from Lock Haven, heading east on Interstate 80 east to 81 north. His ride took him just north of Scranton on Interstate 81 to the exit for Dickson City. He did not have long to wait for a second ride to take him on the next leg of his journey home—north on Interstate 81 to his home. This ride was going to take him up I-81 to the New Milford exit, where he would then get another ride that would be going to his hometown.

Tom recalled that the car that picked him up at this point was a green station wagon, maybe a Pontiac, in good shape and fairly new. He was not sure why he did so, but he noticed the car had 37,000 miles on it. The driver seemed pleasant and, as they headed northward toward the New Milford exit, asked Tom about his major—which was special education—and what kinds of courses he was taking.

The landscape along I-81 north from the Scranton area gradually changed from urban/suburban to rural as the interstate moved out of Lackawanna County into Susquehanna County and beyond. As they drove along, the driver mentioned that he needed to find a restroom. With nothing but wooded land along the route at this point, the driver pulled the vehicle off the highway onto the margin and stopped, indicating he was going into the woods to relieve himself—an act that did not particularly upset or disturb Tom. The driver returned soon, but instead of getting back into the car, he came up to the passenger's side—the window was open—and asked Tom to get out. He wanted to show Tom something in the woods, he said. At this point, Tom realized that something was not right and told the driver he would get another ride. The driver responded, "I asked you nice." To which Tom replied, "And I told you nice." Looking up then, he saw that the driver was pointing a gun at his head. "Now I am telling you," the man said, "get out of the car." With the driver still holding the gun to his head, Tom walked toward a fence that separated them from the woods; anyone going into the woods would have to crawl over this fence. Tom began to climb the fence but stopped, and in so doing probably saved his life. He said, "If you want to shoot me, shoot me here. I'm not going over."

At this point, the former young student remembers the situation as quite surreal. Here he was, frightened for his life, while life in general continued all around him. A steady stream of vehicles passed by on the highway the entire time that this incident was playing out. The day remained as sunny and bright as it was before. It was as if nothing were amiss. At this point, the man, now Tom's assailant, felt the need to explain why he wanted Tom to go into the woods with him and used a vulgar expression that implied homosexual activity. However, at Tom's refusal to do this, the man, still talking and still holding the gun on Tom, walked him back toward the car. For his part, Tom recalled moving his hands while he talked and walked, thinking that this might catch the attention of passing motorists who might help. He was ready to try anything to get away, from grabbing his assailant—Tom estimated the man was about his size—to just taking a chance and running off back down the highway. He even warned his assailant that he had been tested recently for hepatitis (which he had when a friend came down with the illness). "You don't want to do anything with me," he told the driver. Maybe this had something to do with the man backing off, maybe not. With the gun still aimed at Tom's head, the assailant told the student to get back in the car.

Thinking this could be his last chance to escape, Tom planned to jump out of the car as soon as it started up. However, at this point, an elderly couple pulled onto the margin ahead of them. Now Tom thought that if he tried to escape or did anything that would call attention to his assailant and himself, and if the couple did try to help or do anything, the driver might kill them. There seemed to be no option but for Tom to stay in the car, which he did, and they drove off. Still talking, the driver said that "it wouldn't have hurt; it would have been fine." The driver asked Tom if the next exit was his (the New Milford exit); it was not, but Tom said it was. To his surprise, the driver took the exit, pulled to the stop, and told Tom to get out, saying, "How about if you and I forget about this?"

Tom Nasser did not forget—has indeed never forgotten—about what happened to him on this day. Later police would ask him to identify the man who had assaulted him, showing Tom a picture of a man they were investigating for a murder that took place on November 1 in Scranton, just six days after Tom's ordeal. Tom identified his assailant as that man. This time the victims were two young boys from Scranton, Paul Freach and Edmund Keen, ages thirteen and twelve. Apparently abducted on their way home from school, the boys were sexually assaulted and murdered. After shooting them in the head, the murderer disposed of their bodies in a desolate area in Wyoming County—a relatively short distance from the hitchhiker incident—where police subsequently found their remains.[1]

I

MISSING BOYS

The crime still described as the worst in the history of Scranton began on a very ordinary day in the late fall of 1973. The local paper described November 1, 1973—All Saint's Day in the Catholic Church—as a somewhat cloudy day with a chance of showers that represented a worsening weather pattern begun two days prior and suggested the end of what had been a warm and beautiful fall in northeastern Pennsylvania. This signified, the paper suggested, the onset of winter.

November 1, 1973, was a Thursday and, as for most school-age youngsters, began for Paul J. Freach, age thirteen, and Edmond Keen, age twelve, with preparations for school. The boys were friends who lived near each other on Colliery Street—on opposite sides of the street—in the Minooka section of Scranton. Both attended South Scranton Junior High School, located about a mile and a half from their homes. Paul was in eighth grade, and Edmond in seventh grade.

Both boys were lifelong residents of Scranton. Paul Freach was the oldest child in a family of five, with four younger sisters. Also in a family of five, Edmund Keen was the youngest, with four older sisters.[1]

Paul J. Freach Sr., father of the missing Freach boy, said in a 2011 interview that, since the city of Scranton did not offer school bus service, he usually gave the boys a ride to school on his way to work at the Northeastern National Bank (now PNC Bank) in downtown Scranton. The boys' parents, who were close friends, had arranged for rides to and from school between them. Mr. Keen often provided the boys a ride home if he were home from work on time, or, if not, another parent would drive by the school to see if the boys needed a ride. The boys also had the option of walking home, which they sometimes did. If they were in a hurry to get home and go out to play, or if the weather was bad, the boys usually had money to take a city bus.[2]

On this particular school day, Thursday, November 1, according to statements given to police, Mr. Keen's car had gone into a garage for a new transmission, and he was unable to stop for the boys after school.[3] According to later testimony by parents at the trial, they were all aware that Mr. Keen would be unable to pick up the boys after school due to car trouble. The families assumed the boys would walk home or take the city bus. Although the walk was a fairly long one, the boys were young, healthy, and athletic, and the route home was a well-traveled, busy city street occupied by a number of businesses and homes. According to Mr. Freach and others who lived in this region, the area from the school to the boys' homes on Colliery Street was thought of as safe, in spite of a mine fire section between the school and Minooka. Moreover, South Scranton Junior High School was a large school with a substantial student body, served by numerous teachers, administrators, and staff. When school was dismissed, around 3:30 p.m., students usually walked home in groups. The boys would not be the only children walking homeward.[4]

On his way home from work on November 1, Mr. Freach drove by the school in case the boys needed a ride, but they weren't there. When he arrived at his house, he recalled asking his wife where their son was. When she told him Paul had not yet returned, he said, he and his wife assumed their son was at the Keens's house. The boys were good friends and often got together at each other's homes. Or perhaps Mr. Keen had decided, as he had one other time, to take them to the garage with him—presumably the garage where the Keen car was being repaired.[5] When Paul had still not returned by dinnertime—around 5:30—the family grew concerned. When driven home, Paul usually returned between 3:45 and 4:00. When he walked, he typically returned between 4:00 and 4:15. He walked home one day out of the week—Friday—because he had an eighth-period study session that kept him in school later. When the boys walked home from school, they would walk south through South Scranton along Cedar Avenue, a long street that runs north and south from the school. Cedar Avenue intersects with Davis Avenue in Minooka (now an exit from I-81). Before this, the boys would turn off Cedar in order to get to their homes on Colliery Avenue, a street that paralleled Cedar Avenue and connected with Davis as well.

Now alarmed by his son's absence, Mr. Freach called the Keen home. There was no answer. Eventually they found out that Mr. and Mrs. Keen were at the garage, and their daughters were at 5:30 Mass. Assuming the boys were with the Keen parents, the Freach family sat down to eat dinner, unaware both boys would never return home and were by now the victims of a deadly murderer. Around six o'clock, Mr. Freach said he called the Keens again, and one of the Keen daughters told him that the boys must be with her parents at the garage.

At 6:30, now back from the garage, Mr. Keen called the Freach home and said he did not pick the boys up. P.J. was not at their house. Furthermore, his own son had not returned home either. He and his wife assumed their son was at the Freach home. It was at this point that Mr. Freach asked his daughter, who was one year younger than Paul, if she had seem them after school. She told him she had, that the boys were sitting on the porch of the hotel/restaurant on the corner of Cedar Avenue across from the school—a common place for kids to sit or wait for their rides.[6]

After hearing that their son was not at the home of his friend, who was also unaccounted for, Mr. Freach went to the Keen home, and he and Mr. Keen went looking for the boys around South Scranton. The families also began contacting friends to see if anyone had seen the boys, but no one had. "I knew he [Paul] was in trouble then," recalled Mrs. Freach at the trial.[7]

As the hours passed, the Freach and Keen families became more alarmed but still clung to the hope that the boys *might* have become distracted somehow after school. Mr. Freach and Mr. Keen continued to walk down to and through Scranton's south side looking for the boys. They stopped along the way at spots where they thought the boys might have delayed to play, such as along the Lackawanna River, where kids threw rocks into the water. They walked and walked, but no boys. Turning back, the two fathers walked up through the mine fire area where firefighters had been spraying water to extinguish the fire. The fathers thought perhaps something there had interested or engaged the boys. No one was around. By this time it was dark out.[8]

Between 7:00 and 7:30, the parents called police. The police counseled caution and urged the parents to remain calm. They cited similar cases of missing children in which the children were later found. Kids typically failed to return home simply because they lost track of the time or decided to run away from home. The families of the missing boys knew this was not the case with P.J. and Buddy, who were known as well-mannered, happy boys. The boys came from loving and caring families. These boys, their parents asserted, were not the sort who would run away.

Mr. Freach recalled that he and Mr. Keen went to Scranton Police headquarters later that evening to report the boys missing. They wanted an alarm put out for them. But, following procedure, the police told the anxious fathers that "officially" they couldn't do that—that they would have to wait twenty-four hours before the boys would be declared "officially missing." Seemingly trying to comfort and calm the fathers, someone suggested that the boys had probably "gone fishing, or something of that nature." Knowing their sons as they did, this was not particularly helpful—and Mr. Freach had told the police, "They don't do that." They left with at least a promise from the police that they were going to put the word out to keep a look out for the boys.[9]

As the hours of that first day passed into the next, November 2, there was no doubt in anyone's mind, including police officers', that the failure of these boys to return home was a grave matter. Detective Captain Frank Karam, who headed up the investigation for the Scranton Police, recalls that from the beginning he was certain the boys' disappearance was very serious; he believed that neither boy was the type that would worry his parents, and his investigation confirmed this early on. Neighbors, friends, schoolmates, and teachers confirmed to the police that these boys were "good kids," "nice boys," boys who were respectful of their parents and who lived in loving families.[10]

That day, a Friday, the fathers went down to Scranton Junior High and spoke to someone—either a principal or teacher—and asked if that person would question the students to see if anyone had seen them the night before. As word spread that the two students were missing, fellow students and the school confirmed that the boys had left the school at dismissal around 3:30 p.m. The police, now actively involved in the quest for the missing boys, began questioning teachers and students at the school and people in the neighborhood. Some friends reported they had seen P.J. and Buddy sitting on a wall near the school waiting for their ride—sightings that were confirmed by P.J.'s sister; others said they saw the boys walking toward home. Later, at trial, it was made known that two girls had made similar reports to the police, saying they had seen the boys alive after school in the vicinity of the local restaurant/bar called Biff's, approximately two blocks from the upper section of Cedar Avenue.

When the twenty-four-hour window passed, an all-out, massive police investigation began, with the Scranton Police soon joined by the Pennsylvania State Police and the Federal Bureau of Investigation. Police went to the school to speak with students—eliciting a story from a schoolboy who knew both missing boys. He claimed to have seen the boys accepting a ride with two people, a man and a woman, near the school on Cedar Avenue and Maple Street. The boy, who said he had been walking home with Paul and Edmund, told police that a car passed them heading up Cedar Avenue toward Minooka, then turned around and returned heading toward the center of Scranton. According to this account, the car then made another turn, came up to the curb, and stopped near the boys. The couple, a man and a woman, in the car called to the boys to "hop in." According to the eyewitness, Paul and Edmund did, but he refused, asking, "Are they your grandparents?" Paul or Edmund answered, "No," and the car drove off.[11] The boy provided police with a description of the man and woman and the automobile. He described them as a "middle-aged pair" in a 1966 Chevrolet with a blue body and white top. The police prepared a composite sketch of the couple based on the boy's description and circulated the sketch to local law enforcement offices and the press.

This created a theory that two people (or more) were involved in the murders of the two boys. Incidentally, some local people still relate this idea with confidence, in spite of police and law enforcement disclaimers to the contrary. According to this story, one of the murderers was apprehended and convicted; the other escaped detection and was never brought to justice. The facts of the case, as they were later discovered, fly in the face of this theory. Indeed, the eyewitness who provided the account of the man and woman in the car later acknowledged that he had fabricated the story to get attention. As a result, police discounted the entire incident the eyewitness described. Later still, the murderer himself denounced this story as untrue.

On this second day since the boys had gone missing, however, police were still gathering their first clues. Unfortunately, after the last sightings by schoolmates, the boys disappeared from view in the investigation. The two were gone or taken, seemingly in broad daylight, in a heavily trafficked and busy section of Scranton.

However, the police's efforts weren't entirely in vain. Their investigation produced a second important story. This one was from a boy who said that a man had tried to abduct him the previous March when he got into a car driven by the middle-aged man, who refused to let him out. The boy managed to escape. This child provided police with a description for another composite drawing. Reportedly, this second composite drawing closely matched the first of the couple spotted by the other boy on November 1.[12]

When told of this report, Mr. Freach was dubious, as were others, including some of the investigating officers.[13] Freach told the police that P.J. and Buddy had been told not to take rides with strangers and would not do this.

Nonetheless, the hitchhiking story was all the police had to go on at this point, and the clock was running. On November 3, the police sketch of the suspects described by the schoolboy began to appear in local newspapers.[14] People of the region that day (and for days afterward) opened their papers to see this depiction of a strange and somewhat sinister-looking couple, one clearly a man and the other who looked like a man dressed to look like a woman. Almost immediately an undertone of whispers began that suggested this "couple" was really two male persons impersonating a man and a woman in order to entice children or hitchhikers into their car for some deviant purpose. Under the homophobic thinking more common in this period, it was suggested that these two males were probably homosexuals, who would be more likely to do this. With the publication of the sketch and this information, people throughout the region and even beyond Scranton and Lackawanna County began watching for the blue and white Chevrolet occupied by the odd couple. Fear struck the hearts of many parents and children, worried this couple was trolling the region to pick up unsuspecting children or anyone else who might be inclined to accept a ride with a man and a woman, thinking that a married couple would not be a danger to them. The schoolboy's story had changed the climate of the investigation entirely. Now beyond a simple missing persons case, this had become something far more fearsome and threatening, creating a collective fear for children of the region.

This case marked a subtle turning point in the thinking of people of this region about the safety of their children and safety issues in general. Prior to November 1, 1973, there was an air of complacency in the region. This was an area that had little crime, at least nothing of the type that was to unfold with the Freach and Keen boys' case. After this, people in northeastern Pennsylvania felt less secure in their homes and neighborhoods. One resident said it this way: "Before this, we hardly ever locked our doors; afterward everything was different."[15]

2

INVESTIGATION AND A CAMPER'S DISCOVERY

The *Scranton Times*,[1] "2 Missing City Boys Abducted?" November 3, 1973

City, county, state and federal police agencies sparked an intensive search today for two Scranton boys reported missing Thursday.

While there was no immediate evidence the pair had been abducted, authorities were moving on the theory the case involves a presumed kidnapping.

Arrangements were being made to press a state police helicopter into service. . . .

Detective Captain Frank Karam said police are trying to arrange for use of a privately owned aircraft. . . .

Composite pictures of a middle-aged couple were made by Detective James Hart. The couple, police learned, may have enticed the boys into their car.

Meanwhile, police centered part of the search operation near the remote No. 5 dam area, some distance from Lake Scranton on the property of Pennsylvania Gas & Water Co.

The boys were known to have visited there with their fathers on occasion.

District Atty. Paul Mazzoni, appeared at police headquarters and said he was cancelling his campaigning for re-election for the weekend to join in the search. . . .

John Meade, an FBI special agent, joined Capt. Karam's force late this morning.

Asked why the FBI had been called in, Mr. Meade explained his agency is working on the possible theory of a presumed kidnapping.

Police Supt. John McCrone was on hand and was high in his praise for the city detectives, several of whom, he said, worked overtime on their own on the case. . . .

The FBI issued a description of what it said is believed to be the pickup car . . . based on eyewitness description furnished by . . . the unidentified youngster who saw the boys get into the vehicle. . . .

The car is a four-door sedan. . . .

The Freach boy is described by police as 5 feet, 2 inches tall, weighing 110 pounds with blond hair and a fair complexion. He was in maroon pants and white jacket.

The Keen boy is 5 feet, 4 inches, 100 pounds and has a fair complexion. He was wearing dungarees, a green jacket and black and white shoes.

Both boys wear eyeglasses. . . .

Both boys, police said, are very stable youngsters and neither has a record of disappearing before.[2]

The man who, along with other law enforcement persons, played a leading role in the investigation of the missing boys and who would ultimately prosecute their murderer was Lackawanna County District Attorney Paul R. Mazzoni. Thirty-eight years old, married, and the father of four children, Mazzoni had been elected district attorney in 1969, and in the fall of 1973 he was nearing the conclusion of his first term in that office and was running for reelection—an election campaign that, at the time of the boys' disappearance on November 1, was nearing its conclusion, with the election on Tuesday, November 6. Mazzoni recalls this period vividly: "The boys were missing on Thursday, November 1, when they failed to return home after school. A schoolmate described the boys getting into a Chevrolet car driven by a man with a woman in the passenger's front seat—a story that ultimately proved to be false by police. The car's description and that of the man and the woman were carried in the newspapers, and a massive search ensued."[3]

Mazzoni remembers going with police to talk with parents Gail and Paul Freach and Dorothy and Edmund Keen in order to get some information about the boys. Then, as the police investigated, his office waited and waited, closely following events. As the hours ticked by and no word was heard of the boys, the police continued to check details and concentrate on the only substantial lead they had—the eyewitness account of seeing the boys accept a ride with the man and woman in the sixties Chevrolet. Along with the fear and concern generated by this story, people, including most particularly the boys' families and friends, were struck by a sense of how incredible it was that something like this had happened, that these two boys could so easily and seemingly in plain sight simply vanish. Police, however, began to suspect the worse.

Local newspaper coverage of the search for the missing boys, still presumed to have been kidnapped, continued, giving local residents information about the investigation being waged by the police and providing details, such as they were, of various leads the police were checking out. With a lack of anything else that might lead to the missing boys, the investigation continued to center on the story told by a student about his seeing the boys getting into an automobile near South Scranton Junior High School.

On November 5, with the boys missing now since Thursday afternoon, November 1, papers reported that, as "far as could be determined," there had been no ransom demands but that "it was evident" that the police believed that the boys had been abducted.[4] Investigators, the *Scranton Times* noted, were manning a twenty-four-hour "command post" at Scranton Police headquarters, checking out tips and holding telephone lines open. Police at this point released additional details of the supposed kidnappers' vehicle: It was said to be a 1966 Chevrolet Impala with a blue body and white top. The four-door sedan was described as "shabby," with faded paint and rust spots on the body.[5] The newspaper account said that ground and aerial searches were continuing, with the Scranton Police and the Federal Bureau of Investigation (FBI) cooperating in both. It also reported that DA Paul Mazzoni meanwhile was pressing his investigators and staff into duty and assisting in the investigation. The paper reported that Paul Freach and Edmond Keen, fathers of the missing boys, remained at police headquarters until late Saturday night, November 3, "watching anxiously as police efforts gathered momentum."[6]

As the search for the missing boys continued, it was reported that some law enforcement persons were beginning to theorize that the middle-aged couple said to have picked up the boys could have really been two homosexuals, one male and the other disguised as a female, who could have been "the types that would pick up young men, molest them and then kill them to prevent them from implicating them."[7]

As time passed, the public began to react to the fact that these young boys had seemingly vanished in broad daylight from a busy area of the city of Scranton as they left school and began walking home. Newspapers joined in with comments about the heightened level of public anxiety and concern people of the region were expressing about children and their safety. Nowhere was this more evident than in the various neighborhoods that make up the city, and particularly in South Scranton, the region where the boys had been last seen, and in the Minooka section of South Scranton, where the boys lived. It became a matter of course to walk or drive young and not-so-young children to school or to the school bus stop. Parents began to have serious talks with their children about the dangers of talking with strangers and never accepting a ride from a stranger. People who were youngsters at this time remember being frightened about what happened to Paul and Edmund, even those who did not know the boys, and recognize that their parents were equally frightened and concerned.

One particular manifestation of these concerns involved the issue of school bus transportation for Scranton schoolchildren, or as was the case in the Minooka section of the city where they boys lived, the lack of it. Some parts of Minooka were located a long distance from the nearest Scranton school—as was the case, for example, with South Scranton

Junior High School, a distance of one-half to two miles from where the boys lived. The school transportation issue for Minooka children was not a new one. Residents of Minooka had requested school bus transportation to Scranton schools, but to no avail. In actuality, at this point in time, the district provided very little bus transportation for any of its school children. Now the school bus issue became a major cause célèbre as Minooka residents zeroed in on the fact, as they regarded it, that the lack of transportation was a prime factor in the boys' disappearance or kidnapping. Papers reported that on Sunday night, November 4, three days after the boys disappeared, about one hundred parents met at the Connolly American Legion Post on Birney Avenue (near the boys' home area in Minooka) to draft a petition to the Scranton School Board requesting that bus transportation be provided for students from that area attending South Scranton Junior High School. Spokesmen from the meeting summarized the issue, saying, "The disappearance of the Freach and Keen boys has underscored the determination of the neighborhood parents to see that busing is provided for the youngsters."[8] In other sections of the city, parents of schoolchildren joined in with requests for school bus transportation—an early effect of the Freach and Keen tragedies.

The story of the missing boys continued to be front-page coverage as the days passed. Police continued asking for tips and running the twenty-four-hour hotline.

Then, on Sunday, November 4, three days after the boys went missing, a breakthrough occurred, and an entirely new nightmare began.

A Scranton resident, identified as Joseph McNamara, had been camping at the How Kola Campgrounds, a privately owned campsite located in Falls Township, west of Scranton and just across the Lackawanna County line in Wyoming County. Leaving his camp to return home, he discovered some books and papers at a dump near the camp. Mr. McNamara said he knew nothing about the search for the missing boys. At the dump he noticed some schoolbooks that looked in good condition, so he picked them up and found they had Scranton School District stamps on the insides. He took the books with him and began the drive home. While driving, he heard a news account on the radio about the missing boys. He had looked through the books and found some papers with names on them. Looking them over, he now saw that these names were those of the missing boys. On returning to Scranton, he reported his findings to the police that day.

That day, Sunday, on receiving McNamara's information, the police responded immediately to the report and went out to the dump, but the onset of darkness made it impossible to search the area. They returned the next day.

The search for the missing boys had been in the hands of multiple law enforcement agencies from the second day of November: Scranton Police, with personnel from all ranks; Pennsylvania State Police from several local barracks; the FBI; and the Lackawanna County District Attorney's Office. In addition, Scranton Mayor Eugene Peters, Scranton's director of public safety, and other city government officials were actively involved. Now as police undertook a search of the dump where the schoolbooks had been found, law enforcement personnel from neighboring counties joined in. A preliminary search early on Monday, November 5, turned up nothing, but, as Detective Captain Frank Karam remembers it, he and his men and all involved were so intent on finding the boys that after asking a local clergyman to pray for the boys, he urged his men to go back over areas at the dump they had already searched. It did not take much to get cooperation from all involved, he recalls, because many of the men had children of their own, and, although professionals, this was unlike any other case they had ever had—or as it turned out for many, would ever have again.[9] Nothing in their policing experience prepared them for what they found at this obscure, out-of-sight dump, so near and yet so far from the homes of these two youngsters.

Later, Detective Frank Glynn testified to the events leading up to the discovery of the bodies of the missing boys. Going back to Sunday, November 4, Detective Glynn said he received the call from Joseph McNamara about the books at the dump site near the How Kola Campgrounds. After talking with McNamara, Glynn and other members of the Scranton Police, along with agents from the FBI, went to the dump. They found nothing but returned the next day, Monday, November 5. Early on,

Detective Glynn, searching the roadway leading to the dump, found a pair of eyeglasses that appeared bloodstained, and were later identified as belonging to Edmund Keen.[10]

Pennsylvania State Police Captain Lawrence O'Donnell and Scranton Chief of Police John McCrone put out a call to Wilkes-Barre Police in nearby Luzerne County for the use of two trained German shepherd dogs to assist in the search. The dogs, recalled Detective Frank Karam, almost instantly began sniffing and scratching one section of the dump.[11] Although later police would say that this area did not immediately turn up anything, it was apparent that the dogs were on to something. Then one of the investigators, FBI Agent Wayne Smith, noticed an old red rug on the dump near an embankment. He pulled it back, and under some plywood and other rubbish, he found the concealed, partially clothed, and apparently mutilated bodies of Paul Freach and Edmund Keen.[12] The sight of two young boys so brutally murdered, lying there amid debris and trash in this cold and remote area, was an image that would remain in the minds of those present for the rest of their lives.

Soon various law enforcement personnel as well as others who would be instrumental in the ensuing investigation into the murders of the boys began converging at the dump site. State Police–marked cars, unmarked cars from the Scranton Police, a State Police helicopter, and a private helicopter lined the dirt road leading to the dump and the nearby field adjacent to it.

Wyoming County Coroner Bryce Sheldon; Dr. Hollis Russell, a pathologist from Wyoming County; and Dr. George Hudock, Luzerne County coroner and a pathologist joined others at the site, as did Lackawanna County District Attorney Paul Mazzoni and county detectives. Scranton Mayor Eugene Peters arrived a little later, accompanied by Scranton Public Safety Director Anthony Batsavage.

District Attorney Mazzoni recalls this part of the case: "On Sunday, November 4, as a result of Mr. McNamara's finding of the books belonging to the boys at the dumping site, I became aware of the possibility that the boys may have been put there."

Although the search could not be continued on Sunday, Mazzoni describes the scene Monday at the dump where the boys were found: "There was sort of a roadway that led into the dump site and we got down there—there were trees all around and you could see where vehicles were dumping their trash, but there was a road where you could get to walk into the dump."[13]

Emotionally, Mazzoni recalls that the finding of the boys' bodies was "terrible."

He remembered, "They [the boys] were rolled into a carpet and buried under rubbish about four or five feet." Describing his reaction to seeing the two boys, he said, "I immediately thought of my kids, including my twins, who were eleven years old, and in my mind all I can picture was what if those were my boys buried there, and I just broke down in tears."[14]

Finding the boys' bodies, said Mazzoni, made him "determined to get the persons responsible for this." He added, "I say persons, because at the time we thought it was two people in that car."[15]

Mazzoni, speaking about this later, noted the importance of McNamara's finding:

> I am convinced that but for the camper we would have never found the boys and if that were the case, to this day we would not know what happened to them. There was no evidence in this case that would have led us to search this dump in Wyoming County. Most people involved in the case did not even know of the dump's existence, let alone connect it to the disappearance of the boys from a street in South Scranton. The accidental finding of the schoolbooks by the camper, his connecting them to the missing boys, and his immediate reporting [of] this information to the police was a major break in the case and led to the discovery, apprehension, and conviction of the murderer of the boys. To repeat, but for the camper, we would still be wondering what had happened to Paul and Buddy and the murderer would have been free to murder again.[16]

Indeed, after working without letup since the previous Friday—the day the boys were officially declared missing—the accidental finding of the boys' schoolbooks had led the police—city, county, and state—and the FBI to this deserted site, where, as one *Times* reporter noted, a "raw wind whipped up snow devils of dust" along the area.[17]

Law enforcement personnel briefed reporters at the scene, who subsequently reported that all present were "visibly appalled" and that DA Mazzoni "wept openly" and "wiped his eyes" but "regained his composure."[18] The murders of the two schoolboys became the focus of all news and regional attention. The *Scranton Times* reported on the reaction of the police on finding the boys' bodies. Under the headline, "Rage, Sorrow Evident at Site," a staff writer described the scene at the dump site: "It was a grim group that shuffled around the windswept narrow dirt road Tuesday afternoon. . . . There were veteran police officers, a handful of newsmen and photographers. . . . A number of them were white-faced with anger. . . . One wept openly and unashamedly. . . . A Scranton detective emerged from the small woodland plot muttering epithets through clenched teeth."[19]

While still at the site of the discovery of the bodies, Mayor Peters, who like DA Mazzoni was also involved in a reelection campaign, conferred with Detective Captain Frank Karam and Chief McCrone and passed an order on to Director Batsavage and the officers that all persons connected with the investigation were to be on a twenty-four-hour duty to apprehend the murderer or murderers.[20] Scranton detectives and other police had already been working around the clock to find the missing boys; now they were ordered to continue to do so. The police were ordered to "pull out all stops" and launched an investigation that promised to be one of the most intensive in local history. Captain Karam was told to request whatever he needed—manpower, equipment, anything—to carry out the investigation.

Meanwhile, as these orders were being issued and reporters were briefed, a lone station wagon containing the bodies of the boys quietly inched down the dirt road, heading out toward the highway. Its headlights cut into the night, leaving those gathered at the dump behind in the increasing darkness of night. The bodies were taken to Tyler Memorial

Hospital near Tunkhannock in Wyoming County, where the boys were subsequently identified by their fathers.[21]

The dumping site where police found the missing boys was located just off the Schultzville-Falls Road, a few miles from the Scranton Municipal Airport at Schultzville, near the border between Lackawanna and Wyoming counties. The site was near the junction of a two-lane paved road and a dirt road near a small white church, the Bethel Church of the Evangelical United Brethren. The bodies were found a little more than five hundred yards up the dirt road that leads to the How Kola Campground—a private campsite. Since the area was in Wyoming County, Wyoming County officials became involved in the subsequent investigation with authorities from Lackawanna County.

The following day, Tuesday, November 6, the *Scranton Times* carried the shocking headline, "Kidnap-Slaying Probe Pressed: 2 Minooka Area Schoolboys Sexually Assaulted and Shot to Death." Written by four of the paper's leading newsmen—Gene Coleman, Robert Flanagan, William Mang, and John O'Hora—the article reported that the boys were found at the dump site in Wyoming County, shot and mutilated, on Monday—murdered by a gunshot wound to each of their heads.[22] Public response to this news was immediate and intense. People had continued to believe that the boys would be found safe, but news of the discovery of their bodies had ended that hope—now replaced by a deep sense of sadness, loss, and not a little anger that such a terrible thing could have happened in a place known for its friendly and peaceful people. Moreover, this news article that described the bodies of the boys as having been mutilated served to lay the foundations for a long-standing speculation about the nature of this "mutilation." Later, at the trial, it would become clear that "mutilation" was a poor and inaccurate word choice.

William Koscinski, a criminal investigator with the Pennsylvania State Police stationed at the Wyoming Barracks who had been assigned to investigate the missing boys and later their homicide, testified that he was present at the dump site on Monday, November 5, 1973, the day the boys' bodies were found. He arrived at the site after 3 p.m., after the boys' bodies were uncovered. Later, he went to Tyler Memorial Hospital, where the bodies had been taken. He attended the autopsy of Edmund Keen the following day. He also attended the autopsy of Paul Freach, which was performed by Dr. Hudock. He was present when the doctors removed one bullet each from the two bodies. The bullets—spent projectiles—were given to him, and he was able to identify both bullets as coming from a .25-caliber weapon. Officer Koscinski took the bullets to the crime laboratory in Harrisburg and turned them over to the ballistics expert at the laboratory, Trooper Dale Allen.[23]

Testifying at trial as to the condition of the bodies when found, Joseph J. Gorski, a criminalist with the Pennsylvania State Police at the Wyoming Barracks, said that he had conducted a preliminary investigation of the two bodies after they were uncovered. He noted that both boys were unclothed—their clothing pulled over their heads and around their ankles. Both bodies had numerous marks and cuts and abrasions, some of which, he indicated, looked like animal bites. Trooper Gorski further testified both boys had been brutally assaulted sexually.[24]

Wyoming County Coroner Bryce Sheldon examined both bodies at Tyler Memorial Hospital and said that the bullet wounds were the "immediate and primary cause of death in each case."[25] The coroner conferred with two pathologists who helped conduct the autopsies and reported that the boys were believed to have been dead three to four days before their bodies were found. He said the bullet wounds caused lacerations of the brain in each case and other "massive injuries."[26]

Hollis Russell, MD, was one of the pathologists who worked on the case. A practicing physician in Tunkhannock, he was on the staff of Tyler Memorial Hospital in 1973. Called by Coroner Bryce Sheldon to perform an autopsy on Edmund Keen on November 6, he testified in 1974 that he removed the bullet from the left portion of the sphenoid sinus, the base of the brain.[27] The bullet had lodged in the left side of the base of the skull. From the location of the entry wound, he determined that the youngster had been shot in the midportion of the forehead, below the hairline in midline.[28]

Dr. Russell testified further that he had found several contusions and lacerations of the abdomen and multiple contusions of the left and right hip regions, along with multiple contusions of the back, below the level of the seventh rib.[29] Dr. Russell confirmed that the cause of Edmund's death was the bullet wound of the head and that the boy had died momentarily after the shot was fired.[30] The doctor testified as well to the fact that the victim had been sexually molested.[31]

Dr. George E. Hudock Jr., county coroner of Luzerne County (located south of Lackawanna) and a pathologist, performed the autopsy on the body of Paul Freach on the morning of November 6, 1973, at Tyler Memorial Hospital. He was present when the boy's father identified his son's body, according to his testimony and at the dump the previous day when the bodies of the two boys were found. He testified that his autopsy revealed a gunshot wound to the head with entrance in the left parietal region of the scalp, located on the left side of the head above the ear. The bullet had traveled downward toward the front of the body through the brain toward the base of the youngster's skull, coming to rest in the area behind the throat on the right side, lodged in the right tonsil at the right rear of the mouth.[32] Dr. Hudock said the bullet had caused destruction of the brain with subdural and other hemorrhage—as was the case with Edmund Keen. Death, said Dr. Hudock, was instantaneous.[33]

Dr. Hudock testified at the trial to the fact that his examination revealed sexual molestation as well as multiple contusions and abrasions and lacerations of the skin. He identified the causes for some of the wounds to the youngster's sexual organs as consistent with an act of sodomy.[34]

Asked to give an opinion in regard to the cause of the bruises and markings that he found throughout the body, Dr. Hudock said that in his opinion they resulted from coagulation of blood and force and trauma being subjected to the skin and could be the result from a fall at or near the time of death or blows to the body.[35] Later, in cross-examination by Defense Attorney John Dunn, Dr. Hudock admitted that the bruises could have been caused by pressure from the weight of the rug that covered the body and not necessarily by blows inflicted by another person.[36]

Bryce Sheldon, the Wyoming County coroner, told newspapers that the conditions of the internal organs indicated the boys had been slain from eight to twelve hours after they were abducted. In other words, released from school at 3:30 and walking toward home, they could have been abducted anytime after this. This would mean that they could have been murdered between 11:30 the night of November 1 and 3:30 the morning of November 2.

The case of the missing boys had been broken due to the remarkable accident of Mr. McNamara finding the boys' books and papers. As a result, the boys had been found—dead and sexually assaulted, their bodies wrapped in a dirty red rug, covered by debris, and thrown or placed in a dumping site located down an obscure road around twelve miles from Scranton. Even more remarkable about this was that the owner of the dump told police it was his intention to plow over the area the next day. If that had happened, the boys would likely have never been found, and no one but the killer would have known what had happened to them.

With the discovery of the bodies, the case that Scranton Police had first treated on November 1 as a routine missing persons investigation and later escalated into possible abduction was now murder and sexual assault.

3

WHO MURDERED PAUL FREACH AND EDMUND KEEN?

The discovery of the bodies of Paul Freach and Edmund Keen at a desolate dumping ground in Wyoming County, Pennsylvania, on November 5, 1973, resulted in an immediate intensification of the police investigation—an investigation now targeted on finding the killer or killers of the two young boys, who had been missing since last seen leaving their school on November 1. By Wednesday, November 7, Pennsylvania State Police Commissioner James D. Barger had arrived in Scranton and was reported to be conferring with Scranton Police and his own field commanders on the murders. Included in a meeting held at the office of Scranton Police Superintendent John McCrone on Wednesday were Scranton Police officers Detective Captain Frank Karam and Lieutenant Frank Roche; State Police Captain O'Donnell; and FBI Agents John Mead, Paul Durkin, and Robert DeLoache. Commissioner Barger said that he was "gratified at the cooperation among the police agencies" and cited the "excellent investigative work that had so far taken place."[1] At this meeting, FBI Agent Mead, who was in charge of the Scranton office of the FBI, said that from that point on the FBI would no longer be directly involved in the case but would continue its relationship only in the role of "liaison."[2]

Emotions ranged from shock at the unbelievable nature of this crime to sorrow and loss at the tragedy that befell the boys and their families to anger at what had happened and frustration that the person or persons responsible were still at large. No group felt this more than the police and law enforcement agencies involved in the case. The investigation, which had been in high gear since day two after the boys had failed to return home, now took on an even more intense, heightened effort to bring the killer or killers to justice.

Meanwhile, the Freach and Keen families prepared to bury their sons.[3]

The enormity of the tragedy was evident in daily newspaper coverage of the murders and in the extensive focus on the details of the burial of the boys. Public attention to the unfolding story of the missing boys was drawn to these daily reports of the details of the murders. As a result, memories of these terrible days remain clear in the minds of local people, and friends and neighbors of the boys have full recall of the events and their impact.

One such person is Angela Ceccoli Scalzo, a youngster at the time of the murders who lived near the boys in Minooka and knew them. In addition to the shock and horror she and her family felt about the murders, Angela recalls the evening she and her family went to pay their respects at the wake held for the boys. She describes a scene that is poignant in its depiction of deep sadness, intensified by a heavy rain and the chill of the wet darkness, that infested the people standing in long lines outside the funeral home waiting to go in. It was so damp and miserable that Angela and her family waited in their car to avoid getting wet. It was something that she never forgot.[4]

Others recall the mixed emotions of sorrow and anger that were apparent in comments made by people of the region as well as the general public. Tom Cummings, now a practicing attorney in Lackawanna County, says he is still affected by the tragedy and equates it, as do others, with an "end of innocence feeling."[5] A young child at the time, he remembers feeling afraid and his parents as well as neighbors taking more precautions with protecting their children, especially as children made their way to school. The reality of what had happened seemed almost surreal to the people of Scranton and the vicinity. One person, a neighbor of the Freach and Keen families, summed this up as "total disbelief."[6]

The joint funeral for the boys was conducted eight days after they went missing. As described by news media, the funeral procession began shortly before 9 a.m. at the Miller Bean Funeral Home on Cedar Avenue and was unusually large, according to reports, containing about forty-five to sixty cars and joined at St. Joseph's Church in Minooka, the home parish of the boys, by more than ninety additional vehicles.[7] As the procession proceeded south on Cedar Avenue, the same route the boys had most likely used on their way home the day of their murders, it passed businesses and homes along the way that were flying the American flag at half mast.

Scranton Times reporter Robert Burke described the scene: "Never in its 100-year history had St. Joseph's Church in Minooka witnessed such a somber occasion."[8] St. Joseph's, a Roman Catholic Church of the Diocese of Scranton, was located within sight of the Freach and Keen homes. The boys, who had grown up together and gone to school together, had together, said Burke, become the victims of what had "already been branded the most brutal crime in Northeastern Pennsylvania history."[9]

The young victims were eulogized by the Reverend Thomas E. McCann. Instead of talking about the circumstances that resulted in their deaths, Father McCann talked about the Christian belief that after death there is life, a cause for rejoicing. While mourning their deaths, he continued, there was "reason for hope of a life of eternal salvation." He said, "This earth is nothing but darkness with the light of Christ which leads man down the corridor of life to his goal of eternal salvation. . . . These two young boys have achieved their goal. . . . They are happy with God in Heaven."[10]

A number of dignitaries attended the funeral, including the Most Reverend J. Carroll McCormack, bishop of Scranton; Monsignor James Timlin, chancellor of the diocese; Eugene Peters, mayor of Scranton; John F. Stephens, superintendent of schools; and the Reverend Joseph Corcoran, pastor of St. Joseph's Church.

Classes at South Scranton Junior High School were cancelled for the day to allow classmates to attend the services.

A Boy Scout honor guard and a color guard sponsored by American Legion Post 568 in Minooka also took part in the funeral.

Pallbearers for the boys included friends and relatives of each boy.

Continuing, *Scranton Times* reporter Burke described for his readers the scene that prevailed, saying that at the funeral Mass and burial service at the parish cemetery—where the boys were interred side by side—there were few dry eyes among the "hundreds" who attended.[11]

Burke noted further that it was evident that the search for the killers was still on, because several plainclothes detectives circulated among the crowd at the funeral on the "chance" that the killer or killers might be there.[12] At this time, the Scranton Police investigation was under the direction of Police Superintendent John McCrone. Likewise, on November 9, the *Scranton Times* reported that even as the boys were being buried that day, "state and city police were following up literally hundreds of 'tips' related to the crime," while refusing to discuss the nature of the leads.[13] Meanwhile, a team of city policemen went door-to-door in South Scranton, where the boys were last seen, looking for even the smallest bit of information that might lead to the arrest of the murderer or murderers.

In the ensuing days the press continued keeping the public abreast of the murders and the ongoing investigation on a daily basis. The press coverage included basic and repetitive information about the case as well as detailed information about the finding of the boys' bodies and the state of the bodies as determined from their autopsies. Citing information given them from police and others involved with the investigation, reporters published details that included that both boys had been beaten, mutilated, and sexually molested.[14] According to one reporter, medical and laboratory work on the boys' bodies tried to piece together the murder and indicated that there was evidence the boys had been forced to commit "unnatural sexual acts"; cuts and bruises were found on their bodies that suggested the possibility the boys had been tortured. Later testimony, as noted previously, would dispute this information about torture, pointing instead to the fact that the injuries most likely would have been caused by the bodies being pushed down the incline at the garbage dump and by insect or rodent bites.[15] Nonetheless, the general nature of these details in the press gave rise to a good deal of misinformation, speculation, and rumor, which quickly spread among the public. One reporter's use of the word "mutilated" in particular to describe bruises and other wounds to the bodies of the boys was later corrected in the paper. In a subsequent article appearing in the *Scranton Times* on Saturday, November 10, reporter Bill Halpin clarified, saying, "Contrary to earlier reports, the victims were not mutilated, garroted or dismembered, the coroner said today. . . . However, they were sexually abused, as reported."[16]

In spite of this and later exacting testimonies at trial, some of the details surrounding the boys' murders and the state of their bodies would become oft-repeated "stories." The horror of the community in reaction to this unthinkable crime to two of their young people became perpetuated in everyday talk in the region. As a result, as time passed, additional "details" and "facts" that went beyond the truth became accepted as truth—particularly as to the sexual aspects of the case. Although clearly refuted by experts, these aspects of the case nonetheless took on meanings far in excess of the facts. The rumors surrounding this case were hard to dislodge from the public's understanding and continue to persist to the present.

As the murder investigation continued, offers of rewards began to appear. By Wednesday, November 7, a few days after the discovery of the boys' bodies, the rewards were topping $11,000, and more was to come.[17] The Northeastern Pennsylvania National Bank and Trust Company, where Paul Freach's father was employed in the data processing center, posted a $5,000 reward. Three parent-teacher associations established a Freach-Keen Reward Fund, posting $100 each and naming the Citizens Savings and Loan Association as its depository.[18]

Scranton mayor Eugene Peters called a special press conference shortly after the discovery of the boys' bodies, at which he announced a $1,000 award for information leading to the arrest of the person or persons responsible for the heinous crime.[19]

The American Legion Post 568 offered a scholarship in the boys' memories, the P.J. Freach/Buddy Keen Memorial Scholarships for high school seniors who were residents of the Minooka section of Scranton. By 2010 this award was valued at $1,000.[20] A recent *Times-Tribune* picture showed the scholarship winner in 2013; the amount was still $1,000.[21]

Other rewards and memorials would follow, testifying to the level of emotional attachment the murders had generated with the public and the outpouring of public sorrow for the inexpiable loss of the young men. By November 15, regional officials of Little League Baseball, Inc., announced the establishment of a memorial sportsmanship award honoring the two boys. Called the Freach-Keen Sportsmanship Award, it was announced by Thomas Burdett, district administrator of Little League District 17, and was designed to commemorate the boys and their dedication to Little League and to the sport of baseball. The plan was to establish a panel that would annually choose an outstanding young athlete from candidates of the twenty-three Little Leagues in District 17 and present the recipient with the award at an annual district banquet.

Burdett praised the boys, saying that both youngsters were Little Leaguers who "exemplified the finest aspects of athletic tradition. . . . Both of these fine youngsters were enthusiastic Little Leaguers . . . and I know that their parents shared their deep interest in baseball and the character-building program fostered by Little league competition. . . . Both boys were talented athletes and loved baseball, [and] exemplified the finest aspects of athletic tradition as practiced by our American youth."[22] Mr. Burdett noted that the fathers of the boys were also active in Little League. According to Burdett, Mr. Keen was a Little League manager, and Mr. Freach was a manager and officer.[23]

Joining Burdett at this announcement were several other prominent people involved in the administration of the sportsmanship award, including Vivian Edwards, vice president of the Northeastern National Bank where Mr. Freach, Paul's father, was employed; Jack O'Connor, former District 17 administrator; and representatives of Northeastern National's Trust Department, which had established the Freach-Keen Memorial

Fund to raise $10,000 to support the annual award. Mr. Burdett explained that District 17 was prompted to administer the fund by friends of the two families.[24] Burdett added that the administrators of several independent funds collected since the boys' murders had already indicated to the bank that they were going to direct their donations to the sportsmanship award fund.[25]

In addition to the scholarships and memorial funds, the murders, as mentioned previously, impacted the school busing system of the community. Earlier during the search for the missing boys, parents living in Minooka and South Scranton met at a local South Scranton American Legion hall to plan the draft of a petition to the Scranton School Board demanding that bus transportation be provided for children from that area attending South Scranton Junior High School. On November 12, local papers reported that "fearful parents" were making a concerted plea to the Scranton School Board to provide bus service for their children. According to a school board report dated November 12, 1973, the chairman of the Minooka parents group, John McIntyre, presented a petition to the board for busing with over five hundred names attached.[26] Reportedly, an "edgy confrontation" took place between parents and school board representatives, which included threats of court action by Minooka residents if bus services were not provided for their children.[27] The school board responded that they would "do the best we can to the best of our resources and ability."[28] The Minooka parents' group was represented by Attorney Michael Eagen.

Minooka parents were not the only ones making requests for school bus service for their children. Earlier, parents in the East Mountain area of Scranton had made the same request and, according to this report, succeeded in securing transportation for their children. The meeting with the Minooka parents ended with Albert Sporer, the board president, telling the attendees of the "monumental task'" it would take to protect some fifteen thousand Scranton schoolchildren from the "evil force'" that had befallen the Freach and Keen boys. Adding to these concluding remarks, the parents' group heard from John Stephens, Scranton school superintendent, who urged "reason and calm . . . without panic."[29]

The day following this meeting, the local newspaper reported that a growing number of parents were calling for bus transportation for their children. To handle the situation, Board President Sporer created a committee of three to study the problem. President Sporer chaired this committee. The other members were school board members Donald B. Cahoon and Eugene Donahue. The committee planned to meet with state legislators, officials of Scranton city government, representatives of the County of Lackawanna Transit System (COLTS), and interested parents to find a solution to what was now characterized as a "major problem."[30] Board action was, according to this reporter's view, a response to the overflow crowd that had been in attendance at the earlier meeting and the less-than-satisfactory response of the attendees to the words of the board president. Even as the study committee was formed, however, Mr. Sporer was clear in his comments to the newspaper that he did not want the board to provide the busing the parents sought without considering the busing needs of other sections of the school district. In Sporer's view, one of the primary steps that had to be taken was to pressure the state legislature into changing the reimbursement formula the state used to provide local school districts with cash payments for busing their students. The current formula did not provide sufficient funding for Scranton and some other urban school areas. The problem was related to mileage: Scranton received very little state funding, because it did not run buses over long routes that would accumulate the necessary mileage to meet adequate reimbursement standards.

Meanwhile, the Scranton board was attempting to provide busing with the use of the county public transportation system, COLTS. Integration of the public system would save city taxpayers some money. If the public and school busing efforts were not integrated, according to Mr. Sporer, city taxpayers were going to have to pay for the COLTS operation as well as for the school bus runs, which would cover essentially the same routes.[31] In July 1973, the Scranton school board moved to establish transportation for resident students in grades K–6 who lived at least one and one-half miles from their schools as well as those schoolchildren living a shorter distance away in hazardous areas (as determined by the

Pennsylvania Department of Transportation). In the same motion, the board resolved to provide transportation for students in all grades (elementary and secondary) if no public transportation was available and if their homes were two or more miles from the school and for those living in hazardous areas. These motions were passed unanimously and became effective for the 1973–1974 school year.[32]

One year later, in July 1974, the board restated and reaffirmed this policy for the school year 1974–1975, stating that it would "provide free school transportation for resident pupils in Grades K–6, both public and non-public, if their residence was one and one-half or more miles from the respective school . . . and for those on existing hazardous routes."[33] In the same motion, the board resolved to provide transportation for seventh and eighth grade students "traveling hazardous routes."[34] The previous resolution to provide transportation for all students living distances of two or more miles if no public transportation was available presumably continued. Kids of school age in 1973–1974 from Minooka and South Scranton who were interviewed for this book recall that following the Freach and Keen murders they were given transportation to school. So ultimately the parents' petition met with success, and school bus service for Scranton students became a reality—but too late for Paul and Edmund.

The city of Scranton was, in the 1970s, a city composed of many different neighborhoods, with many divisions based on ethnicity, culture, and religion. Class distinctions also served to divide the grid of the city, evident in the many different varieties of homes, suggesting a wide range of income levels ranging from affluent to solid middle class to blue collar and lower income. Political affiliation was another divider. Certain political wards and sections favoring one political party or the other were easily discerned and regularly targeted by aspiring political parties and candidates. To a certain extent, these distinctions are true even at present. However, the city today is in a poorer economic condition, and neighborhoods have changed to become more integrated and, in some cases, poorer in appearance, with derelict housing and increased crime.

Minooka, the home of Paul and Edmund, was one such distinctive place. Known as a particularly family-oriented, close-knit community, Minooka is located at the southernmost tip of the city. Historically it had once been a separate town and not part of Scranton. But since 1949, Minooka has been the twenty-fourth ward of Scranton. Although more ethnically diverse today than it was in the 1970s, Minooka has retained strongly Irish Catholic and Democratic. Loyalty to the Democratic Party goes far back in its political history. The story persists that when Alfred E. Smith ran for the U.S. presidency in 1928, out of the 1,100 or so votes cast in Minooka, 1,099 were for Smith. Some Minookans claimed they "knew" who voted against Smith.[35] Minooka covers an area of about five square miles and has long been associated with a number of proud ethnic groups and social and recreational activities.[36] It is a place of neighborliness and friendly associations. It is also a place that has never forgotten two of its own young citizens, building the Freach Keen Memorial Park to honor and remember the boys. The park stands today not far from the boys' homes, the area where they once played Little League baseball, and the cemetery where they are buried.[37]

Author Michael Bracey has written with feeling about his hometown of Minooka. He describes it as "not just a series of streets, houses, yards, and stores. They are full of character and characters, both old and young, living and dead. Their actions, imperfections, deeds and savings live on forever in barroom chatter. . . . Name the subject, any subject, and someone will not only voice their opinion, but may title himself or herself a self-proclaiming expert on it."[38]

In Bracey's work, Minooka is a unique community, so much so that folks identified strongly with it, feeling that "anything beyond Pittston Avenue [meaning Scranton] was the great unknown."[39] Bracey and others say that Minooka was more than just a place to live; it was their world. It had everything. It was a place where kids ran the streets at night and played without fear, just as their parents had before them. Bracey, writing in 2004, tells of feeling safe inside the "borders" of Minooka because neighbors watched out for kids and would scold them when necessary. It was truly a "village" that offered nurturing and protection to those who lived within it—at least that was the perception. As Bracey notes, this perception might have been mistaken in view of the Freach and Keen murders. In a chapter on the murders, titled, "The Town Mourns," he calls the crime "perhaps the most tragic event that occurred in the town."[40] Recalling that time, Bracey tells of how the search for the missing boys and their murders affected his town: "During those unnerving days when they were still unaccounted for, mothers were fearful to let their children outside to play. . . . A surreal unsettling aura blanketed the town as police helicopters hovered over the area searching for the boys. Minooka lost its innocence as a result of these murders. In a way, the untimely deaths of these children banded the town together even closer than before."[41]

As the families of the murdered boys mourned their incredible loss—the only sons of each family—a massive search was under way, a search that included multiple agencies of law enforcement and included all manner of criminal investigation.

As the investigation of the crime that was now called the most shocking in Scranton's history continued, it first looked like the police might be able to break the case quickly. With few other leads to follow, the police continued to concentrate on the story offered by the eyewitness of seeing the boys getting into a car occupied by a man and a woman. As they had earlier, the police were considering the possibility that the "woman" was actually a man in disguise. Once the boys' bodies were found, the police believed they were dealing with two brutal murderers. The supposition was that these two were likely to be two homosexuals, who might be the sort who would pick up two young boys, molest them, and then kill them to prevent them from talking.[42] Based on this, a widespread manhunt began. Joining in this as well were many watchful, concerned, and now frightened and angry citizens of Lackawanna and neighboring counties who were on the watch for the two persons driving the beat-up 1966 Chevrolet Impala who had abducted the boys. The investigation focused on likely suspects for this type of crime that might be in the area, with particular emphasis on people who had previous histories of sexual crimes, child molestation, and murder.

With their investigation centered on the information provided by the eyewitnesses, the police investigation sought leads to the identity of the two persons said to have been driving the automobile the boys entered. The witness last saw the boys getting into the car on Cedar Avenue near Elm or Genet Streets. In another account, they were last seen on Maple Street.

Police were stopping to question anyone who looked remotely like the two people in the composite drawing and running down lists of persons known to be "sexual deviates" for questioning. Thousands of tips were called in to the police and checked—but to no avail. The mystery couple was nowhere to be found.[43] Some speculated that perhaps they were drifters, long gone from the area.

By November 15, a little more than two weeks from the day the boys disappeared, newspapers were reporting that the police continued to work around the clock on the investigation and that it was proving to be protracted. Despite the open hotline and canvassing efforts, police had no new leads, and the investigation was still based on the story that the boys had been hitchhiking home on November 1 and had been picked up by the car. After finding the boys murdered, the police assumption was once the boys entered the automobile, the man and woman had taken them from Scranton to a cabin or vacant cottage in the area near the dump where their bodies had been found five days later. Based on this, police were searching that area in hopes of finding some clues to the identity of the killers.

As a result of the location of the bodies of Paul and Edmund—a remote dump site in Wyoming County in an area not visible to travelers on the adjacent rural road, not easily noticed, and only people very familiar with the area near the campgrounds would know—police theorized that the person or persons they were seeking must have knowledge of this area.[44] The police investigation soon concentrated on the dump area where the boys' bodies had been found. They questioned the wife of the owner of the campground located nearby, identified in local papers as Mrs. Howard Eckel. Mrs. Eckel told the police she never told campers to use the dump—it was about ten street blocks away. According to Mrs.

Eckel, there were only three guests at the campgrounds at the time the boys went missing. One camper told Mrs. Eckel that he and his wife were from Scranton but were traveling from Connecticut to the South. This couple had checked into the camp on October 31, the day before the boys went missing, and checked out on Sunday afternoon, November 4, one day before the boys' bodies were found in the dump. The owner's wife described the man as having a beard that covered a scarred face; they were driving a blue Chevrolet and hauling an eighteen-foot camper. Police checked the Scranton address the couple had provided and found that it did not check out. Unfortunately, the camp did not require guests to provide license plate numbers, so it was impossible for the police to check on this. While the description gave promising support to the eyewitness account of the couple in the blue Chevy, with a lack of any further information about the campers, the police were unable to follow up with the couple from the campsite. Although police put out appeals for this couple to come forward, they never did. Meanwhile the manhunt had spread nationwide, with Scranton Police headquarters receiving information and pictures of criminals from police in neighboring states.

Adding to the police's problems was a lack of manpower for an investigation that was rapidly becoming much larger than the immediate area of Lackawanna and adjacent counties. Moreover, the special agents of the FBI who had been on the case at the beginning were withdrawn with the discovery of the bodies of the two boys.

Scranton Detective Frank Karam detailed the criminal investigation for reporters, saying that the police were continuing to run down hundreds of leads provided by citizens—leads that were largely the result of the composite sketches of the middle-aged couple seen in the car the boys had allegedly entered. This was slow, tedious, and emotionally draining work that included checking files and auto registrations as well as sorting out tips in order to eliminate duplications.[45] Every now and then a tip was obtained that suggested the possibility of major movement in the case. For example, on November 9, what was described in the local press as an "excellent clue" was received at police headquarters, the day of the burial. A car matching the description of the white and blue 1966 Chevrolet had been sighted in the Keyser Valley area of Scranton. The caller told police there were blood spots on the rear seat. Unfortunately the sighting proved to be false—just another "tip" from a concerned citizen that, like so many others, went nowhere.[46]

The days passed. Timothy Thomas, who authored an article in 1976 in *Startling Detective* magazine, reported that the parents of the dead boys were becoming increasingly impatient with the police investigation. Thomas further asserts that this impatience began on day one, with the police's initial lack of concern for the missing boys. The parents' first concerns, he points out, were met with the reply that the boys would likely show up, that they were just late coming home, or delayed playing, or even that they might have run off somewhere—all suggestions that were unacceptable and implausible to the caring, increasingly frightened parents. Of course, the police position was based on standard statistics that, more often than not, people reported missing are not really "missing" and often turn up. As a result, it is normal operating procedure for official investigations of missing persons to begin after a twenty-four-hour period has passed. Even on the second day (November 2) that the boys were missing, Thomas said that the police continued to hold to the view that the boys had probably gone to "a friend's house or something akin to that."[47] Actually, as police have indicated and as previously mentioned, as early as the evening of November 1 and early on November 2 during this pre-twenty-four-hour period, Scranton Police were unofficially moving on the matter of the missing boys, and police throughout the city and county were instructed to be on the lookout for the two boys. Especially by the second day, when the boys had failed to return to their respective homes, police involved in this case recall that they had uneasy feelings about the boys and were beginning to think that something was indeed wrong and that the boys might have come to some harm. Indeed, it was this second day that the boys were missing that police received the eyewitness account that was to be their first big (if ultimately false) lead from the schoolboy.

According to reports, it was evident that the investigation was "beginning to take its toll on investigators," many of who were said to have been putting in "20-hour days."[48] Detective Captain Frank Karam acknowledged the magnitude, scope, and intensity of the investigation as he talked with reporters on November 14. In this interview, Captain Karam told the press that, even as the investigation concentrated on the area where the bodies of the boys were found in an effort to try to locate places nearby where the boys might have been held and killed prior to their bodies being put in the dump, police still held out the hope of finding the car used by the people said to have picked up the two boys as they were hitchhiking home from school. At the same time, an important part of the investigation included the follow-up on numerous tips coming in to police headquarters. Many of these concentrated on numerous sightings of the old Chevrolet.[49]

On November 24, the local newspaper reported that city and state police were continuing to check out all possible leads in order to track down the killer or killers. Detective Captain Frank Karam had indicated to reporters that a witness to the abduction was going to be hypnotized in order to see if that person had any additional information that might be helpful to the investigation. This person, it was later reported, was hypnotized, but no further information had been gained except that the earlier information he had provided had been confirmed. This detail is interesting, because, later, when this witness's account about the abduction of the boys by the two persons in the white and blue Chevrolet was discredited, it left authorities and the public with disturbing, conflicting, and unanswered questions about what really happened to the boys after they left school and who had abducted them. This state of doubt and confusion would continue when, still later, a suspect in the case confessed to murdering the boys—if not in the minds of law enforcement, then in the minds of those closest to the boys.

The Scranton Police scuba team checked some small ponds in the Wyoming County area near the dump site on the chance that the car used in the abduction and murders may have been dumped there. This met with no success. This did not stop the police from hoping that a "good" lead would come up that would lead to the location of the 1966 Chevrolet Impala, which was still viewed as the car used by the "killers."[50]

Meanwhile the "flood" of tips had begun to decline somewhat. Still police continued to check and cross-check everything that might be relevant, and the now "hundreds" of leads were put on file. In order to do this, Captain Karam acknowledged that police officers were volunteering to work around the clock on the case and had been since the grisly discovery of the boys' bodies.[51]

Police believed that finding the car driven by the deadly couple was their best chance at discovering the identity of the murderers. Police continued to urge regional citizens to remain on the lookout for the old Chevrolet. All available manpower of the Scranton Police and the Pennsylvania State Police—particularly troopers from the Wyoming Barracks (where the dump was located)—continued to work twenty-four hours a day, according to reports. The FBI was also fully engaged in the investigation, as was other law enforcement and government officials from Scranton, Lackawanna County, and other neighboring counties. It was an investigation that many agree the likes of which the region had not seen before—at least in their memories. In addition, off-duty detectives and uniformed police from the entire region worked on their own time to track down leads provided by people in the area who were anxious to bring the murderer or murderers to justice. All this took endless hours, and the going was slow. Manpower was stretched beyond all possible limits. Meanwhile, a frightened, angry public held its collective breath amid increasing rumors about the details of the murders and the alleged two killers.

On November 25, 1973, the *Scranton Times*'s Joseph Flannery reported the account of a woman who had "seen" the murders of the two boys in her crystal ball. One of "thousands" of leads being checked out by the police, in what this reporter termed was at this point, "the futile attempt to solve the case."[52] Emphasizing that the police, increasingly frustrated in its efforts to break the case, had continued to plea for the public to report any information that might be helpful, no matter how slight. As a result, the woman called the office of Paul R. Mazzoni, the district attorney of Lackawanna County, to report the information that she had "seen" in her crystal ball. According to Flannery's report,

She "saw" the boys with their two captors and "saw" them being shot. The most interesting part of her story, however, was that she claimed that the crime occurred in a large dwelling of some kind along a lake, river of [sic] other body of water. [The woman also reported that the] rug found at the Falls area dump with the bodies was actually from the dwelling where the crime occurred (and just an old rug that had been disposed of in the dump). She claimed that the killers rolled it up and took it with them as they drove to the dump.[53]

Not surprisingly, the police, said Flannery, were "reluctant to comment on the report" but said the most interesting part of the woman's vision of the crime had been that the boys had been murdered in a cottage or some type of "seasonal" building. This seemed to support the theory the police had about the killers' choice of the disposal site of the boys' bodies, the theory being that the killers abducted the boys in South Scranton and took them out of Scranton, perhaps to a deserted cottage or house that they had broken into somewhere in the region of the dump. In the event that an owner of a home in the Falls area (a region near the dump site) had had a break-in and possessed a red rug that was now missing, they were urged to contact police immediately.[54] This information could break the case, said the reporter, adding that if this did break the case, it likely "would also increase the number of persons who believe in crystal balls."[55] Unfortunately, the police did not report any information as a result of its appeal, and as the days passed, none was forthcoming.

Even without the crystal ball story, the rug found on the dump covering the bodies of the boys had already warranted some serious checking.[56] It had been sent to a crime laboratory for study for clues right away, but, said Flannery, police were reluctant to comment on preliminary lab findings, and ongoing laboratory tests were continuing.[57]

Meanwhile a parallel state police investigation was underway and had been since shortly after the boys went missing. Retired Pennsylvania State Trooper Jerry Gaetano recalls the incident:

> I can still remember this. . . . I was a young trooper just called into headquarters to work in the crime room. That was an honor back then. I may have been at Dunmore [Barracks] for a month or so, when one

day, about a week after the murders, Sgt. John Noel walked over to my desk at the end of a workday. He gave me a copy of an Initial Crime Report, which was completed by a uniformed trooper working out of the Gibson station. He then asked me to look into the [Nasser] incident and see if there was any connection to the Freach and Keen homicides. . . . It wasn't an investigation out of Dunmore [Barracks] and while we were provided with some facts, we didn't know everything. It was a PSP [Pennsylvania State Police] Wyoming investigation. He really didn't give me any direction, except to tell me that the Susquehanna County [Nasser] incident occurred one week before the Freach and Keen homicides and there probably wasn't any connection, but he just wanted to be sure. . . . Billy Wright's name had been "common" knowledge as having been a suspect early on in this [Freach and Keen] investigation, but . . . he was ruled out.[58]

The incident that Trooper Gaetano was asked to investigate was the attempted abduction and probable assault of Thomas Nasser, a young college student and hitchhiker, that had taken place on Friday, October 25, 1973, along I-81 in Susquehanna County.

After being set free by his would-be attacker, hitchhiker Tom Nasser received a ride on the interstate from a young woman, a college student who, like himself, was heading home for the weekend. She had actually seen the assailant with Tom, and she had honked her horn as she passed the two of them. To her, it looked like they were engaged in some sort of argument. She told Tom later that she thought something was wrong when she passed and had turned around and passed by the scene a second time. Then she called the police. After Tom got in her car, he told her about the situation. On hearing Tom's story, the woman took him to the State Police Barracks at Gibson, something that Tom was not particularly keen to do, because he still wanted to get home in time for his brother's soccer game. He never made the game; instead he told the state police what had happened on the highway and accompanied the police to the site of the encounter in Susquehanna County, right over the Lackawanna County line. After identifying the location, he went back to the State Police Barracks, completed the report, left, and hitchhiked home.

At home, Tom told his father about the incident. At this point, Tom's thinking was that what had happened to him was some type of homosexual advance that, even with the gun involved, probably wasn't as bad as it had seemed. His father may or may not have agreed with this assessment, but he did think that it was important for Tom to try to identify the type of gun involved. With the help of a gun collector friend of his father's, he was able to do this. Tom identified the gun as a .25-caliber automatic. Tom thought the incident was over, but he was wrong. It was just beginning, and Tom's acute awareness and keen powers of observation were to play an important link in solidifying the case against the man who, as it later turned out, would be accused of the murders of Paul Freach and Edmund Keen.[59]

Tom returned home from college the following weekend (November 3) and heard about the missing boys in Scranton—never connecting the two incidents, aside from some minor suspicions. Retuning to Lock Haven College to resume his studies, he received a call from Trooper Gaetano, as he recalls it, probably the week the bodies of the boys were found or soon after. Trooper Gaetano had received orders to conduct an investigation of Tom's incident to see if there was any possibility it might be connected to the Freach and Keen murders. Following these orders, the trooper met with Tom and his father the next weekend at the Gibson Barracks. Tom recounted his story, and Trooper Gaetano showed Tom some composite sketches depicting the couple who were driving the car that the Freach and Keen boys were said to have entered on Cedar Avenue. Tom told Trooper Gaetano the kind of gun that his assailant had held to his head and particulars about the car the man was driving, including the mileage. Tom later said he was sorry he had not looked at the license number as his assailant's car drove away from him—knowing if he had, the driver might have been found; and if the man was the same one who killed the boys, their murders might have been prevented.[60] After meeting with Tom, Gaetano continued his investigation of the hitchhiker case, and the police investigation into the murders of Freach and Keen continued.

DA Paul Mazzoni tells of working on the murder investigation. He had county detectives working with Scranton Police and Pennsylvania

State Police. He was active with Scranton Police and kept in the loop with the investigation. As the time passed and no sighting of the Chevrolet or its occupants were found, according to DA Mazzoni, police began to discount the story told by the schoolboy. Mazzoni said, "We were on a wild goose chase for two or three days and some of the story that the boy had told started to not make sense; he was just looking for attention."[61] The police were thinking along the same lines and soon after the discovery of the boys' bodies, they "found out he [the eyewitness] was not telling the truth. He confessed that he made up the story."[62]

All this time, one man had been particularly in the sights of the police as a likely suspect—William Wright. Wright was a confessed murderer and attempted rapist who, until a recent work release, had been a patient at Pennsylvania State Hospital for the Criminally Insane at Farview, located in Wayne County. According to Trooper Gaetano and others, Wright had been questioned and eliminated because of time constraints. His work activities on the day of the Freach and Keen murders placed him in locations that would have prohibited his moving to and from the South Scranton area to the dumping site where the bodies were left. Although this seemed to rule him out, he still remained a possible suspect because of his prior history.

Gaetano looked at this man in relation to the Nasser incident as well but was perplexed that the suspect did not own an automobile. Nevertheless, going on the possibility that he might have gained access to one, he talked with a member of Wright's family and was informed that, at the time of the Nasser incident, Wright had borrowed his brother's car—a car that perfectly matched the description provided by Thomas Nasser. By this time police had identified the type of weapon used in the murders of Paul and Edmund—a .25 caliber automatic, the same type of gun identified by Tom Nasser. With Wright in the sights of police on both cases and the weapon matches, the two cases eventually began to intersect.

The final piece of Gaetano's investigation fell into place later, after Wright was again in the picture for the murders of Freach and Keen. According to a report on December 8, 1973, Trooper Gaetano showed Tom a group of pictures of men, one of which was Wright. Without hesitation, Tom picked out William Wright as the man who had threatened his life.[63] According to Gaetano, this information was passed to State Police at the Wyoming Barracks, who were already building a case against Wright in the murder of the two boys, and Nasser's identification helped them to cement their case against Wright.[64]

4

THE MURDERER

In July 1980, *Scranton Times* reporter Francis DeAndrea recounted the 1973 story of the hitchhiker incident on Interstate 81 and told his readers how this had been connected to the murders of Paul Freach and Edmund Keen. This account told how, shortly after the disappearance and murders of the two boys, Pennsylvania State Police Trooper Jerry Gaetano began to investigate the hitchhiker matter with an eye to any possible connection it might have to the murders of Paul Freach and Edmund Keen. Meeting with the hitchhiker, on December 8, 1973, Thomas Nasser, a young college student, proved fruitful indeed. Nasser was able to pick William Wright out from a photo lineup as his attacker as well as identify the weapon Wright used as a small-caliber automatic handgun. Gaetano and his superiors were convinced that Nasser's close call was connected to the murders of the two Minooka boys and that the information Nasser provided would be crucial to the murder investigation and to the outcome of the trial.

Indeed, ten days after Nasser identified Wright as his assailant, a group of law enforcement officers confronted William Wright, who was at this time in custody in the Scranton area on charges of breaking parole. Confronted with evidence linking him to the Freach and Keen murders, Wright confessed and later entered a guilty plea.[1] Wright also acknowledged that he had attempted the molestation of Thomas Nasser but had "let him go."[2]

Soon after the bodies of the boys were discovered, rewards for information that would lead to the arrest of the murder or murderers had been established. Tom Nasser recalled that in 1979 or 1980, at the urging of Trooper Jerry Gaetano, he applied for the reward.[3] He recalls this period as a difficult episode, because not everyone involved in the case agreed that Nasser's information had been instrumental in bringing the murderer to justice. As a result, Nasser had been forced to hire an attorney to petition the Lackawanna County Court for the award and had to go to court as the plaintiff in a hearing held to determine whether or not he was eligible for it. Some parties connected to the award contested Nasser's claim, arguing that a statute of limitations had run out on claims to the reward. The judge determined otherwise, finding that Nasser's information had contributed 50 percent to the case by helping establish a "pattern of illicit activity" of Wright that led to securing his arrest and conviction. Nasser had furnished information that provided a "significant link in the chain of circumstantial evidence." The judge said further that many factors had resulted in the arrest of William Wright and that the work of many law enforcement agencies was significant in the case.[4]

In July 1980, almost seven years after the murders of Paul Freach and Edmund Keen, Thomas Nasser, now a young teacher, was awarded half of the reward that had been collected in the Freach and Keen case for contributing significant information to the police that led to the arrest and conviction of the murderer—a sum of $15,150.[5]

Although the murder investigation was to eventually focus exclusively on William Wright, as late as early December 1973 the police investigation was still centered on the "eyewitness" story of two middle-aged people in a white and blue Chevrolet who had picked up the boys while they were hitchhiking home from school. In pursuit of clues to what had happened to the boys, on December 8, the *Scranton Times* reported that City and State Police were that day searching a wooded area in the Minooka section of Scranton looking for a location where the two boys had been shot and killed after being abducted on November 1. Citing information that he had received from a child in the area who claimed to have heard gunshots in the wooded area along Interstate 81 near the Davis

Street exit in Minooka on November 1, Detective Frank Karam said that this youngster had seen a car resembling the Chevrolet the police were seeking.[6] Because of the two-person focus of the investigation, Wright was not considered a serious suspect at this point in time.

Based on police investigation of the dump area where the boys' bodies had been found and autopsy information, investigators were in agreement that the boys had not been shot and killed at the dump. Seeking information that might reveal the site of the murders, the police followed up many rumors, but now one month and some days after the murders, police acknowledged that they had few leads and were not near an arrest. Finding the location of the killings, they thought, might provide a lead to the killer or killers of the boys. Earlier the police had asked persons who had cabins or homes in the Falls region near the dump to check on their properties to see if they might have been the site for the killings. But nothing had come of this, and as a result, the investigation had turned back to the Minooka region as a possible site for the murders.

As police continued to focus on the story of two middle-aged people in a Chevrolet, the article detailing the search for the location of the murders revealed that the police had been looking at several persons of interest. Included in this were people whom police turned to as "usual suspects" for this type of murder, particularly those who had some history of child sexual molestation; those who had records or who had purchased or were in possession of a weapon like the weapon used to kill the boys; and those who, because of other factors, might be involved. However, *Times* coverage of this period indicated that if the police had anyone of special interest, they were not disclosing it to the press.

Over the course of the investigation, one person in particular continued to attract the attention of some parties involved in the murder investigation—William J. Wright, a thirty-six-year-old former patient and trustee at Farview State Hospital for the Criminally Insane in Waymart, Pennsylvania.[7] Wright, who had a history of crime and violence beginning as a youth, had served time in a juvenile facility and, later, in a state penitentiary for murder. He had been sent to Farview as a result of a sanity hearing that had found him insane after an attempted rape. At

Farview, he admitted to another murder, but this crime remained unproven. In 1973 Wright took part in an early release program offered at Farview that subsequently placed him in the Scranton community, living on his own with little supervision from the hospital. He worked for Vector, a rodent-control agency that serviced a number of municipalities in Lackawanna and surrounding counties, including neighborhoods in the city of Scranton.[8]

Wright was known to police but had remained under the radar during the early stages of the murder investigation for a number of reasons, in addition to the two-person theory of the murders. Wright didn't resemble the composite drawings of the pair in the Chevrolet, and he did not own a car—although he had access to the Vector van that he used for his work. He was also not linked to a woman or anyone who might have dressed as a woman. He had been questioned about the missing boys but was able to establish an alibi for the afternoon of November 1; he was working as a rodent exterminator outside Scranton, and at the time the boys were thought to have been picked up after school, he claimed he had not yet returned to the area. Although some police personnel had knowledge of his criminal background and the release program from Farview, it was clear that, overall, few knew his complete history or the violent nature of his prior crimes. Ironically, Wright was also someone often seen around city hall in Scranton, where the Vector agency had an office and where the Scranton Police headquarters was located. A number of police even knew him by name. Adding to this irony was the fact that Wright had actually assisted Scranton Police in the apprehension of an escaped prisoner who took off while being questioned at police headquarters. Wright's assistance in this attempted escape resulted in his being awarded a letter of commendation from the Scranton Police.

Thus, in spite of Wright's criminal history, he was not considered a possible suspect early on. In fact, on Tuesday, November 6, Election Day in Lackawanna County and the day after the bodies of the murdered boys were discovered, Wright worked at the election polls. While everyone in the region was focused on the horror of the murders, Wright went on in a calm, collected manner. The night of the election, as Scranton Mayor

Eugene Peters met with supporters to acknowledge his reelection—an event that was considerably toned down due to the murders—the mayor told supporters that finding the guilty person or persons was the major priority of his new term. William Wright was reported to have stood a short distance from the mayor as he spoke.[9]

According to later testimony at Wright's trial for the murders of the two boys, Paul J. Farrell, the Pennsylvania district supervisor of the Wilkes-Barre office of the Pennsylvania Board of Probation and Parole, had contact with Wright starting soon after his release from Farview.[10] Asked what Wright's status with him was, Farrell replied that he was on parole under "our" (Probation and Parole's) supervision. According to Mr. Farrell, Wright had been under this jurisdiction since the latter part of May or early June 1973 at the time he was released from Farview. It appears from this testimony that, at this point, Wright was on a day-release program and returned to Farview each evening. Sometime in the summer of 1973, Farview authorities gave Wright permission to move to his own apartment in Scranton, a decision probably related to the distance (about nineteen miles) involved in traveling from Farview to Scranton on a daily basis. According to the terms of this release arrangement, Wright was to maintain weekly contact with Farview—in person or by telephone. Farrell acknowledged that his agency only became aware that Wright was living on his own (as opposed to day release) and residing in Scranton on or around July 20, 1973. Wright was then assigned to the caseload of one Frank Walsh in the early part of August 1973.[11]

Asked if Farrell had ever had any contact with Wright, he said that he had. He also testified that he had talked with Wright prior to November 1, the day the boys went missing. Farrell had interviewed Wright in the Scranton Probation and Parole Office sometime in the early part of September.[12] According to Farrell, he had thought of Wright immediately when the bodies of Paul and Edmund were found.

Farrell said he contacted the Scranton Police and the Wyoming Barracks of the State Police after the boys went missing and after their bodies were found. Earlier Farrell said he "brought to the attention of the police various people under our supervision that [he] wanted them to be aware of that could possibly be involved in this [the abduction of the boys]."[13] Once the boys' bodies had been discovered and there was clear sexual molestation involved in the crimes, Farrell testified that he told Scranton and State Police of "numerous" individuals that his agency had "under supervision . . . who had committed aggressive acts or sexual molestation."[14] On November 8, Farrell brought Wright's "particular case to the attention of Detective Karam of the Scranton police . . . the only file that he brought to Karam's attention at this time.[15]

Farrell testified at the trial that he talked with Detective Karam about Wright and as a result of this talk went to see Wright—around the fourteenth of November. They met at Wright's apartment on Pittston Avenue.[16] Farrell wanted to ascertain Wright's activities around the date that the boys were missing. Farrell described Wright as calm and collected when interviewed by police about the murders, with the result that he was not seriously considered a high-priority suspect.

Farrell's interest in Wright as a possible suspect in the abduction and murders had been the result of his conversation with Detective Karam, who had told him that the police had information that Wright had purchased a gun—information that Karam had asked Farrell to keep confidential and not disclose to Wright. As a result, when Farrell met with Wright, their conversation was about Wright's activities and associates around this time. Farrell said, "It appeared that he had been doing well."[17] However, Wright's gun purchase, which was illegal according to Wright's status, led Farrell to wonder if his assessment of Wright's appearance at this meeting might have been in error.

According to Farrell, he and Wright had a long conversation during which he found out that Wright had been in the Tunkhannock area of Wyoming County on November 1. Wright had been working there and could substantiate his time. Wright told him that he had come back to Scranton with a fellow Vector employee. Wright also told Farrell that he had been dating a woman (something Farrell did not know), and he gave Farrell her name.[18] Farrell told Wright that he was conducting an investigation into the murders of Freach and Keen and that he was questioning Wright to find out if he was involved. Farrell subsequently checked out

Wright's alibi by talking to the other Vector employee who, according to Wright, was with him on November 1. This man acknowledged that Wright's story was true. Farrell also went to the home of the woman Wright had named as his "girlfriend." While Farrell was speaking with her, Wright telephoned her and spoke with her in Farrell's presence. After talking with him, the woman gave the phone to Farrell, and he spoke briefly with Wright, who was "upset" that Farrell had contacted her—upset to the point that Farrell had to tell Wright to calm down and that he would talk to him at a later date.[19]

Soon after, Wright's cool collapsed totally, and he fled. Agent Farrell went to Wright's apartment on November 19, prompted by a telephone call earlier in the day from Wright's counselor at Farview.[20] According to Farrell, the counselor had phoned Farrell to relay the information that Wright's immediate supervisor in the Vector control program had called to tell him that Wright had "taken off."[21] Farrell and Parole Agent Frank Walsh contacted Wright's roommate. Meeting with the young man at his place of employment, a shoe store on Penn Avenue in Scranton, the roommate acknowledged that Wright had indeed left. Farrell and Walsh then went to Wright's apartment to check it out. Finding that Wright was not there and seemingly had left without his personal belongings, Farrell contacted his superiors in Harrisburg and received authorization from them to issue a Wanted for Parole Violation Teletype. Farrell then went to the Scranton Police Department to alert them to the situation. It was then, November 19, 1973, that Scranton Police Department issued the Wanted Teletype. Wright's flight gave police their first major break in solving the murders of Paul Freach and Edmund Keen. Farrell and other law enforcement officers interpreted Wright's action as indicative that he had something to do with the murders.[22] Flight, under Pennsylvania law at the time, could be used as evidence against a person charged with a criminal offense as consciousness of guilt.

It turned out that Wright had fled to Florida, but there he was quickly apprehended by Florida police and was returned to Pennsylvania on December 6 or 7 by extradition officers. He was confined to the State Correctional Institution at Graterford, located in Montgomery County, Pennsylvania, about thirty-one miles west of Philadelphia. Founded in 1929, Graterford is Pennsylvania's largest maximum-security prison. It is about one hundred miles south of Scranton. Owing to Scranton Police's interest in talking with Wright about the Freach and Keen murders as soon as possible, arrangements were made for Wright to be transferred to the Pennsylvania State Correctional Institution at Dallas, Pennsylvania, known more commonly among law enforcement personnel as "Chase," a medium-security facility located near Wilkes-Barre, in Luzerne County (about thirty-five minutes south of Scranton). Wright arrived there on December 13, 1973.

In addition to trying to find the murder site, the investigation had been heavily concentrated on finding the .25-caliber gun used in the killings of Paul and Edmund, the car or vehicle driven by the killer or killers, and anything else that could tie in with the murders. The police followed routine procedure in checking for the gun—recent purchases of guns similar to the type used to kill the boys. Police revealed to the public that they had the slugs from the .25-caliber automatic weapon that killed the boys, but they did not have any cartridge cases. As they searched the Minooka woods, they were hopeful that they might turn up some casings that would provide evidence of the location of the murders and pinpoint the murder weapon. The police knew that if a revolver had been used, the spent castings would have stayed in the gun. Police, according to a reporter, were quite convinced that the gun used to kill the boys was a semi-automatic, which ejects the empty shell casing after being fired.[23]

Even as they were now focused on William Wright police, suffering from lack of clues, were still uncertain if the murders had been committed by one person or more than one person. When questioned by reporters, police indicated that they were still heavily invested in the search for the middle-aged couple in the 1966 Chevrolet and the thinking that this car could lead to the murder or murderers. Thus, as late as one month after the discovery of the boys' bodies at the Falls Township dump, a December 8 *Scranton Times* article contained extensive details from the police about the Chevrolet, the model of the car (an Impala), and other specifics of this particular model, including the Impala symbol behind the front wheel and on both front fenders and the particular tail light arrangement (three lights arranged in horizontal line on each side, directly above the rear bumper). Following the "eyewitness" description from early on in the investigation, the police told the reporter that the car was rusted along the bumper panels on the right side and had oversized real bumper guards with rubber inserts.[24] But in spite of the continuing search for the car and numerous sightings, neither the car nor its occupants were ever found.

Meanwhile, William J. Wright, now the main suspect in the murders, was being held at Chase Correctional Institution in Dallas, Pennsylvania, for violation of parole. At the time of his arrest for the murders, *Scranton Times* reporter Robert Flanagan wrote that Wright had come to the attention of police in the Freach and Keen murders after the bodies of the boys were discovered on November 5. At that time, according to this reporter, Wright's name came up as Scranton Police detectives began investigating "known homosexuals, persons with prior records and persons who had purchased a .25 caliber pistol or ammunition for such a weapon."[25] Wright had been brought in for questioning by police detectives at this point in the investigation—just one of several persons of interest that were being checked out in a process designed to eliminate suspects. Wright, who had an alibi for the day of the murders, was not regarded as a "prime suspect" though. All this changed when he fled to Florida.

After Wright was returned to the Scranton area, he continued to deny involvement in the case, and although police became increasingly convinced that he was the murderer, they still did not have any physical evidence against him that connected him to the crimes. Police were willing to accept any help in the case they could find and continued to check countless tips—all to no avail. In addition to the crystal ball evidence mentioned earlier, they accepted what might be considered other fairly extreme offers of assistance, including one offered by the Reverend Walker Wescott, a parapsychologist psychic scientist and evangelist from Brooklyn, New York, who came to Scranton with his wife to review the case and assist in solving the murders.[26] Although police discounted Wescott's assistance, he would later claim that he did provide police with "much helpful information."[27] Nothing came of these avenues of investigation, and more and more the police zeroed in on William Wright as the right person. According to reporters who were covering the case, police acknowledged that in Wright they had a clever person with a high IQ and a history of violence, which contradicted his appearance as a calm, meek person.

Meanwhile, Wright, held at Chase, was continually interviewed by Pennsylvania state and local police. On December 18, 1973, he confessed to the murders of Paul Freach and Edmund Keen during questioning by Pennsylvania State Police Trooper William Koscinski and Scranton Police Detective Frank Glynn. His confession was duly recorded by police officers that day and presented later at his preliminary hearing in Scranton and at his trial in September 1974.[28]

In his confession to the dual murders, Wright said that there had been no truth in the story about the couple in the blue and white Chevrolet—that, in fact, he had acted alone. He said he had worked at his job all day, and after he had dropped his coworker off at a local tavern, he went home. He then called his girlfriend, but she was not interested in seeing him. He said he had come home that day sometime after 3:30 p.m. After being rejected by his girlfriend, he took the yellow Vector van and went "driving around." Eventually he came to the deserted area off Cedar Avenue in Minooka—a former mine fire dump (located adjacent to Cedar Avenue and west of where the boys lived).[29] He went there to see if it needed any poison and to shoot rats, which was part of his work with Vector. He denied having seen the boys prior to this or at any time before November 1, although his apartment was located near the school the boys attended, and the mine fire dump was an area he covered for Vector. He told police that his first sight of the boys was as they walked up to this area on their way home. They were alone. Wright readily admitted to murdering the boys at the mine fire site after having forced them at gunpoint into the back of the van. He denied having beaten them, but he did admit, somewhat reluctantly, to having sexually molested them before he shot them. He refused to describe his acts of molestation to the officers. Then he mentioned an incredible fact that was not public knowledge: a Scranton Police officer who Wright later said was off duty, stopped at the van, presumably to inquire what Wright was doing on the site at that time of day. While this exchange was occurring, Wright said, the boys were still alive inside the back of the van. Wright killed the boys, according to this statement, less than five minutes after the policeman left. By this disclosure of the policeman at the scene and in keeping with his later defense and characteristic of his makeup, Wright attempted to lay fault on the policeman for failure to look into the van. What he said in essence was if the policeman had seen the boys in the van, they would not have been murdered. The truth is that all evidence points to the boys already being dead by that time.

Wright told the police that after murdering the boys he drove from the mine site looking for a place to dispose of the bodies. After driving around for some time, and as it was beginning to get dark, he came across the dumping area in Wyoming County where the boys' bodies were eventually found. Once he arrived at the dump site, his actions suggested calm, self-directed, and purposeful efforts to hide the evidence of his crimes and avoid discovery. To conceal the boys' bodies, he threw a rug he found at the dump over them. He threw a pair of eyeglasses, later identified as belonging to Edmund Keen, out of the van as he left the site along the exit road. He acknowledged throwing the boys' schoolbooks into the dump as well.

Wright's actions at the dump site begs the question: If Wright was so careful and calculative to take the bodies of the boys to such a desolate area of a dump many miles away from the boys' homes, bury them deeply as he had done, and cover them in a rug, then why was he so reckless in throwing the schoolbooks on top of the dump and discarding the eye glasses on the roadway near the dump in plain sight? It is almost as if Wright intentionally did this to leave a trace of the boys for someone to find.

Yet Wright did attempt to further cover up his crime. He told police that he cleaned and washed out the van. Although it is not clear from his statement, it appears he did this at the dump site. Then he returned to Scranton. He disposed of the murder weapon by throwing it under a bridge into what was identified as Roaring Brook Creek, a tributary of the

Lackawanna River, near the Elm Street overpass in Scranton. He said he had left the shells along with the gun's clip there as well. He disposed of some other shells that he had in his apartment by throwing them into the rubbish the next day. The one mistake Wright made—one that turned out to be most grievous for him—was throwing the boys' schoolbooks onto the dump, in plain sight. Later found by Mr. McNamara, the camper, these books provided the key to police finding the missing boys' bodies, beginning the intense search for the murderer.

With the exception of the schoolbooks and the glasses, Wright's account of his actions at the dump suggests that he acted with perfect control of his emotions and with thoughts of covering up his murders. Wright even went to the Viewmont Mall outside Scranton shortly after disposing the bodies to withdraw money from a bank account he had at Northeastern Bank in order to purchase some clean clothes. Moreover, while at the mall he ran into a guard he knew from Farview, and they talked briefly. He then returned to his apartment.

During his confession, from time to time, Wright seemed intent on explaining to the policemen questioning him that he needed help—presumably psychiatric help. He related that sometimes he was able to get control of his actions—as in the hitchhiker episode—and sometimes not. He said he had hoped he would be found out after this incident so he could be stopped from doing it to others. He seemed to believe that by confessing he would receive treatment for his actions—actions that his account suggests were those of someone who possessed a logical, if diabolically controlled, mind; calm emotional demeanor; and a desire for self-preservation.

Reporters covering the murders noted on December 19 there had been "strong indications" that a "charge of murder may be lodged against a man already in custody" and that a "meeting of law enforcement officers, which had been in progress since early morning broke up." "Newsmen," reports indicated, "were told to remain at the hotel [Hilton]" and that District Attorney (DA) Paul Mazzoni "would return there to make any statement he might have regarding the case."[30] At the time of the announcement by DA Mazzoni, reporters knew an interrogation of Wright had been ongoing from the time of his return to the region. During this period reports had been circulated that the Scranton Police were conducting searches with metal detectors of the Lackawanna River near the Elm Street Bridge in South Scranton, searches that suggested to reporters that Wright might have told police he got rid of the murder weapon in that area. All in all, reporters noticed a stepup in activity around Scranton Police headquarters, including meetings with State Police and city officials, suggesting that something was up. In his report in the *Scranton Times* dated December 19, Robert Flanagan asserted, "Some newsmen had known that Wright was in custody and [that] he had become the real suspect . . . that word about his possible involvement in the case was leaking out."[31] Intensification of activity in and around city offices, such as a reported late-night meeting held with Mayor Eugene J. Peters and Public Safety Director Anthony Batsavage; Police Chief John McCrone; Detective Captain Frank Karam; Detectives Thomas Baggott and Frank Glynn; Dr. Richard Huber, director of public health; and Acting Public Works Director James B. McNulty gave support to such speculation. According to Flanagan, Mayor Peters announced after this meeting that "he had also been in contact . . . with D.A. Mazzoni and [Peters] confirmed that some action was likely, but . . . requested that the man in custody not be identified," although this news account noted that the man in custody was known to newsmen and went on not only to identify Wright but to include some details on his previous criminal history and more recent activities.[32]

Both DA Mazzoni and Mayor Peters were concerned at this time that premature publicity about Wright might endanger the case. In accord with this concern, the December 19 news account in the *Scranton Times* carried Mayor Peters's statement that the "police had a suspect in custody and that a charge of murder might be made today [the nineteenth]"—WDAU, Channel 22, a local television station, identified Wright as the suspect in its 11 p.m. news program.[33] News reporters believed that the meetings being held were for the purpose of bringing all law enforcement together to tie up the case they had against Wright—a view that was subsequently substantiated by people involved with the investigation. It was clear from later comments made by the mayor and others that the case was close to being resolved—especially so when the mayor requested that the press "note his thanks to all of the police agencies involved for their full cooperation in the many facets of the investigation."[34] Indeed, the next day, December 20, newspapers reported that Wright was charged in the murders of Paul Freach and Edmund Keen.

William J. Wright was formally charged and arraigned on Wednesday night, December 19, with two counts of murder, two counts of kidnapping, and two counts of involuntary deviate sexual intercourse at a hearing before District Magistrate Joseph Eiden. The news coverage reported that Wright, "bespectacled, crew-cut, . . . listened with bowed head and manacled hands as the charges were read."[35] Security was, according to news reports, "extremely tight."[36] The scene outside of Magistrate Eiden's office was filled with police officers and several hundred spectators who stood on snow-covered sidewalks to catch a glimpse of the accused murderer. Wright emerged from the police car dressed in "wine-colored" prison garb and a "brown corduroy prison coat," his hands and legs shackled.[37] He was escorted by two plainclothes detectives and rushed into the court. Inside, he sat quietly with his head down and his hands folded. When told to stand before the magistrate, he did so silently and heard Magistrate Joseph Eiden read his rights and the six charges against him.[38] Wright appeared confused and, according to reporters, looked as if he hadn't slept, staring ahead, emotionless, through black-rimmed glasses. His public defender lawyer, Attorney John Dunn, appeared several minutes after his arrival. When the hearing commenced, Magistrate Eiden asked Wright if he wanted a hearing, and Dunn responded that Wright was indeed requesting a preliminary hearing. The hearing was set for Friday, December 28, at 1:30 p.m. The arraignment concluded at 6:35, and Wright was returned to the Chase Correctional Institution.[39]

The Policeman's Story: As Narrated by DA Paul R. Mazzoni

In the course of attaining Wright's confession of the events of November 1, another story unfolded, the story of the police officer who came across the murder scene, as told by Wright himself. The police officer, shortly after Wright's arrest and his confession, had learned of his presence at the scene at the time of the murders.

It would have been better for this policeman if Wright had left the incident out of his statement. Now everyone in the Scranton Police Department, as well as other law enforcement agencies who worked on this case, knew the identity of this officer. In that statement, Wright relates a quarrel that ensued at the scene between this officer and himself. However, Wright failed to disclose what sparked the quarrel.

Wright, by bringing this policeman into the mix, created yet another victim. Wright claimed that at the time this officer arrived and spoke with him, the boys were alive inside the van. On learning of Wright placing him at the van before murdering the two boys, the officer began to blame himself for their deaths for not looking in the van.

I remember clearly Captain Frank Karam meeting with me at the DA's Office concerning this Scranton policeman and the guilt he was undergoing for his not looking in the van. He believed if he had done so, the boys' lives would have been saved.

Captain Karam and I together did all that we could to put this officer at ease. Our approach in comforting this good police officer was to convince him that we didn't believe Wright when he said the boys were alive at the time he arrived. Our reasoning, which we still hold today, was that the boys would have cried out for help or made a sound to be heard by an outsider. If a quarrel developed as Wright said there was, the boys would have known of another person outside the van besides Wright and would have sought that person's rescue.

Moreover, considering the person we knew Wright to be, his characteristic shirking of responsibility is clear. For instance, when he murdered his great-aunt in Pittsburgh, he claimed she was going to report him to the authorities, leaving him no choice but to kill her. Then, at the van on

November 1, he wanted everyone to believe a quarrel between him and the officer is what caused him to destroy the evidence by killing the boys.

In addition, Wright put much of the blame for his actions on his mental illness. During his trial for the murder of the two boys, Wright asked the judge to order tests and examinations on his brain to support his defense of an impulsive disorder that made him lose control of his actions, which his experts labeled a discontrol, or discontrolled, syndrome. The judge denied his request.

As for the policeman, Wright implied that, had there not been this quarrel, the boys would have been released. In order to lend credence to the supposed reason for the killing of the boys, Wright had to fabricate a quarrel that triggered this outcome. Wright was never able to identify the nature or subject of this impasse between the officer and himself. I related this to the police officer. We wanted him to believe that the boys' lives were already taken at the time he arrived at this van. Moreover, at the time there was no obvious cause for the policeman to have done a search or even looked into the van.[40]

I never saw the police officer again in or out of uniform. A tragedy in it's own right, he will carry the burden of this incident through the remainder of his life—this eternal, unfair, and self-imposed guilt for not looking in the van on November 1, 1973.

5

WHO IS WILLIAM J. WRIGHT?

William J. Wright—the thirty-six-year-old accused murderer of Paul Freach and Edmund Keen and former patient at Farview State Hospital for the Criminally Insane in Waymart, Pennsylvania, Wayne County—had, at the time of the murders, been on a work release program from Farview, working for Vector Control, a rodent control agency, and living in an apartment on Pittston Avenue in Scranton's south side. Later, following his arrest for the murders, police acknowledged that Wright had been a strong suspect from the onset of the murder investigation and was described by those close to the case as a "classic case of a ticking bomb getting himself lost in the bureaucracy of justice and being turned loose time after time on an unsuspecting public."[1] Nonetheless, there is some doubt that Wright's previous, not inconsiderable, criminal history and dangerous mental and emotional proclivities were well known to police and others with whom he was involved while he lived in Scranton following work release from the mental hospital.[2]

Born on August 13, 1937, Wright came from Collingdale, Pennsylvania, a small borough located in Delaware County outside of Philadelphia. Although records concerning him remain classified and unobtainable to the authors, newspaper accounts depict Wright as having had a troubled youth. He got into trouble with police as a teenager for theft and running away from home. His actions were serious enough for authorities to remove him from his home and send him to George Junior Republic Correctional School, a low-security juvenile facility located in Grove City, near Pittsburgh in Allegheny County.[3] In 1955, one year after being sent to the juvenile correctional facility, he fled.[4] That day, January 26, 1955, he murdered his great-aunt, Mrs. Evelyn Leonard Thomas, in her home in Pittsburgh.[5] Some time later he was arrested for the murder. Accounts vary as to Wright's age at the time of this murder, but given that his birth date was August 1937, he would be seventeen years old in January 1955 and would turn eighteen later in August of that year—one fact in a fateful chain of events that put him in Lackawanna County on a loosely monitored probation in 1973 and gave him the opportunity to murder again.

When questioned by police about his actions at the time of the 1955 murder, Wright was said to have "calmly" admitted killing Mrs. Thomas at her home. She had been bludgeoned to death. Wright told police he had run away from the juvenile facility and went to his great-aunt's home to ask her for money. Wright told authorities that he had never seen Mrs. Thomas prior to that day; he had only learned of her a few months before in a letter written him by his mother. When he left the juvenile facility he got her address from a telephone book and found his way to her home.[6] Instead of giving him money, Mrs. Thomas pleaded with him to return to the school. He refused to do this, and, according to his account, she started to call his family to find out why he was at her home. He said he feared she would call the police, became angry, and stopped her by beating her to death with a hammer—a hammer she had given him when he asked for something to remove a nail from his shoe. After killing her, he continued to hit her. He then ransacked the home, stole money, took bonds, and, in an effort to cover up his crime, set a pile of clothes afire to burn the house down.[7] According to authorities, at the time of the murder, Wright had been absent from the juvenile detention school for eight hours.

Prior to Wright's arrest, the Pittsburgh Police had come to a dead end in their investigation of Mrs. Thomas's murder and had no idea that the teen, who returned to George Junior Republic after the murder, might be involved. This all changed as a result of a tip given to Delaware County Police by Wright's father, Robert. When he and Wright's mother first learned of the murder of Mrs. Thomas, they noticed that it had happened on the same day their son William had run away from George Junior Republic School. Soon after, William was released from this facility and returned to his home. Wright's family noticed that he had some bonds that belonged to Mrs. Thomas. These details led Wright's parents to notify their local police in Delaware County. The seventeen-year-old Wright was brought to Pittsburgh for questioning where, as reported, he readily admitted to the murder.[8] He was arrested and charged with Mrs. Thomas's murder on March 5, 1955. A *Pittsburgh Post Gazette* reporter writing about Wright provided some explanation for the murder. According to this report, Wright's act was the result of his learning the night before the murder that he was not going to be released from the juvenile facility. The next day, January 25, he began pushing some boys around, and before the day was over he would leave the facility and murder Mrs. Thomas.[9] Wright was described in one newspaper as a "baby-faced, bespectacled" young man; they also described him as a "brilliant" boy with an above-average IQ of 134.[10]

William Wright's behavior at this point was summarized by William D. Gladden, superintendent of George Junior Republic in March of 1955 for the *Pittsburgh Post Gazette*. According to Superintendent Gladden, "Billy failed to complete the ninth grade. He ran away from home and school. He stole money from an employer . . . in Collingdale and was sentenced to George Junior."[11] Continuing, Mr. Gladden told reporters that at the juvenile school, Wright was placed in the ninth grade but did so well that he was moved ahead to the tenth grade immediately. He made the honor roll and was evaluated with a high IQ. Describing Wright as "very extroverted, but in a nervous way," the superintendent said it was his belief that Wright "wanted attention." Gladden also noted that Wright experienced emotional "peaks and valleys" but never attacked anyone.[12] Gladden said Wright was not released because conditions at his family's home were not helping him. When told that he was not going to be released, Mr. Gladden said Wright showed no anger initially but gradually, as the reality settled in, began lashing out. At this point Wright ran away from the facility and arranged for transportation to Pittsburgh.

Gladden summed up his statement to reporters by saying William's crime came as a complete surprise to him and that he had "no feeling . . . that this would happen."[13]

Wright's relatively young age at the time of the murder of Mrs. Thomas played to his advantage. On June 16, he was sentenced in criminal court in Pittsburgh for eight to twenty years, a surprisingly light sentence for such a brutal murder. According to the *Pittsburgh Post Gazette*, Judge J. Frank Graff, who sentenced the youthful murderer, said that he had little doubt that this sentence was necessary in view of the "shocking and horrible crime . . . [that Wright gave his victim] five different blows [that] would have killed [her]—in addition to the other blows that were struck." The judge continued by saying that this murder was in the first degree and that the punishment called for was necessary "in light of the interests of society and preventing like crimes from being committed."[14]

Wright went on to serve the minimum sentence of eight years in a Pennsylvania state correctional facility and was released on parole on March 9, 1963, at the age of twenty-five.[15] This date is important, since if he had been given a longer sentence or the maximum, he would have still been in prison as late as 1975 and, therefore, would have not been in Lackawanna County or had the opportunity to murder Paul Freach and Edmund Keen in 1973.

An interesting aspect of Wright's history—one to which he himself attached a good deal of importance in his later defense in the Freach and Keen murders—was that, in 1956, while in prison for the murder of Mrs. Thomas, he received a psychiatric examination that he claimed revealed an unnamed brain disorder. Prison authorities, however, in Wright's view, failed to provide him with the results of this study, and he never received any treatment for a mental problem or problems while incarcerated. Once again Wright had attempted to lay fault on others for his actions. In a later comment about his mental state, he would return to this matter, asserting that if he had received treatment, he might not have committed future acts of violence. According to one report, based on an interview with Wright at the time of the Freach and Keen case, Wright felt that, as a result of the failure of the criminal justice system to provide him the necessary treatment for his "brain disorder," he was also a "victim"; and the state, having failed him, had been responsible for "ruining his life."[16] Wright's continued focus on himself and his tendency to place blame for his actions onto someone else was a pattern. Nowhere in any of his recorded statements, prior to or after 1973, does he accept any responsibility for his actions or remorse for those he harmed. Rather, his actions point to a psychopathic personality: someone who acted to get what he wanted when he wanted it. Wright was a person who, when confronted with his crimes, confessed and, while doing so, recited his crimes to authorities with no evidence of human reaction or acceptance of culpability. As in the murder of his great-aunt, Wright blamed someone else for his killing of Paul Freach and Edmund Keen—the policeman who came across the scene.

In both cases—the murder of Mrs. Thomas and the murders of the two boys from Minooka—his real motivation for murdering may have been a simple effort at covering up his crimes. He simply did not want to be caught. Regardless of whether the Freach and Keen boys were still alive at the time the policeman stopped, Wright's description of the crime suggests that as soon as he forced them into the van at gunpoint, he began molesting them. Given his reluctance at admitting to acts of sexual deviance, as is clear in his confession to the killings, this type of aggression would motivate him to hide his actions. Killing his victims so that they would be unable to identify him and disclose what had happened would appear to be in accord with this effort—as would his later effort at hiding the bodies of the murdered boys.[17] Wright's earlier release of the hitchhiker he held at gunpoint on Interstate 81, an act that saved that young man's life, might have been because this event took place in daylight on the side of a busy interstate highway. Any number of passing motorists could have witnessed Wright holding a gun to Nasser's head and been able to identify Wright. Wright's claim that he "let him go" was not due to any kindness on his part, even though he might have wanted to convince authorities otherwise. Wright's release of the hitchhiker would later add to the difficulty of convincing the court of his defense of discontrol syndrome in the Freach and Keen case.

In 1963, still on parole for Mrs. Thomas's murder, Wright was living with some family members. He was not considered mentally ill by the courts at this time. Nine months following his release from prison, Wright attended a New Year's Eve party in his hometown of Collingdale. Accounts vary about this incident. News reports of this case say that Wright met a couple at the party who had an eleven- or twelve-year-old girl at their home babysitting their three-year-old child. However, the trial testimony states this differently. According to this record, the couple's daughter was the babysitter.[18] In any case, Wright noticed that at first the father was frequently checking on the babysitter by phone, but as the evening progressed, he checked less often. Taking this opportunity, the now twenty-six-year-old Wright left the party and went to the couple's home. Apparently he gained entrance with little difficulty and found the babysitter asleep in bed with the three-year-old. Wright then attempted to rape the babysitter and in the process caused her some severe injuries. He stopped, and without inflicting further harm to either her or the baby, he fled the scene and went to his home.[19] The girl, however, knew Wright and identified him as her attacker to the police. He was arrested soon after, still wearing the bloodstained clothes he had on during the attack. This crime, which police and others maintained was "attempted rape," resulted in the Delaware County Court ordering that Wright undergo psychiatric testing to determine his sanity. Actual records of the results of this testing are not available, but a summation of them was provided at the Freach and Keen trial. According to testimony at the trial, the examination revealed the following findings: Wright was upset by people (family members, neighbors, anyone) arguing even as a youngster, and this was a reason why he often ran away from home; Wright had uncontrollable urges to sexually molest children; Wright had uncontrollable urges to murder anyone who irritated him; and Wright had spells of depression and euphoria.[20] As a result of this mental evaluation, on January 28, 1964, the Delaware County Court ordered Wright be sent to Farview State Hospital for the Criminally Insane.

Wright, now in his twenty-seventh year, was once more confined.[21] This time he was officially a "patient," at Farview State Hospital for the

Criminally Insane, a Pennsylvania state mental hospital that was then classified as a "therapeutic institution for the criminally insane run by the Pennsylvania Department of Welfare." This facility was built in the early years of the twentieth century. At the time of the laying of the cornerstone on July 24, 1909, Dr. Charles G. Wagner, superintendent of the State Hospital for the Insane at Binghamton, New York, described the hospital's establishment by saying, "If there were places of this kind available, there would be no longer any excuse for the deplorable practice of placing the insane even temporarily in common jails where, often, regardless of sex or mental disturbance they are grossly ill-treated. . . . Concentrated effort on behalf of the individual patient will be the watchword of the future. . . . [All the facilities here will] help banish the idea of prison bars and . . . make an environment that tends to aid the recovery of the patient."[22]

Farview was designed as a maximum-security hospital for the treatment of those determined to be "criminally insane." By the 1970s the hospital was benefitting from more modern efforts at the treatment of mental illness, including the use of medication to control some mental problems and behaviors. It had also by this period earned a certain local reputation as a less-than-secure facility. Communities in its area complained at the laxness of its staff and the fact that its patient trustees were rumored to have been seen walking the streets of Carbondale and Honesdale, the two largest communities near the hospital, without guards. There were also whispered stories of abuse of patients by overzealous and even brutal guards. Passersby to the region driving on Route 6 in Wayne County near the rural town of Waymart were often struck with the vision of Farview as a large, somewhat foreboding three-story brick structure, representative of early twentieth-century institutional construction design, set on the edge of a beautiful, idyllic mountainous area. For people in the region, it was a major employer. Numerous local medical and mental health professionals, staff, guards, and the like worked there. Locals, in general, usually kept their distance from the institution; it was rumored to be the home of some of the most notorious murderers in the state. In the mid-1970s, the hospital was the subject of a major scandal, exposed as a result of the investigative reporting of *Philadelphia Inquirer* reporters Acel Moore and Wendell Rawls Jr. "The Farview Findings," was a three-month investigation by the two newsmen, printed in June and July 1976. The findings exposed the facility for inhumane treatment by guards and others of patients and resulted in a massive, long-going formal investigation and ultimately the creation of a special grand jury and the appointment of a special prosecutor.[23]

At Farview, Wright, according to some later testimony, appeared to have some initial difficulty adjusting to his confinement but soon became, in the words of some who knew him during this period, somewhat of a "cock-of-the-walk," someone who knew how to use the system to his advantage.

Sometime fairly early in his stay at Farview, Wright, seemingly out of the blue while being interviewed by psychiatrists or psychologists, calmly revealed that he had committed another murder—a murder that no one had attributed to him. According to later testimony from Farview authorities, Wright confessed to them that on February 10, 1954, one year before the murder of Mrs. Thomas on January 26, 1955, while home on a furlough from the George Junior Republic facility, he had murdered a four-year-old child in Collingdale by shoving a plastic gun down his throat. At the time of the death, the police in Delaware County had thought that the child had accidently fallen on the gun with the result that the plastic barrel fractured his larynx and ripped his trachea. Wright's confession presented authorities with a dilemma: Ten years after the child's death, someone now had confessed to the murder of the little boy. Authorities had a confession to a killing that they had long since accepted as an accident, but it came from a person who had been judged insane, and, to add to the problem, the confession was given by a person who had not received any of the Constitutional warnings of his rights. The doctrine of doctor-patient privacy also applied, given the circumstance of Wright's confession. In "explaining" what had led to this brutal murder, Wright told his interviewer that the child had pointed the gun at him and repeatedly yelled, "Bang, bang." This had annoyed Wright to the point that he grabbed the toy pistol and jammed it down the boy's throat. He then walked away, leaving the choking child to die.[24]

In spite of the legal questions involved with Wright's confession to murdering the little boy, Delaware county officials did try to bring charges against him but eventually decided that they did not have a case sufficient to hold up in court. Wright, who had been taken to Delaware County, questioned, and held in this matter, was returned to Farview, where he would continue to be treated for criminal insanity. According to reports, Delaware County authorities thought at the time that, knowing the state had filed a parole detainer against Wright for the Pittsburgh murder of Mrs. Thomas, Wright would be kept in custody at least until he had served his maximum term of twenty years (until 1975).[25] This was not to be the case. Once again, Wright was in a position to receive advantage at the hands of the criminal justice system in Pennsylvania.

Eight years after Wright was sentenced to Farview, authorities there determined that he was sufficiently sane to bring to trial—in this case for the 1963 attempted rape charge and for the earlier 1954 murder charge of the child. However, once again luck was on his side and, owing to the fact that Wright had now served a term of eight years at Farview, Delaware County law enforcement officials decided that it was useless to bring him to trial on the attempted rape charge. They reasoned that, even if he were convicted, the sentence would be retroactive, and the maximum term had already been served. The attempted rape charge from 1963 was dropped. As for the child's horrific murder, charges were similarly dropped. In this case, Delaware authorities determined that the circumstances related to Wright's "confession" of this murder would never hold up in court. One wonders if Wright was just lucky or if he knew the law and its application as related to his eight years served and the Constitutional issues involving his rights. Did he seemingly "confess" to the little boy's murder as he had in order to shield himself from any possible attempt to bring him to justice for the crime? We will never know the truth about this, but the coldly calculating nature of this supposed highly intelligent person suggests that he not only understood the law involved in these matters but also knew how to use it to his advantage.

As to the parole detainer against Wright, Farview officials, in spite of describing Wright as sly and cunning, did not honor this restriction against Wright. According to reports, he became a trustee and was housed in a separate building for such patients on the grounds of the hospital. He became one of those inmates who as a trustee was permitted fairly free use of the facility and from time to time was able to travel, presumably always accompanied with staff, to towns near Farview for services and provisions. At Farview he was involved in a number of vocational and recreational training programs, including one involving rodent control that provided the background for him to later work for the Vector rodent control agency and live in the Scranton community.[26]

Wright was freed from Farview to work in the Alpha House program on June 15, 1973—four and a half months before the murders of Paul Freach and Edmund Keen. William Wright was thought by those in charge of him at Farview to be ready for release. They believed he would benefit from work release and a transition into a community setting. He remained somewhat connected to the hospital by way of various weekly meetings with hospital social workers, with the option of phoning if he needed to connect for a particular reason. This arrangement reveals that Wright was more on his own than connected to the hospital and was excused from more personal contact with the hospital because he had a busy work schedule and found it hard to return for meetings with counselors or staff. It is suggested by these facts that the decision to place him under supervision by the Pennsylvania Parole Board was due primarily to one person, Paul Farrell, and was not part of any official procedure or arrangement prior to his release. These circumstances were such that William Wright was in a situation where he was only loosely supervised by Farview.

During the December 12 day of Wright's trial for the murders of the Freach and Keen boys, a number of witnesses were called that shed further light on Wright and his days at Farview. Much of this testimony was geared toward disproving the defense position that Wright suffered from a type of uncontrollable behavior. But this testimony also reveals the type of person Wright was at Farview and suggests reasons the administrative and professional staff of Farview were inclined to transition Wright to a level where he would be considered for work release into the community. A therapy activity worker at Farview who worked with outpatients at the hospital and who had been working in that capacity there for about sixteen years testified for the prosecution and told the court that he had worked with Wright when Wright was assigned to occupational therapy. He said that he worked with Wright on a daily basis in the period from 1964 to 1968. Wright was assigned to the craft shop at the hospital where he worked for about five hours a day, five days a week, according to the therapist. He described Wright as very good at craftwork and "very talented." When asked by the prosecution the kind of individual Wright seemed to be, he said Wright—whom he referred to as "Billy"—"seemed to be the type of person that was well-planned . . . always had his facilities [sic, faculties] . . . [and] was shrewd."[27] When asked to elaborate on his use of the word "shrewd," he said that he had worked with fifteen to seventeen inmates in his shop and over time got to know all of them quite well. Wright, according to his testimony, was always assisting others and always in front "running everything." The therapy activity worker testified that he couldn't say Wright was manipulative but indicated Wright used every advantage he could get, was something of a "teacher's pet," and was "constantly with us."[28] During the time he worked in this shop, according to this witness, Wright never exhibited any "uncontrollable rage" or any other kind of violent or antisocial behavior but, rather, "he treated everybody well" and had a level temperament without changes in disposition and never gave the therapist any trouble.[29]

However, on cross-examination, this witness testified he had not heard any reports of Wright's behavior in general at the facility but that he had at one time known that Wright was removed from the occupational therapy shop and transferred to the D ward—a disciplinary ward. Asked if he knew why Wright had been moved to D ward, he said that he believed it was because of a spoon. It was his understanding that Wright was found in possession of a spoon—spoons were collected as patients returned from dinner. Wright had told the therapy worker that he had a missing spoon and turned it in to security. He did not, he said, know the exact nature of the problem, but Wright had asked him to intercede for him. The witness said he told Wright he could not do this, as this was a "security problem" and out of his jurisdiction.[30] Later Wright was returned to his shop. When asked if he had any thoughts about this situation and the discipline Wright received, the therapist said he thought Wright had tried to present himself well while he was in A ward—a low security area—and the spoon had provided him an opportunity to prove himself trustworthy. The therapy worker said he thought Wright had taken it with the intention of turning it back in to security so security would see he was indeed trustworthy, but it did not work out well for him. According to him, the spoon incident was a factor in Wright's being removed to the D ward. Other than that, this witness had no knowledge of why Wright was removed to the more secure ward.[31] Asked if he had ever heard any other rumors about Wright involving uncontrolled behavior, he said he had not.

Two other employees of Farview also provided information during Wright's trial about their involvement with him while he was at the hospital. One had been employed at Farview for three years, from 1968 to 1971, in the maintenance and Vector Control area of the facility. Here, he said, he had very near daily contact with Wright. He, like the therapy worker, testified that during this period of time Wright exhibited no unusual behavior, was "normal," and did not show any uncontrollable rages or aggressive physical or sexual attributes.[32] A second person, identified as a mechanic employed by the hospital for some fourteen years, testified that for about a month in October of 1971, Wright worked in the auto shop with duties involving washing cars and changing tires. According to him, Wright was as normal as any other person and did not display any rage or passion, never causing any difficulty in the shop, and was a "better than average individual in his employe [sic]."[33]

Paul Farrell, who was district supervisor of probation and parole of Northeastern Pennsylvania, was in charge of the Lackawanna County Adult Probation and Parole Office, which covered Wright's parole in Scranton. Farrell testified later at the Freach and Keen murder trial about Wright and how it was that he was released from Farview in May or June of 1973 to live and work in the greater Scranton community.[34] Asked as to how long he had known Wright, Mr. Farrell said that he came in contact with him in 1967. He had, however, only learned of his release from Farview in July 1973. According to Farrell, at the time of his release, Wright had been participating in the Alpha House graduated release program, which had been initiated by the social work staff at Farview with presumably the support of the authorities of the hospital. Farrell was uncertain of the exact date of Wright's release, testifying that it was sometime in late May or early June. According to Farrell, at first Wright had been coming into Scranton to work on a daily basis but returned each night to Farview. Then, said Farrell, Farview authorities released him from the obligation to return after work to the hospital and permitted him to live in Scranton. He could return to Farview whenever he wished or contact advisors or counselors there any time. Although the Pennsylvania Parole Office had carried Wright since the early sixties, Farrell said that his office had not been "actively engaged in the supervision" of Wright, because he was committed to Farview by the court. Farrell said that his office was "monitoring the progress of this case to determine when or if he [Wright] would become available to this agency again." According to Farrell, in the meantime parole made "routine contacts with the hospital."[35] In 1972, around the time that the Alpha program was created, it was Farrell's belief that Wright's original commitment to Farview (for the attempted rape in Collingdale) was terminated nol. pros. (will not prosecute). As a result, Delaware County turned Wright over to Farrell at Parole and Probation.

At this point, Farrell said, the Executive Board of the Pennsylvania Board of Probation and Parole "took action to return him to the State Correctional Institution" and to ask for an updated psychiatric evaluation "to determine whether or not he should remain confined in the penal system or should be allowed to return to the streets at that point." Farrell recalled that he had been contacted by the Social Work Department at Farview, which told him "of the formalization of this new program." Farview and its social work area had requested that Wright be "allowed to continue in this program as opposed to being brought back to the State Correctional Institution at that time." As a result, Parole and Probation rescinded the original action and took the action that, "in effect, said, 'we have no objection to the participation of Mr. Wright in this program, which would be a graduated release program to the community.'"[36] About this time, Farrell believed Farview started the Alpha program, "with phase one an intensive counseling type of thing." Farrell said that the agent from Parole and Probation continued to go to the hospital but made "no personal contacts with Mr. Wright."[37]

In the early stages of the Alpha program, Farrell said that Parole and Probation made contacts at Farview with various staff persons to "determine progress and in January 1973, Mr. Wright was still in the initial phase of that program."[38] The next time that agents from Probation and Parole went to Farview was in March 1973, and, according to Farrell, Wright had obtained employment with Vector Control, a rodent-control agency that serviced a number of regions in and around Scranton and neighboring counties. At this point Wright was still at Farview, but authorities there told Parole and Probation that Wright was going to leave Farview to "go to the community as a worker." Even so, he would still remain "on the active counseling of the hospital." Farrell said Parole and Probation "didn't interfere at that point."[39]

The Northeastern Pennsylvania Vector Control Association, Wright's employer, was identified at Wright's trial as a "federation of six local rodent-fighting agencies . . . [that included] the Scranton unit . . . supervised by Dr. Richard Huber, the city's health officer."[40] The program, managed by the central association, was financed by federal and state funds, with each unit's supervisor serving as a director.[41] The main headquarters of the association was in Dupont, Pennsylvania, a community a few miles south of Scranton. The Scranton unit of Vector had an office at the Scranton Municipal Building, or city hall, a floor above police headquarters. At the time that Wright was at Vector, according to newspaper accounts, he was paid $6,500 a year and was one of forty employees in the rodent program.

In 1974, the executive director of the program and "the person who accepted Wright's referral for employment from the Bureau of Employment Security," provided a reporter with details as to Wright's work in the program.[42] Although it seems fair to say that some people in the rodent control program and some city officials knew Wright's background, it is very unlikely that the general public in the Scranton area knew anything about Wright when, as writer Timothy Thomas said, "he was turned loose in their midst."[43] Even the local parole officer testified that he had no knowledge of Wright's release until he learned of it "by accident" and when he provided supervision without any real official authorization. Living on his own, Wright functioned well in the Vector program and living in the Scranton community. He was given a "special" police badge and according to later information was deputized as a special patrolman for Vector in order to have the authority to police certain illegal dumping areas in Scranton. Wright's job provided him with sufficient money as well as the use of a van, a van that was supposedly owned by the city of Scranton. Wright was able to avail himself of a gun, a used .25-caliber pistol that he attained illegally. His superior at Vector found out about the gun and was said to have warned Wright to get rid of it, but Wright paid no attention. It is said that a number of other persons with whom Wright had contact knew he had a gun and, according to some who had no knowledge of his history, accepted Wright's explanation that he felt that it was necessary in the work that he did for Vector to shoot rodents in addition to poisoning them.

At the time of the Freach and Keen murders, Vector had six vans and three cars, including the van that Wright was said to have used in the murders. Federal guidelines, according to the executive director, required that Vector employ "disadvantaged" persons, and in an effort to do so, their hiring was done through the Bureau of Employment Security (BES), which included hiring employees referred through the Pennsylvania Department of Welfare. Wright had taken courses in rodent control at Farview, and Farview staff referred Wright to Vector with the cooperation of the BES. According to one newspaper account of Vector's executive director's testimony, the director knew William Wright's history of murder and other violent crimes when Wright applied for the position. It was his understanding that, at the time Wright was hired by Vector, the "Farview staff had cleared him for freedom and the Welfare Department and the BES both vouched for his skills and reliability."[44] Hired in March 1973, Wright first served Vector in the capacity of trainee but in September was promoted to the level of Vector controller number one. This was his status at the time of the murders and at the time he reported off sick following the murders, fleeing to Florida. This account said that, according to the executive director, Wright was the only worker hired with a history of "criminal insanity."[45]

Wright's job with Vector was to "bait any and all complaints," meaning that his job required that he respond to any complaints, surveyed the property, determined the cause of the problem, and then baited it.[46] In addition, Vector cleaned up properties where there was garbage and such not taken care of by city collection agencies. At the end of October 1973, Wright was sent to deal with two serious rodent problems in Towanda, in Bradford County, and Dushore, in Sullivan County, two small picturesque communities located sixty-three and fifty-six miles, respectively, northwest of Scranton. On November 1, Wright was in Towanda and Dushore taking care of these problems. He was using a yellow Ford van, the newer of two vans Vector used in their work. A supervisor and another worker went with Wright. On the day of the murder, Wright and the others completed their work, and, driving the yellow van, Wright and a coworker returned to Scranton after dropping the supervisor off at his home in Tunkhannock—a drive that usually took between thirty and thirty-five minutes, depending on traffic, according to the supervisor.

While employed at Vector, Wright worked out of the Public Health Office in Scranton's city hall. His job took him in and out of city hall, frequently going from the Vector office to the Vector van, which, according to reports, he often parked in an alley behind the municipal building. As a result, Wright became a familiar person in and around city hall, someone that many persons, including police officers and city employees who worked in the building, knew or at least recognized. He became even better known, in fact, by the odd twist of fate mentioned previously, when Wright was involved in helping police apprehend a prisoner attempting to flee. As the story goes, Wright, on his own, helped police apprehend this person. For his assist he was awarded a citation and, by some accounts, a

Scranton Police badge, which Wright was said to have carried with him always. Might this badge, if it existed, be something that Wright had used on November 1 to encourage Paul Freach and Edmund Keen to believe that he was someone either connected to the police or a police officer and, therefore, someone who could be trusted? Unfortunately we will never know, and nothing further was said about the badge after Wright was arrested for the murders.

After it was revealed that Wright had been employed by Vector, that agency came under a great deal of criticism, and its executive director, speaking with *Scranton Times* reporter Joseph Flannery in January 1974, made every effort to provide details about the agency and its good record, in spite of Wright's hire. Asked about Wright's supposed police badge, the Vector director asserted that if Vector employees required police powers, "they must obtain them from the governmental unit which operates them."[47] In other words, if Wright carried a Scranton Police badge, it had been issued by the city of Scranton—not by the Vector organization.[48]

Returning to the curious set of circumstances that had resulted in Wright being released from Farview in the first place and the nature of his relationship with the state parole board in Scranton, Paul Farrell clarified the situation during Wright's 1974 trial by saying that Farview never turned over actual control of Wright to the State Parole and Probation authorities. When Wright entered the Scranton community, Parole and Probation took on their "legal responsibility for him and we became actively involved in the supervision process . . . a dual type of supervision. [Wright] was still being counseled by a social worker from Farview but was living in the community."[49] This arrangement was not, in Farrell's view, "what we [Parole] had originally agreed to. We agreed to the plan; but we wanted to know when he would be out so that we could begin carrying his case actively."[50] This dual control arrangement of Wright had been set in place around August 1973. Farrell said that it was his view that the Alpha House program, "although not specifically stated . . . [was] a parole plan . . . he [Wright] was recommitted by our board to the Correctional Institution but allowed to continue here [under the

Alpha program]." Asked specifically if the Alpha House program was a program of the Pennsylvania Parole Board or a program of the Farview State Hospital, Farrell answered that it was a Farview State Hospital program, a type of parole program and not a part of the state parole program and not administered by the State Parole Board.

To clarify Wright's position as regards the parole agency, Farrell was asked to state Wright's exact designation vis-à-vis his agency. He responded that "statistically, he was classified as an unconvicted violator in a mental institution," committed to Farview by a court decree that was never terminated.[51] At the September 1974 trial of Wright, there was some discussion as to whether or not that decree had ever been terminated and, if it had not, why state probation was involved with Wright. According to Wright's defense lawyer, Attorney John Dunn, because of Farview's ongoing jurisdiction over Wright, the Pennsylvania Parole Board should not have had any jurisdiction over Wright, and he should not have been released without returning to court.[52] Dunn, in questioning Mr. Farrell, had asked him about his contact with Wright prior to November 1, 1973, the date of the murder of Paul Freach and Edmund Keen. Farrell acknowledged that he had had contact with Wright and that Wright had objected to him becoming involved in the supervision of his case. Asked why Wright had expressed this position, Farrell said that Wright told him he felt he "had been making progress with the people at Farview and he didn't see any reason for our [the Pennsylvania Parole Board] becoming involved." Wright also warned Farrell that one of the reasons he did not want to have the parole board exercise any control over him was because he could not guarantee what he might do if they maintained this control over him. Farrell went on to say that, Wright's views notwithstanding, Parole and Probation had been involved with him "all along."[53] This involvement included restrictions on Wright's travel (in August, September, and October of 1973), even though apparently this did not take into consideration trips Wright might make to Farview, as was part of his release plan. It also did not seemingly consider that Wright's work for Vector took him to a wide geographical sweep outside the city of Scranton, into Wyoming and other nearby counties, giving him some opportunity to learn about the region, including, as it turned out, the dumping area in Wyoming County where he disposed of the bodies of the boys he murdered on November 1, 1973.

How did local news after Wright's arrest cover his early release plan, and what was the public's understanding of it? *Scranton Times* reporter Joseph X. Flannery wrote in March of 1974 that his paper had learned that, following questioning for the murder of the young boy in Collingdale, Delaware County authorities understood that Wright would remain at Farview until further order of the court after having been found mentally ill in January 1964 in relation to his attempted rape of a Collingdale girl. The "until further order" part of the court's decision, says Flannery, was apparently violated when Wright was released from Farview in 1973. Flannery also reported that the Pennsylvania Board of Probation and Parole had filed a warrant with Farview, which in turn charged Wright with a violation of his parole. The Probation and Parole warrant required that he be kept at Farview until March 1975. Flannery informed his readers that no legal action could be taken in the case of the child's suspected murder for which Wright had confessed, given Wright's status as insane and the constitutionally inadequate nature of his confession. He went on to write that in February 1972, Dr. John P. Shovlin, superintendent of Farview (who was retired by 1974), "sent an unsolicited petition to Delaware County stating that Wright was able to participate in a trial and that he had the capacity to understand the charge against him and that he could cooperate with his counsel."[54] Nonetheless, continued Dr. Shovlin, Wright still had a "sociopathic personality disturbance" and "antisocial reaction with psychotic reaction."[55] According to this reporter, as a result of Dr. Shovlin's letter and evaluation of Wright, Wright was brought to Delaware County and charged with the 1954 murder of the child and the 1964 attempted rape of the eleven-year-old girl. It was at this turn that Delaware County determined they could not go forward with either case and that the judge's order stood since Wright was under a parole warrant until 1975. Then, continued Flannery, without notice to Delaware County, in 1973, Wright was released on the Alpha program, which placed him in the Scranton community and afforded him the opportunity to murder Paul Freach and Edmund Keen a few months after his release.

The Alpha House program, which ultimately provided Wright a route to freedom from the confines of the state hospital, is an area of particular continued interest and scrutiny. More than one person then and now has asked: How could it happen that a person with William Wright's history of crime and record for murder and violent behaviors be released from a high-level security mental hospital to live freely in a community?

Identified as a program run through the social work services at Farview, the Alpha House program began in the early 1970s and was approved by the highest administrative professionals of Farview State Hospital, from the superintendent on down through the psychiatric and psychological staff, who, according to those involved with the program, retained the authority of approval of all decisions made in relation to the program. The first director of Alpha House was a social worker at Farview who began work there in 1969 and worked there for a period of five and a half years. On the last day of Wright's trial in December 1974, DA Mazzoni read a statement from this supervisor to the court in which the supervisor said that he had supervised William Wright for a period of ten months and during this period had opportunity to observe and work with Wright, who became a candidate for the program upon recommendation of the hospital staff.[56] Wright was subsequently placed in the program about 1972. This supervisor said he observed Wright up until August 1973, when he [the supervisor] left Farview to pursue advanced graduate work. According to information from his testimony, Wright was given an option to stay at the hospital under the Alpha House program while he awaited job placement or to be "put out on the street under the supervision of the Parole Board."[57] Wright chose to stay at Farview but was still under the supervision of the parole board. According to testimony at Wright's trial in December 1974, this supervisor was "instrumental . . . in getting him [Wright] a job through the employment security office in Vector Control in the City of Scranton."[58] In this testimony, the social worker said that Wright had "some Vector Control experience while at Farview working with one of the hospital's vocational staff." He said further that he "saw him every day in the last ten months before his release" and that Wright "appeared to be normal in all respects, as normal people would be by definition."[59]

The Alpha House supervisor testified further at the trial that Wright had been under his personal supervision at Farview during June, July, and August 1973. He said he believed Farview notified the parole board in July 1973 that Wright had left the hospital and was working for Vector in Scranton. Given that, the Alpha program was "set up in various stages" during which Wright would be "leaving the hospital grounds and returning at night." But that he was unsure without notes if Wright was still in this phase of the program in August or if he had transitioned to living off the hospital grounds in Scranton. Asked if he was familiar with Wright's activities, including his "behavioral problems," if any, this witness said that he was, but added, "[In the] period . . . I knew Mr. Wright, I would have to say that he didn't have any particular behavioral problems that I was aware of."[60] He clarified for the court his responsibilities as a social worker/counselor to Wright. In response to a question from the defense as to if it was not important that he know Wright's previous history at Farview in relation to the Alpha program, he explained the program as one designed as a "prerelease program. At that particular state, when an individual went into the program, the focus was on his future and not on his past."[61] Asked by the defense attorney if it wouldn't have been necessary to review a patient's past in order to help plan out his future, the social worker said that might be the case in terms of occupational placement, but "other than that we try to avoid going into an individual's past. When an individual came into this discharge plan or [at] this point in the program, he had already gone through that process with the other hospital personnel."[62] The meaning is clear here that at this point, prior to release, the patient had gone through other avenues of scrutiny and found to be ready for the release transition.

As with the previous Farview staff witnesses, this witness was asked questions about Wright's previous history at Farview and, specifically, if he had any knowledge that Wright had attempted suicide in the past. The witness said that he had no knowledge of this, that in fact when he did hear of this, he was surprised. The witness was asked to read aloud for the court some 1964 "ward progress notes" from Farview of Wright, particularly a section that included items from March 8, 1964, to March 17, 1964. These notes indicated that on March 8 Wright had been transferred from H ward to Q ward for closer supervision, and on March 9 he was again transferred from Q ward to R ward for observation. The notes indicated that on March 10 Wright was involved with a "series of patients being accused of mishandling of pills" and, because of this, was moved back to Q ward. After this transfer, Wright, "in immature judgment," broke his glasses and was said to have swallowed the glass. He was sent to R ward again for observation.[63] The report went on to describe Wright as "cunning, shrewd, evasive, and suspicious whenever questioned and evasive in answering, a cunning white male, well accustomed to prison life. He needs constant supervision, shows no remorse for any of his activities. Mental status remains stationary."[64] Later, the report continued, on March 12 Wright was transferred from R to Q ward and noted as "improved"; on March 16 he was transferred back to R ward as "disturbed"; and on March 17 he was transferred from R to H ward, having "improved."[65]

This witness had not worked at Farview during the period covered by these notes. He started at Farview in 1969 as a ward counselor working under a federal grant program. It was in that capacity that he first met Wright. When this grant ended, he was employed by the state as a caseworker, a job he held for about a year and a half. He was then upgraded to caseworker supervisor. It was at this point that he took over the direction of the Alpha House program. Asked if he, as counselor to Wright from the beginning and during the Alpha House program period, had ever seen or heard about a biography Mr. Wright was said to have written that was in the official records at Farview, he said that he had, but that at this point he did not recall it "in detail."[66] He said he did, however, know about "the incident involving the young child and the gun that William Wright was alleged to have injected into the child's throat."[67]

Thomas Glacken, who became the second head of the program, was one of several social workers at Farview State Hospital for the Criminally

Insane at the time Wright was a patient and during the period prior to the murders when Wright was with the Alpha program and working for the Vector agency. Mr. Glacken provided some information about the work of the Social Work Department there. At this hospital, according to Glacken, social workers dealt with patients on a daily basis. Caseworkers had assigned patients and wards and performed a multitude of tasks, including compiling social histories and dealing with the courts, family relations, and such. Glacken noted that the 1970s marked a turning point in the field of mental illness; it marked the beginning of psychopharmacology, the use of drugs to help patients achieve and maintain some form of order in their lives. At Farview, social workers worked alongside psychologists and activities and recreational staff, as a team, so to speak.[68]

As far as the Alpha House program was concerned, and although he would eventually head up this program, Mr. Glacken said that he was unhappy with it from its onset in the early seventies. His disagreement with it centered on the mission of the program, which, designed as it was to achieve release of patients, he viewed as incongruous with the status of the hospital as a maximum-security facility. He recalled the meeting when the program was first discussed; at this point, the idea of a transitioned release program was being referred to as a "new beginning," and, interestingly, he suggested that if it was a "new" program, "Alpha something" might be an appropriate title.[69] According to Glacken, he believed the idea of a transition work program to a community setting was not in itself a bad idea, but he believed that if a patient was going to be sent outside the facility to work, he should be assigned to his home area so as to better prepare for return to his own community. At the time of its creation, the program was under the jurisdiction of another social worker. In an odd twist of fate, Glacken was placed in charge of the Alpha program after the previous director left. Considering Mr. Glacken's opinion of the program and his wish to see it closed down, his elevation to director seems strange indeed. As he recalls it, his supervisors gave him little choice about whether or not to take over this position. In the long run, Glacken did in fact see the Alpha House program closed. Its demise took place about six months after he took over. The Freach and Keen murders by one of the program's released workers and another incident on the grounds of the hospital were primary in the institution's decision to close it down, according to Mr. Glacken.[70]

As indicated in Glacken's testimony in the Wright trial, at the time when he assumed leadership of the Alpha House program, Wright was already in the program, living in Scranton, working for Vector Control, and not returning to Farview. It was unclear from the testimonies of both Mr. Farrell and Mr. Glacken when Wright became officially covered by the Pennsylvania Parole Board. The Alpha House program was small, with about ten participating, according to Mr. Glacken. Most patients, though not all, lived in Alpha House, which was in a section of a separate building on the grounds of the hospital.[71] Patients had their own rooms in this area and may have taken meals in the building as well, apart from the main facility. Some patients had jobs in Honesdale or Carbondale—each community about four miles from Farview. In the beginning, patients involved in the Alpha program, including Wright, returned to Farview after work. It is not clear how many patients, however, like Wright were eventually permitted to reside in the community.

Even before the Alpha program began, Wright was a Farview trustee—staying in Z building (the separate building that eventually housed the Alpha program). A number of people said that Wright was well known at Farview—the kind of inmate who had become well acquainted with the institution and accepted as a calm, intelligent, even helpful patient. As a trustee he was given fairly free rein of the hospital and was able to travel to neighboring communities with staff members for needed services. Although Wright, according to the trial record, had a troubled earlier history at Farview in the 1960s that included a suicide attempt and evaluation as cunning and manipulative, this man whose even earlier history of violence and murder was by 1973 believed by Farview psychiatrists, psychologists, and others in the hospital's administrative staff to have successfully adjusted and progressed to a point where he was a good candidate for transitioned work release. According to Thomas Glacken, Farview would have had a good deal of paperwork on Wright that certainly would have included his prior history and detailed information about his crimes or alleged crimes, and such records would have been available to parties and departments that had contact with him. Asked if the Social Work Department would have known Wright's past history, Glacken reiterated that all past history would be on patients' charts.[72]

There were some indications to the contrary, however. For example, the chief psychologist at Farview offered a statement at the December 1974 Freach and Keen trial indicating that he had seen Wright over the years as a patient. Wright, according to him, had a high IQ but was a "shallow and manipulative person . . . had a personality disorder but was not psychotic; he was emotionally shallow and immature [and] had a high level of physical and mental activity."[73] The psychologist said that he never knew the patient to dysfunction or to be uncontrolled or to perform bizarre acts."[74] He also noted that Wright had "repressed sexual inversion, [with] latent underlying homosexuality and that he practiced homosexuality."[75] The psychologist said that Wright's sexual situation had been discussed with the staff at Farview. "Wright," said the doctor, "was not closely supervised toward the end of his stay at Farview and allowed freedom of the grounds, [and] had trustee status."[76] At the time of his release into the Alpha program, he said, he had warned Wright "this would be his last chance"—that if he did not work out in the program, he would be "immediately returned."[77]

In his testimony at Wright's trial, Mr. Glacken testified that he was currently an employee at Farview, having first begun work there in 1971 as a social worker.[78] At the time he replaced the previous social worker as director of the Alpha House program, Wright was enrolled in the program and "out in the community,"[79] "technically under the supervision of the parole board."[80] Glacken testified that he knew Wright worked for Vector Control and had kept in touch with Wright, seeing him about four or five times from August to the beginning of November 1973. These meetings were at the hospital, and Wright drove himself there. The meetings involved discussion of Wright's living, work, and parole situations; his activities; and any problems he may be having. In general, these meetings allowed Glacken to see how Wright was getting along and were to provide support "if he [Wright] would need it."[81] Mr. Glacken said that Wright gave no indication he was having any serious problems and that the meetings with Wright were "more or less a requirement."[82] Although he had seen Wright in person at the August, September, and October meetings, the November meeting occurred by phone.[83]

Although Glacken could not recall the specific date of the November conversation, he recalled that it was some time after the first of November. "[It had] come to my attention from the Parole Office . . . I believe it was Paul Farrell that that office was providing the police department with a list of their people that they were working with in this investigation [the Freach and Keen murders] and certainly Mr. Wright's name came up in that context," said Glacken. He added that he "knew Wright's name would come up in relation to the murders and did not know what kind of problem it was going to create for him."[84] When Glacken talked with Wright, he found that Wright was aware of the situation and knew that he would probably be questioned by police, but Wright, recalled Mr. Glacken, told him that "there wasn't any problem" and that he was, in fact, "waiting for them to pick him up for questioning."[85] In Mr. Glacken's recollection, Wright had seemed calm about this impending situation and indicated to the social worker that, because he was not in Scranton at the time the boys had disappeared—he was in fact in the Tunkhannock area—he had nothing to fear from police.

Mr. Glacken explained some further circumstances of Wright's life during this period. The program director said that while Wright was working in the community "there was considerable demand on his [Wright's] time," with the result that Farview's oversight of him was "somewhat loose; [that] Mr. Wright came to the Hospital when he had time to get to the hospital . . . [and that] averaged out about every three weeks."[86] During this time, Wright also reported regularly to the Pennsylvania Parole Board. According to Glacken, at one time Wright had phoned him and invited him to attend a group session offered by the parole board. Glacken could not make it but said he knew that Wright intended to attend. Wright's phone calls to this social worker—which were not frequent—were most often directed to particular issues but, in

Glacken's recollection, involved nothing of any really serious import. He recalled, for example, that one of his calls involved Wright going "up state . . . [to] New York, or something like this."[87] Wright had called on this occasion to change an appointment that was in conflict with this journey. Glacken said that this trip had been cleared with the parole board, although he did not recall if Wright had said anything about this in their conversation. Mr. Glacken responded to questioning about whether or not Wright had been put under the jurisdiction of the parole board for supervision from the onset of his being in the Alpha House program. Glacken thought that he had not, but didn't really know. However, he did recall an incident at no specific date when Wright had been under the parole board. At that time Mr. Glacken said that he had had a talk with the psychologist at the Alpha House and Paul Farrell at the hospital sometime, he thought, in August 1973 about probation.[88] Wright at this time was in the Alpha program and working in Scranton. Afterward, Glacken recalled that he received a telephone call from Wright and that Wright told him he had had a visit from the parole board. Glacken indicated that Wright was "irritated" about this visit.[89] The defense asked Mr. Glacken if Wright had told Glacken that he was afraid after this visit, but Glacken had no memory of this (and there were no notes kept of these contacts).[90] Moving on, Glacken said that the meeting he had with Farrell and the hospital psychologist, had to do with Wright being an "unusual situation," because both the parole board and the hospital had "some interest" in Wright and thought the parties should "coordinate what we [they] doing" for better oversight of Wright.[91] No specific policy or procedure seemed to result from this meeting; it was decided that both the hospital and the parole board would continue to maintain some contact with Wright. At the same time no decision was made as to which agency, hospital or state board, had responsibility for Wright.[92]

Glacken, who had not been part of the patient selection process for participation in the Alpha program, said the social work group at the hospital discussed selection and who might be eligible for it, but the final decision about placing individuals in the program with the intent of transitioning them out into the community was not finally done by the social work group. That decision, according to Glacken, would go to the clinical director or the superintendent.

The director of social services at Farview Hospital at this point was not called to testify in person, but his statement was stipulated to the court at the Wright trial in December 1974. According to this, from August 1971 to 1973, the director said he had seen Mr. Wright many times at the hospital, though not in a professional capacity. Mostly he observed Wright as they passed in the hallway. His statement said that he felt that Wright was "clear, normal, highly intelligent . . . [and] exhibited no lack of control and . . . no unusual behavioral pattern."[93]

We might ask: How could an inmate be given such liberties and trust when it was known that he was a convicted murderer who had killed at least twice previously? This man was given to violent, unpredictable, murderous, and increasingly sexually deviant behaviors, who had already served one sentence for a vicious murder and had only escaped by legal circumstance being tried for another equally vicious murder, and who had readily admitted attempting rape, an offender who had been judged criminally insane and sent to a maximum-security state hospital in Pennsylvania for the criminally insane. So how was it that by the summer and fall of 1973, William Wright was living relatively freely, on his own in South Scranton; employed in a job that provided him with a van and sent him to areas in and outside the county; and given the opportunity to take advantage of his freedom and purchase an illegal weapon—a weapon that apparently a number of colleagues, including his supervisor, knew he had? The answer to this is hard for a reasonable person to comprehend, but given the curious set of circumstances that prevailed, understandable, if unsettling. How indeed, could this killer be free to walk among the unsuspecting citizens of this region, free to kill yet again? Clearly Wright feigned recovery and rehabilitation to the satisfaction of the most qualified experts in psychiatry and psychology at Farview for the eight years he was committed there.

Who knows what was in the mind of William Wright as he saw these two young boys walking along with little on their minds but school, sports, and the great experience of being on the verge of young adulthood? Perhaps he saw in them something he had never had or never would have. Or perhaps his actions from this point on were, as he describes in his confession, spontaneous, without thought, and beyond control. Even if further information on Wright was available in the form of records or Wright's own words on the subject, it is doubtful that the exact truth of his motivation would ever be known fully. What we do know is that whatever demons controlled the mind and soul of William Wright that first day in November were released and caused him to molest and heinously murder not once but twice, and when arrested for his crimes, he confessed as he had done before, quickly and easily, with no expressions of remorse.

6

THE INVESTIGATION CONCLUDES

On December 20, 1973, the *Scranton Times*[1] ran the story that William Wright, a former patient of Farview State Hospital for the Criminally Insane, had been charged with the murders of Paul Freach and Edmund Keen. Like the *Scranton Times*, other newspapers reporting on this story rehashed details of Wright's earlier criminal history while covering the murders and describing how Wright had been arrested after fleeing to Florida, ultimately confessing.[2] Earlier, the *Scranton Times* had given its readers a clear indication that Wright was about to be charged with the crime and had said state and local police were questioning the suspect soon after his return from Florida. Reporters knew police were using metal detectors along the Lackawanna River in the area near Elm Street Bridge and surmised that they were looking for the gun that had been used in the murders.[3] This particular article included a large picture of the suspect, seemingly taken at the time of his arrest for parole violation. It showed readers a serious-faced young man looking straight at the camera with a resigned look. He wore large, dark horn-rimmed glasses and a sport shirt. His hair was ruffled. All in all William Wright looked like a very ordinary person—someone a passerby might hardly have noticed, someone who would not be seen as threatening or dangerous.

Although Wright was charged with the murders, the investigation into the boys' deaths continued. A number of issues about the murders remained unclear and unresolved. One concerned the original story that had occupied the investigators for so many weeks—the man and woman in the blue and white Chevrolet who had been "seen" giving the boys a ride after school on November 1. Although the original eyewitness recanted this story, it was still out there; and more than a few people in authority still believed there might be something to it. The other issue was the need for more evidence than Wright's confession to tie him to the murders. In regard to this, the police were focused on finding the murder weapon, the .25-caliber pistol or slugs from it and forensic materials that would tie Wright to the murders.

Many in the community, law enforcement and civilians, found it difficult to believe that Wright had committed the murders alone, particularly in light of the earlier story about the two people in the car seen in the vicinity of the school on November 1. As a result, there was still the possibility that Wright was covering for someone else and that there might be at least one other person involved. Wright maintained that he had acted alone—and he would do so from the time of his arrest to his conviction and, so far as is known without access to prison reports, thereafter to his death in 2000. Still, some found it hard to comprehend how he could have done what he did to the two teenage boys without assistance.[4] Even with a gun held on the boys, as he described his abduction of them, it seemed that Wright, a small, slight man, would have had difficulty with two boys of Paul's and Edmund's size and weight, boys routinely described by friends and family as strong and athletic.

Given this concern, police continued to investigate the possibility of additional suspects. On December 30, 1973, just days after Wright confessed to the murders, Robert Flanagan, a *Scranton Times* reporter, wrote in "City Hall Soundings" that he had been "very close" to the investigation from the beginning and that he and some other newsmen had known about William Wright for some time. He also said that, in his view, the police had come to accept Wright's story that he had acted alone in the abduction and murders of the two boys. Flanagan recounted Wright's story that Paul (P.J.) and Edmund (Buddy) were not hitching a ride and were not picked up, as the earlier account had it. Rather, confessed Wright, he forced them into his van at the mine fire site off Cedar Avenue. Flanagan said that he had also known that the State Police had clearly rejected the entire story of the witness to the abductions, that, to a "somewhat lesser degree," Scranton Police "also appeared to doubt that there was any blue and white car involved" or "that a middle-aged man and woman had picked up the boys."[5] Still, the story about the boys hitchhiking home from school on November 1 and being picked up by two people in a Chevrolet continued to live—if only in the minds of the public and with some family and neighbors.

Detective Captain Frank Karam, interviewed in 2010, recalls these days. He said that he (and presumably other detectives) doubted the eyewitness youngster's story from the beginning, and ultimately, after multiple questioning, the child admitted that he had made it up.[6] As reported in the *Scranton Times*, the youth who had given police the story of the two boys in the blue and white car admitted that the story was not true. The next day Karam issued a statement, which the newspaper said had been approved by Scranton Superintendent of Police John McCrone, that the police were no longer seeking the middle-aged couple in the Chevrolet. Karam, said reporter Flanagan in his December 30 piece, did not say that the investigation was over or that the police would cease to investigate the possibility of another party's involvement in the case.[7]

Reporter Flanagan, continuing in this report, said that the paper had been asked to kill the story that the murderer had been found and that the earlier story had been a hoax. By this time there were two statements claiming that Wright was the single murderer—Captain Karam's and another, issued soon after by the State Police at Wyoming, a statement similar to Karam's statement. To add confusion to these conclusions, however, Public Safety Director Anthony Batsavage made another statement, contained in reporter Flannigan's account on the 30th of December, that called Captain Karam and the State Police statements, "premature," and he maintained the investigation was continuing for the blue and white car.[8]

As late as the time William Wright was charged with the murders of Paul and Edmund, Scranton Mayor Eugene Peters made it clear, according to Flanagan's article, that he wanted the investigation to continue "on the chance that there might be someone other than Wright involved," that he wanted to be sure that there was "no one else involved and still at large."[9] Flanagan offered that the mayor's determination to keep the case open on the chance that Wright had an accomplice was "understandable and commendable."[10] But still, said the reporter, this is puzzling in light that the "eyewitness" had recanted his story.[11] The reporter concluded that the mayor was not ready to move beyond the "eyewitness" story of the couple in the Chevrolet because there was only Wright's word that he acted alone, and perhaps the mayor was not "fully convinced" by Wright's admission of the murders. Interviewed later, the mayor said that at the time he believed that it was too early to close the case and, given the seriousness of the situation, believed that the investigation should continue.[12]

Flanagan had, earlier, on December 23, suggested to his readers a scenario of the crime in which Wright could have been able to molest and murder the two boys alone, in spite of any thoughts to the contrary. Information was leaked to the press by authorities, said this reporter, that the boys were murdered at the Cedar Avenue mine fire area in Minooka soon after they were forced into the Vector van by Wright. If this were the case, said the reporter, it would dispel the earlier thinking that the boys had been sexually molested and then murdered at another place, even some distance from Minooka—a scenario that had surfaced with the two-person and hitchhiking theory. However, lending to the continuation of the two-person theory was the information published by the same reporter that he had found out police were interested in a "close companion" of William Wright's, an inmate and trustee at Farview.[13] This unnamed individual and Wright were said to have "raised birds and tropical fish together" while at the hospital, and as a trustee, the reporter continued, this person enjoyed "considerable freedom of movement and he and Wright had frequent meetings after Wright's parole from Farview . . . even after the killing of the two Minooka boys."[14] Now with the arrest of Wright, Flanagan found out that this inmate had been removed from trustee status and sent to another section of the hospital, presumably a more secure area than that occupied by trustees.

Several years later, in 1978, another reporter writing in the other Scranton newspaper, the *Scranton Tribune*, wrote of an interview police had with an inmate at Farview, said to have been Wright's lover, which took place on February 7, 1974. The inmate, identified in the 1978 article by name, was thirty-seven, and the interview was said to have taken place as part of the ongoing police investigation into the murders of the two boys.[15] According to this person, in a conversation he had with Wright two days after the boys' murders, Wright had said, "They will never find the . . . gun or the second guy."[16] The paper informed readers that there had been some renewed interest in this inmate in 1978, as confirmed by then recently elected District Attorney Ernest Preate Jr., who was, said reporter Bob Reese, checking "a new angle."[17] The inmate, a convicted murderer, had come in for this additional scrutiny at this later date due to the reported homosexual relationship the two men had while inmates at Farview. The initial interest in him shortly after Wright's arrest was for the same reason, and to see, as this later story seems to indicate, if he was the unnamed man mentioned in Robert Flanagan's 1973 account. This interest doubtlessly stemmed from the fact that this person, as a trustee at Farview, and Wright had met outside Farview during Wright's release and parole period.[18] According to Reese, those present at the 1974 interview with this person of interest were Scranton Detectives Thomas Baggott, Frank Glynn, and Eugene Genell, and State Trooper Gene Corbett. At the time of this interview, this inmate was facing retrial at Lock Haven, Pennsylvania, in connection with two murders. At the time of the murders of the Freach and Keen boys, he had been on a dawn-to-dusk parole from Farview and had freedom on the hospital grounds. After the murders, the hospital cancelled his trustee privileges and confined him to a ward—a detail that strongly suggests that he was the unnamed inmate mentioned in the Flanagan article in 1973.

In summarizing the 1974 interview between Scranton and state law enforcement and this inmate, reporter Reese said that the inmate admitted going to Wright's apartment on Pittston Avenue on three occasions with his sister but found Wright home only once. He left a note on one occasion. On November 3, 1973, two days after the murders—Wright came to

Farview to visit him. He told the police that Wright was "well dressed" and told him, "Scranton is a hell of a town with murders and other things."[19] According to this account, Wright's visit to him was to pay him for the sale of some lovebirds he had raised and Wright sold. He said Wright owed him thirty dollars, but Wright short-changed him, giving him only twenty. To compensate, according to the Farview inmate, Wright gave him a bottle of vodka. At this meeting, he described Wright as "uptight" and even "suicidal."[20] He told police that Wright had called a minister who served at Farview from Florida after he had fled the Scranton area and told the minister that he would return "after things clear up."[21] He told the reverend his gun was "involved" in the murders but claimed he had loaned it to friends, and when it was returned, he had "put it in the garbage."[22] According to the inmate's story, when he met Wright on November 3, Wright was cold toward him, and after engaging in sex, Wright became "violent" and "hostile." In spite of bragging earlier that police would never find the gun or the "other guy," Wright told him he had acted alone in molesting and murdering the two boys.[23]

Among other things, the police interview of this inmate also provided some details about Wright's sexual drive. According to this man, Wright could be sexually active with two or more partners at a time and believed in "full moons," at which times he became hostile and sexually driven.[24] At this interview, the inmate provided police with the names of two men who had been Wright's lovers at Farview and stated that there was a third person, who he chose not to identify. He acknowledged that he had made numerous phone calls to Wright while Wright lived in Scranton but denied that he had ever gone to Carbondale with him. The reason for asking about Carbondale was in connection with a story about Wright's involvement with two men in Carbondale. No further information about this matter or the identities of two Carbondale men is known. The inmate offered to take a polygraph if police wished, but no information was forthcoming as to whether or not he did. At the time that this article appeared, in 1978, both Wright and this person were inmates at Western State Prison in Pittsburgh. It is not known if they had contact there. Further investigation of this person and this matter seems to have been ended after the 1974 interview, and, as far as is known, Reese's 1978 story about this did not result in any further formal action—except that it likely perpetuated the theory that Wright had an accomplice in the Freach and Keen murders.

Thus, even as late as 1978, after the trial against Wright had ended, some time after Wright confessed to the murders and police failed to turn up accomplices, either in the form of the middle-aged couple in the blue and white Chevrolet or someone else, this article stirred the belief or suspicion of some close to the case and many people in the community that Wright had an accomplice and he (or they) was still out there—a threat to children of the community. Reporter Flanagan, writing earlier in 1973, suggested that there were those close to the case who felt that it was possible that the child who had been the "eyewitness" may have actually seen what he reported. But, "pressured or convinced" by the police, he grew tired of telling his story. For all these reasons there was to remain a disturbing doubt in the minds of many persons in the greater Scranton community about the single murderer conclusion; over time for some this attitude morphed into a disturbing belief that Wright had not acted alone, no matter what he said.[25]

The police kept the case open and continued to follow any leads they could for an accomplice and the "now famous blue and white car,"[26] following Mayor Peter's dictum that it was better to err on the side of caution.[27] Even if Wright had acted "alone in the actual commission of the crimes," the mayor felt Wright may have had help at some later time in "disposing of the gun used in the killings"—the gun that was never recovered.[28] The mayor's director of public safety, Anthony Batsavage, identified as the person who supervised the operation of the Scranton Police Bureau, had responded to a statement made by Detective Captain Frank Karam that the eyewitness information was "false from the beginning."[29] After Batsavage claimed he had information that led to the belief there was another suspect and a car, reporters asked how it was that the captain of detectives on the case was not providing correct information. Batsavage did not respond but said that the investigation was indeed continuing. After this press meeting, a conference took place in Mayor

Peters's office with Captain Karam, Superintendent of Police McCrone, Director Batsavage, and others. The outcome of this was that Karam, called by reporters a trusted law enforcement officer and someone who was respected by the news media, conceded he had "made a mistake in giving out the story [that the case was closed and Wright had acted alone]."[30] According to the news account, the mayor told reporters the State Police earlier had requested that Captain Karam issue a statement about the murders and that statement was "premature."[31] Reiterating that the investigation was ongoing and still focused on the story given by eyewitnesses about the boys accepting a ride in a blue and white automobile occupied by a man and a woman, the mayor said any further statements dealing with the case would come from "his office and his office only," according to a report in the *Scranton Times*.[32] This news account suggested that some of the leaks in the case had resulted in friction between the Mayor's Office and the police.

On the same day, December 28, 1973, another article appeared in the *Scranton Times* rather strategically located above that of the mayor's announcement. Here, Captain Lawrence O'Donnell, commanding officer of the Pennsylvania State Police Barracks at Wyoming, announced that "every piece of investigative evidence [in the Freach and Keen murders] leads to one man and one man only."[33] Captain O'Donnell's statement was said to have been made in response to Captain Frank Karam's earlier statement that day that a nationwide alert for another suspect in the murders had been canceled. Captain O'Donnell, in what suggests an effort to put forth to the public a united front between state and local police, added that, although it was the police's belief that only one man was the murderer, they were continuing to seek evidence and added, "If there is another guy involved, we certainly don't want to let him off the hook."[34] O'Donnell also said that at this point the Scranton Police would reassume control of the case and, "Jurisdiction for this case lies with the City of Scranton," a point strongly reiterated the same day in Mayor Peters's statement. In response to Captain Karam's "premature" announcement, Captain O'Donnell offered a statement that attested to his agency's experience dealing with multiple levels of jurisdiction: "If that is what the

Mayor says, that's the way it is going to be."³⁵ End of the controversy? Perhaps. End of the multiple murderer story? Not really.

The December 30 edition of the *Scranton Times* carried a lengthy article by reporter Lance Evens titled, "Murder Case Confusion Raises Questions, Doubts," which posed some questions about the Freach and Keen murders that remained unsettled to its readers. Saying confusion had led to more questions about the case than answers, Evans began by detailing Captain Karam's earlier announcement that the nationwide search for a car and another suspect was called off—leading the public to believe the crime had been solved. However, continued Evans, Mayor Peters's statement had effectively repudiated the Karam announcement and with that the case was, according to Evans, in a state of "flux"— something he felt had "marked much of the investigation."³⁶ On the police side of the investigation, which included Captain Karam, Captain Lawrence O'Donnell, commander of the Pennsylvania State Police, and city Police Chief John McCrone, there was agreement that this crime was committed by "one man, working alone." Evans, in an effort to keep the story going, continued reflecting on the possibility that perhaps the mayor had overreacted and that the police, "so well trained in their profession," might be the better side on which to rely. Still, Evans acknowledged that one could understand the mayor's concern, but, said Evans, the real confusion emanating from the Mayor's Office came by way of the acting director of public works who was involved in efforts to get the Karam story about the closure if the case killed. But according to Evans, Mayor Peters had been very involved in the murders since the beginning but until this point had been rather quiet on the investigation. After contradicting Karam's announcement that the case had been solved, the mayor explained his position in terms of his responsibility for law enforcement as Scranton's chief executive. This led to a conclusion by some reporters covering the case who knew and respected Captain Karam that Karam was being cast "to the wolves" and that this was unjust.³⁷ The mayor, however, countered this suggestion by shifting the blame, said Evans, to a premature publication provided by the State Police, designed to take the blame off the local officers. However, State Police Captain O'Donnell was having none of this and stuck to his position that the professionals had carefully weighed all evidence and came to the conclusion that there was only one person involved, adding in his statement a tribute to Karam and praising him as "one of the finest police officers I've ever known."[38] Evans concluded his column by saying that whatever confusion existed over this, it was related to a conflict between the Mayor's Office and the police and asking if it were all just a "battle for public prestige on the administration level."[39]

Former mayor of Scranton Eugene Peters discussed this matter with author Kathleen Munley in August 2014 and said it was his view that the case could not be, and was not, closed with the confession of William Wright. His position was that there was no friction between him, his office, and the various levels of law enforcement involved in the case. Rather, said the former mayor, there were differences of opinion on the situation at this point in time. In the mayor's view, no stone could be left unturned in bringing closure to the brutal murders of the two Scranton teens. The case was finally officially closed shortly after, and, said the mayor, all areas of the investigation worked together in full cooperation to bring about the conclusion of the case.[40]

Nonetheless, it is clear that for a time the investigation was ongoing and that it was still looking for a "second man . . . and for the automobile that was mentioned previously."[41] In early January 1974, District Attorney Paul Mazzoni issued a statement to the press that addressed the state of the case at that point. Saying there was nothing new to report regarding William Wright, who had been charged with the double murders and whose case was bound over to the next term of the grand jury scheduled for the week of January 7, Mazzoni stated he believed authorities had the right person, but the investigation was continuing until all avenues had been checked.[42] This included the ongoing search for the other person and the automobile seen by eyewitnesses as giving a ride to the boys after school. The authority for issuing all news releases at this point, according to this article, had been assumed by the district attorney since the case had gone to the grand jury. Further control over news reporting on the case came on January 10 when President Judge Otto P. Robinson issued an order blocking police, prosecutors, potential witnesses, and city officials from making any further statements to the news media that might "interfere with the rights of [William] Wright."[43] The court also met with news media in order to work out some "common sense rules" on how the Wright case would be "publicized" in the future.[44] Control of news releases from this point on, however, did nothing to dissipate the story that another man was involved in the murders.

Authorities working the case or involved in it came to the final determination that the murders were the work of one man acting alone—William Wright. Wright's prior criminal history supported this conclusion as well. Wright had always acted alone, as was the case in the murder of his great-aunt, the child near his home, the attempted rape of the eleven-year-old girl, and the attempted assault of the hitchhiker. Wright himself in this period remained steadfast in asserting he had acted alone. The only suggestion that another person may have been involved came from Wright's friend and fellow Farview inmate, and that person's claim that Wright had told him that the police would never find the "other guy." The police apparently discounted this assertion in the face of Wright's confession and, after a long and extensive investigation, the failure to find any substantial evidence that pointed to anyone else involved in the murders. Nonetheless, the groundwork for a local legend had been laid. The belief that Wright had not acted alone is still often expressed by local people, and, added to it, is the thought that the other killer was a person known to authorities but whose identity was covered up because of his position or connections in the community.

At this point in the case against William Wright, police and prosecutors were engaged in the important task of finding the gun that Wright used in the killings—a .25-caliber gun. Police had been routinely checking out gun shop owners in and around Scranton to try to find out if such a weapon or bullets for such a weapon had been purchased around the time of the murders. At the time Wright was being held on six counts relating to the murders of the boys, police were conducting an extensive search of the waters below the Elm Street Bridge, where Wright claimed he had thrown the gun on the night of the murders. However, nothing turned up. Weather conditions that caused high and swift flowing waters on the Lackawanna River and Roaring Brook Creek near the bridge further complicated the search.[45] Prior to Wright's confessing to the murders, State Police had examined the Vector control vehicle driven by Wright. According to newspaper reports, a religious medal that belonged to one of the victims had been found in the van, evidence police had shared with reporters, telling them that this evidence had "cemented the case" against Wright.[46] At that earlier date, police suspected the van had been used to transport the boys' bodies to the dump site in Wyoming County. Later, Wright confirmed this in his confession.

The story of Wright's gun—how he got it; the source; and how he, a convicted murderer on parole from a state mental institution for the criminally insane, was able to possess a weapon—began to unfold at the onset of Wright's trial in September 1974. Captain Frank Karam, called to testify, recalled that around November 12, 1973, after speaking with State Parole Officer Paul Farrell, Karam had sent for Wright to talk about the murders.[47] Wright came to police headquarters, to the detective bureau, met with Captain Karam, and was read his Constitutional rights, which, according to Karam, he appeared to understand. Along with Karam were Detectives Glynn and Baggott and Captain Roche. Confronted with the fact that he was a possible suspect in the murders, Wright at first said he knew nothing about it and then went into another room to speak with Detectives Glynn and Baggott. In the meantime, Wright's Vector boss told the police that Wright had a .25-caliber gun, the caliber weapon police were looking for in the murders. According to Captain Karam, when police confronted Wright with this information, he at first denied it. In the meantime, two officers who had been checking out stores that sold guns reported to Karam that they had found that a "William Wright" was on the books at Bill's Sporting Goods, located at Providence Square in Scranton, as having purchased some .25-caliber shells on October 4, 1973. Wright's address on the book was Pittston Avenue—the apartment address where William Wright was living while on parole from Farview State Hospital. The owner of the sporting goods store, Bill Zingle, came to police headquarters on November 12 when Wright was being interviewed. Zingle identified Wright as the man who had purchased the shells from him. Confronted with this, Wright admitted purchasing the shells and having a gun and said he had not admitted to it at first because he was afraid his parole officer might find out.

At the trial the prosecution asked Captain Karam about the police pursuing further questioning of Wright about the gun. Detective Karam said he asked Wright to help the police locate the gun so they could check it with ballistics, whereby it could prove his innocence (or guilt). Police asked Wright where and from whom he got the gun. Wright told police whom he bought it from[48] and claimed he had thrown the gun in his garbage at his house and that it had been picked up in the garbage collection, from there to be dumped somewhere on a city dump in Dunmore, Pennsylvania.[49] Asked if he had ever fired the gun, he said he had. He was not sure exactly where but thought it was somewhere around Greenbush Street. At this interrogation, Karam asked Wright if he would go with the police and show them where he had fired it so they could retrieve a slug or casing. Wright did, and they subsequently found a casing but no slug.[50]

Following the interview with Wright on November 12, Captain Karam testified in 1974 that the police conducted an extensive search of the Dunmore dump area, the site for city dumping of refuse, the next day, November 13. However, due to the vast size of this dump, police were unable to find anything. Captain Karam had also asked Wright to come back on November 13, and Wright did this, asking police if they had found anything in their search of the dump. Karam, asked by DA Mazzoni if police had called Wright back in for further questioning after November 13, replied that police had done so, around November 15, but they were unable to find him. He also testified that police had found out Wright had not reported for work and had fled. Captain Karam also said that, subsequent to this, he had learned Wright was in Florida.

Captain Karam told author Munley he recalled Wright had attempted to phone him around this time—perhaps from Florida. Someone had mentioned to Karam there was a long distance call for him, but for some reason he had not been connected to the call. Karam said that he had a good rapport with Wright and thought he might be able to talk him into providing more details or information about the murders.[51] Captain Karam also alludes to this call in his testimony at Wright's trial.[52]

More information about the gun owned by William Wright came up at Wright's trial in September 1974. Wright's supervisor at Vector explained Wright's job as one that involved baiting any rat complaint area reported to the Vector office.[53] Wright had other responsibilities as well, including determining if the refuse collection wasn't being properly taken care of by city or municipal refuse collection and reporting this. The supervisor said that he had told Scranton Police on November 12 that Wright had a gun. The day after reporting this information to the police, he said he talked with Wright when he came to work that day, November 13. On the fifteenth, according to this testimony, Wright called into work sick and said he was going to get some medicine and stay at home in bed. The next day, Friday, the supervisor did not go to work, and the following Monday, Wright failed to call or show up for work. Wright's coworker told the supervisor that Wright had not reported for work on Friday and had not answered his phone.[54] At this point, the supervisor reported Wright's absence to the police. At the September trial, DA Mazzoni asked this man if he noticed anything "unusual" around November 1 about the yellow van that Wright drove for Vector that day, and he responded that he noticed it had been washed and organized.[55]

After Wright disappeared from the area, the supervisor said he ordered Wright's coworker to move the van to the front of the coworker's home for safety. According to this testimony, at this point, two State Police officers asked the supervisor if they would be allowed to check out the van, and he gave permission to do so. Afterward, they told him that he could use the van for work. Sometime after November 12, when workers ran out of rat bait, they returned to the yellow van to replenish it and, when doing so, found a large red or pink spot under one of the bait bags. The supervisor reported this to the police. At the trial the defense attorney asked this witness if he knew Wright had a history of mental imbalance, to which he answered, "No, sir."[56] He said he had, however, been aware that Wright had been a patient at Farview and acknowledged that he knew

Farview was an institution for the mentally insane. Prior to November 1, the day of the murders, he said the State Parole Board had never consulted him about Wright. He said that, prior to November 1, he had not known that Wright had a weapon. However, four to six week before the murders, Wright had shown him a .25-caliber automatic pistol. The supervisor's statements about Wright's possession of a weapon are contradictory. They suggest that when Wright first showed him the weapon, he did not realize Wright intended to keep it, only finding out later that Wright had kept the weapon.

The supervisor admitted he had Wright sworn in as an additional patrolman to patrol the dumps—a ceremony he thought had been done by Chief John Crone [sic].[57] Clarifying the earlier confusion about the supervisor's knowledge of Wright possessing a gun, the supervisor was asked at this time if he had told any of the police officers about the .25-caliber pistol Wright had. He said he had not. Asked why he had not notified the police about this, he said he had not at this time known Wright's history and thought Wright had shown him the gun because he was a collector of antique guns. Wright had asked him what he thought the gun was worth, and the supervisor told him he would probably pay about fifteen dollars for it—as it was probably worth about thirty dollars, and he would want to make a profit on it. He said he had noticed that there was no clip with it, and Wright had confirmed that there was no clip for the gun. In that case, the supervisor said he would not pay any more than ten dollars for it. He recalled asking Wright from whom he had purchased the gun, but Wright refused to tell him. He told Wright that it was unlawful to carry a gun without a permit and that he should give it back to its owner. Wright told him he was going to return it to the owner that day. Asked if the gun was in good condition, the witness said that it looked like it had been used a long time; there was no serial number on it as far as he could see, the bluing was off, and there was no identification of make on it.[58]

The gun used in the murders of Paul Freach and Edmund Keen was never found. However, a number of other witnesses testified at the Wright trial in September 1974 about the gun, and the prosecution was able to prove Wright's ownership of the weapon.[59] Also confirmed was the fact that Wright had purchased .25-caliber shells from a local sporting goods store for the gun and that the store's owner had witnessed Wright signing his name into the store log for the purchase as required by law. This transaction took place on October 4, 1973, a little less than a month before the murders.

Concluding the investigation and connecting the murders to William Wright included identification of other forensics materials. As was later presented during the Wright trial, police collected enough evidence to make the connections. This evidence included various items of clothing, fibers, hair, and body fluids recovered from the bodies of the slain boys at the time of their autopsies, as well as fibers, hair, and other materials found in the yellow Econoline van used by Vector Control that Wright was driving on November 1 and used in connection to the murders.

This, in addition to Wright's confession, was the case the state would put forward against William J. Wright for the murders of Paul Freach and Edmund Keen. Painstakingly investigated and researched by multiple police agencies, employing the latest scientific tests available at the time, the state was ready to prosecute the former Farview State Hospital patient and self-confessed multiple murderer for the murders of the two boys from Minooka, Pennsylvania.

7

PRELIMINARY HEARING

The preliminary hearing of William J. Wright took place on December 28, 1973, before Joseph Eiden, magistrate.[1] District Attorney Paul Mazzoni called a plethora of witnesses for the Commonwealth; all were key officials from the criminal justice system who had been involved in the search for the missing boys and the subsequent discovery and collection of their bodies in early December.[2] In addition, the Commonwealth presented exhibits in the form of autopsy reports of the bodies of Edmund Keen and Paul Freach. No defense witnesses were called, which is the norm at the preliminary hearing stage of a criminal case. They are usually preserved for use at trial by the defense.

William Wright was charged with two cases of murder, on November 1, 1973, two cases of involuntary deviate sexual intercourse, and two cases of kidnapping. The charges against him were as follows:

> Count One: That on or about November 1, 1973, William Wright, did feloniously, willfully and with malice aforethought, kill and murder one, Paul Freach;
> Count Two: That on or about November 1, 1973, William Wright did feloniously, willfully and maliciously murder one, Edmund Keen;
> Count Three: That on or about November 1, 1973, William Wright, feloniously did engage in deviate sexual intercourse with another person, one, Paul J. Freach, who was less than sixteen years of age;

Count Four: That on or about November 1, 1973, William Wright, feloniously did engage in deviate sexual intercourse with another person, Edmund Keene [*sic*], who was less than sixteen years of age;

Count Five: That on or about November 1, 1973, William Wright, unlawfully and feloniously removed or confirmed [*sic*] by force, one Paul J. Freach under the age of fourteen years without the consent of his parents for a substantial period in a place of violation with the intent to inflict bodily injury on or to the said Paul J. Freach;

Count Six: That on or about November 1, 1973, William Wright, did unlawfully and feloniously remove or confirm [*sic*], by force, one Edmund Keene [*sic*], under the age of fourteen years without the consent of his parents, for a substantial period in a place of violation with the intent to inflict bodily injury, or to terrorize the said Edmund Keene [*sic*].[3]

Asked by Magistrate Eiden as to how he would plead, Attorney John Dunn answered for Wright that he would plead not guilty.

The Preliminary Hearing of William H. Wright, as Recalled by Paul R. Mazzoni

In Pennsylvania, in the year 1973, there was in place then and still exists today the criminal process of a preliminary hearing when one is charged with a criminal offense. This preliminary hearing process is presided over by a district magistrate. An elected minor judicial official, and his or her job is to determine, after hearing evidence presented by the district attorney against the person charged with criminal offense(s), if a prima facie case exists. Prima facie is a Latin phrase meaning at first sight, on the first appearance, on the face of it. In establishing a prima facie case, the district attorney has the responsibility of presenting sufficient evidence to bind the case(s) over for trial. In simple language, the magistrate's function is to determine at the conclusion of the hearing if a probable criminal offense was committed and if the person charged is the probable person to have committed it.

The subsequent trial was presided over by a county judge known as a common pleas judge elected by the people at large in the county. Each county in Pennsylvania is allotted so many such judges, with the number dependent on the number of people within the county.

The county where the crime was committed determines the venue or jurisdiction of a criminal case. In the case of William Wright, the shots into the heads of the boys occurred in Lackawanna County. The bodies were disposed of in Wyoming County. The coroners at the autopsies determined the death of the boys to have been almost instantaneous. Hence, jurisdiction of the cases of the two boys lay in Lackawanna County. The criminal offenses occurred on November 1, 1973.

Joseph Eiden was magistrate of the hearing because the murders occurred in his district in Scranton. Magistrate Eiden read the charges to William Wright aloud in his courtroom. The courtroom was filled with people from Scranton and neighboring communities in Lackawanna County. Onlookers also surrounded the magistrate's building. Many police officers from the Scranton Police Department as well as officers of the Pennsylvania state police were on hand to maintain peace and order; emotions of the people were running high in light of what had happened to the two boys from Minooka.

Minooka was then and remains the southern-most section of Scranton. Most of the residents in that part of town are Irish and held fast to historic traditions. People in that area are personally invested in what happens to their neighbors. The people of Minooka at the time were churchgoing, and many belonged to St. Joseph's Roman Catholic Church, as were the families of the two boys. The common bond that held the people of Minooka together began with their ancestors, who originally took residence in that location because of the anthracite coal industry. The coal industry attracted many people from abroad to American shores. The ethnic groups at the time that lived in Scranton and other parts of Lackawanna County were Irish, English, Italian, Polish, German, most of whose ancestor's arrived to become coal miners.

I, Paul R. Mazzoni, was the district attorney and responsible for presenting sufficient evidence to the satisfaction of the magistrate against

William Wright to warrant being tried in a county court on the merits of the charges.

John Dunn Sr., the county's public defender, defended William Wright at the preliminary hearing and throughout the entire trial that was to follow. At the time of the hearing, I was about to enter my second four-year term as district attorney, an office that was then and remains today an elected, rather than an appointed, one.

I called my first witness to the stand—Joseph Conlan, Scranton city detective.[4] His testimony began with his stating that he received a missing persons report of the two boys on November 2, 1973. Conlan said that he went to the home of the Keen boy to talk to the father, Edmund Keen. The father told Conlan that he regularly picked up the boys after school to drive them home. The two boys lived several doors away from each other on Colliery Avenue and were close friends. They both attended South Scranton Junior High School and were one year apart in age, with P.J. Freach thirteen years old and Edmund "Buddy" Keen twelve. But on this particular day, November 1, Edmund Keen's car was at a local garage for repairs. The boys were let out of school that day at 3:30 p.m. and were last seen by other students at 3:45 p.m. when they were walking home from school, some two miles away. Both fathers explained that the boys never ran away from home before, and it was doubtful that this was the case this time. Detective Conlan then talked with Mr. Edward Walsh, the principal of South Scranton Junior High School, and the vice principal, Mr. John Murphy. School was in session at this time on November 2, so the administrators, speaking over the public address system at the school, asked anyone who had seen the boys the previous day to please come forward. Several boys came down and told Detective Conlan they had seen the boys walking homeward along Cedar Avenue. The school administrators confirmed that the boys were in school on November 1 and that school had been dismissed at 3:30 p.m.

On cross-examination, Defense Attorney Dunn elicited information from Detective Conlan that a fellow student said he had seen the boys get into a car after school.[5] This boy described the car as a 1966 blue Chevrolet with a white top and said that this had occurred between Genet and

Brick Streets around 3:45 p.m. Later this youth gave juvenile detectives a description of a woman and man in the car. As a result, the police prepared a composite sketch of these suspects. According to Conlan's testimony, after he had completed this initial investigation, his captain turned the matter over to other detectives. It was later learned that this young boy concocted this story to get attention.

Following Detective Conlon's testimony, I called Scranton policeman Lieutenant Frank Roche to the witness stand.[6]

Lieutenant Frank Roche served seventeen years as a Scranton policeman. He testified to the ages of the two boys and said the Detective Bureau had gone into full operation on this case, because it seemed to be an abduction. Police obtained pictures of the two boys from their parents and distributed these to other policemen and law enforcement agencies to help identify the boys when found.

Lt. Roche recounted the events of Sunday, November 4, when they received a call at or about 1:30 p.m. from a Mr. McNamara of Scranton, who had been camping in the Falls area, a township that is a rural area in neighboring Wyoming County some fifteen miles northwest of Scranton. The camper, in leaving his campsite to go home, went to a nearby private dump site to discard something when he noticed two schoolbooks with papers in them at the top of the dump. The schoolbooks appeared to be in good shape. He took the books and put them in his vehicle to take home. The camper noted that the papers in the books contained the names Edmund Keen and Paul Freach, the names of the missing boys. At the time that he found the books, Mr. McNamara had not heard about the search for the boys. He was unaware of the boys being missing, but on his way back home, he heard about it on his car radio and recognized the names as the same as the names listed in the books. When he returned to his home, McNamara contacted the police. FBI Special Agents Paul Durkin and Bob DeLoach were in the police office at this time, as were Detective Frank Glynn and another officer. They met with Mr. McNamara at his home. McNamara gave the books to the police officers. The books were clearly identified as belonging to the Scranton School District, South Scranton Junior High School, and the names of the boys were written on assignments and examinations papers located inside the books. According to Lt. Roche, there were six books in all, and these were turned over to the criminal laboratory for investigation. Lt. Roche, the camper, and other law enforcement personnel, including FBI agents, proceeded to the dump site where the books had been found. It was dark when they arrived. Lt. Roche stated that the police search that had begun on Sunday, November 4, had to be put off until the next day due to darkness. Captain Karam ordered a full search of the dump and the surrounding area. Police returned the next day, November 5, around 9:30 a.m. The search included taking pictures and protecting what was already determined to be a crime scene.

Taking part in the search of this remote site was a large number of police officers from the Pennsylvania State Police, the Scranton Police, and the FBI. In addition, the canine corps of the Wilkes-Barre Police Department was requested and joined the search group. Around 12:30 Detective Frank Glynn found a pair of glasses near the dump site that were later identified as belonging to Edmund Keen.[7]

The Wilkes-Barre canine corps dogs were trained to detect evidence through their natural scenting ability. Police first allowed the dogs to sniff some of the boys' clothing the police had obtained in order to familiarize the dogs to the boys' scent. Following this, the dogs almost immediately began to dig frantically into the debris in the dump, and as they did so, the police pulled away one layer of debris at a time. The canine corps led the police to a part of the dump about twenty feet high, so the police divided up their search team, with Lt. Roche and FBI Agent Durkin searching from the top downward and FBI Agent Lane Smith and a state trooper searching from the bottom upward. Then the evidence appeared. A large red carpet was found. Special Agent Wayne Smith picked it up and found the dead boys' bodies underneath and partly rolled into the carpet. A large amount of rubble, metal objects, and rubbish were spread on top of the red carpet so that the bodies were actually submerged below, no more than six or seven inches, according to Roche's testimony.[8] The boys' bodies, said Lt. Roche, appeared to be wrapped in the red carpet and to be "well mutilated because of the rubbish and the weight of the things that were on the dump."[9]

Continuing with his testimony, Lt. Roche said that after the bodies were found, the Wyoming County coroner was notified, and the Pennsylvania State Police Criminal Identification Division of the Wyoming Barracks handled the remainder of the procedures from that point.

The bodies of the boys were taken from the scene of the dump to nearby Tyler Memorial Hospital, which was equipped with the necessary equipment to conduct the autopsies of the boys to determine the cause of their deaths.

Lt. Roche's testimony further established that the books and papers of the boys were found in plain sight at the top of the debris in the dump, not buried in the dump as the boys were.

I called Bryce Sheldon, Wyoming County coroner for some twenty-eight years and a funeral director of some thirty years, to the witness stand to establish the maintenance of the chain of custody of the boys' bodies, which were considered evidence.[10] He was at the dump site where the boys' bodies were found and removed them from the dump to his official vehicle to be taken to Tyler Memorial Hospital. Sheldon began his testimony by recounting that State Police of Tunkhannock called him to the dump on Monday, November 5, around 3 p.m. After arriving and reviewing the scene, he called Dr. Hollis Russell, the pathologist he used in Wyoming County who was affiliated with Tyler Memorial Hospital, to come to the dump. In the meantime, Dr. George Hudock, a pathologist and coroner of Luzerne County, arrived.

Mr. Sheldon testified that before the bodies were removed from the dump to be taken to the hospital, two doctors who were to conduct the autopsies saw the bodies at the dump site to identify them in advance of their autopsy work. Once again, this was necessary to assure the bodies on which the autopsies were to be done were those of the two boys seen in the dump. I was at the dump site when the boys were found. I directed the policemen at the scene as to the manner in which the evidence was to be attained and maintained in order to assure that the legal processes of gathering the evidence, including the boys' bodies, was followed. I also had to assure that this evidence was legally and properly maintained in the chain of its custody from the time it was gathered to the moment it was to be used at a court proceeding. This was a major concern to me in that I had to keep in mind any future defensive maneuvers of suppressing the evidence due to the manner in which this evidence was attained and maintained. During this, Dr. Hollis Russell from Wyoming County and Dr. George Hudock of Luzerne County were present at the crime scene; both pathologists would later perform the autopsies.

Mr. Sheldon testified that he observed the pathologists and police personally wrap the hands of the boys. He also said that he witnessed seeing their bodies placed on stretchers to be removed from the dump. The bodies were placed in his station wagon, and he took them to Tyler Memorial Hospital about three miles west of Tunkhannock. This occurred between 6 and 7 p.m., according to Sheldon. He also testified that the same procedure was followed on arrival of the bodies at the hospital: they were x-rayed and then removed to the autopsy room. Sheldon was present when the fathers of the two boys, Edmund Keen and Paul Freach, arrived at the hospital to identify their sons before the autopsies began. The following day, Sheldon witnessed the autopsies performed on both boys, Edmund Keen first and then Paul Freach.[11] The autopsies were performed on November 6. Dr. Russell performed the autopsy on Edmund Keen, and Dr. Hudock the one on Paul Freach. The two pathologists performed their respective autopsies on the boys at different times, because there was only one autopsy table at the hospital.

The autopsies revealed that the causes of the death of the two boys were identical. Both died from a single gunshot to the head. A bullet was removed from each boy's head, and the bullets were identified as coming from a .25-caliber gun. Both boys had been sexually molested and sodomized.[12] According to Coroner Sheldon, the autopsy reports of both boys did not indicate time of death. However, the pathologists who examined the bodies and conducted the autopsies indicated it was "possible [that it] could have been around eight to ten hours after abduction."[13]

On cross-examination, Attorney Dunn referenced that Coroner Sheldon had testified both bodies contained multiple contusions, but it was later determined these were consistent with the exposure of the bodies to the elements. Neither of the two doctors who performed the autopsies testified at the preliminary hearing.

The next witness I called to maintain continuity in the manner this case developed was Trooper William Koscinski.[14] He testified he had been a Pennsylvania State Police officer for twenty-three years. Trooper Koscinski was stationed in the criminal division of the Pennsylvania State Police in Wyoming. He was present during the autopsies in order to attain any evidence removed during the autopsies that played a part in the boys' deaths. In this case, doctors removed one bullet from each boy's head and gave them to the trooper at the moment of removal, in order to keep each separate from the other. The trooper, trained and experienced, then marked which boy each bullet came from and placed the bullets in properly marked and tagged evidence bags. The trooper then testified that he personally transported the .25-caliber slugs to Dale Allen at the Pennsylvania State Police Ballistics Laboratory. I had used Dale Allen as an expert witness in ballistics in a number of my criminal cases, and he was an exceptional expert in his field. Dale concluded after examining the slugs that they had come from a .25-caliber firearm.

At this point, in the absence of the gun that had been used in the murders, Dale Allen was limited to only making an opinion of the caliber of the firearm.[15] There was no evidence yet of the suspected firearm from which the bullets were fired. It was hoped that the weapon used in the murders would be found and testified about by the witnesses later. As it turned out, the murder weapon was never found, but the prosecution was able to place the murder weapon in the hands of William Wright by chain of custody of witnesses. The next witness was the person who originally owned the gun.[16] His testimony was to confirm the beginning of the ownership of a .25-caliber pistol that ultimately ended up in the ownership and possession of the defendant, William Wright.

By the hard work, good police training, and experience of the Scranton Police and the Pennsylvania State Police, we were able to trace the exact weapon used in the killing of the two boys to William Wright. And it began with this initial owner of the gun that Wright had later purchased.

This man bought a .25-caliber pistol sometime in the middle of the summer of 1973 from a man named "Bill" (not Wright) who lived nearby in the Pocono Mountains. He said he bought it from "Bill" at the Waco Diner on Keyser Avenue in Scranton. He paid $45.00 for it. There was no serial number on the pistol. It was removed. As part of the sale, he was given a box of .25-caliber shells. He testified that he had the pistol for a couple of months and sold it. He said he fired the pistol into a tree near the town of Tunkhannock in a rural community in Wyoming County of East Lemon.

He took two Scranton policeman, Detective Tom Baggott and Detective Frank Glynn, to the very tree into which he fired the bullets. The police officers were able to remove the bullets and send them to the Harrisburg ballistics lab for identification and comparison with the two bullets that had been removed from the heads of Paul and Edmund.

I then called the next owner of the weapon to the stand in order to establish he bought the subject pistol from this previous owner, whom he had known for over twenty years, for $20.00 in the latter part of August 1973.[17] This witness testified he kept this weapon—which he described as a German make with serial numbers punched off, made of blue metal with a black handle—for about two or three weeks and then sold it to William Wright. William Wright told him he wanted the pistol to shoot rats for his job. The person said he knew Wright casually and had met him when Wright was working for Vector Control and putting out poison at various sites in the region. Wright, on occasion, visited his house to watch TV. This man never fired the pistol and had mainly purchased it as a showpiece. He had never purchased or possessed bullets for it. He said he had never seen the weapon again after he sold it to William Wright, although he continued to see Wright on occasion.

I then called Detective Frank Glynn as the next witness. Detective Glynn, in talking to William Wright, had learned that Wright bought the pistol from a gun owner.[18] From there, working backward, we were able to trace the ownership and possession of the gun to the previous gun owner and then, going forward, to Wright. In other words, it was through the gun owner who sold the weapon to Wright that we found out about the previous owner. That owner was then summoned to the Detective Bureau of the Scranton Police Department and questioned. Detective Glynn said the gun owner volunteered his time to show the police the exact location and the tree that he fired shots into.

Glynn described how, on December 11, 1973, by use of a metal detector, we learned there were slugs in the tree the former gun owner indicated. The police cut the tree down and, with a wood chisel, cut out a section of about seven feet three inches. This section, with the bullet still in it, was then sent to the Pennsylvania State Police Crime Lab in Harrisburg on December 13, 1973, once again giving more evidence to the ballistics expert, Dale Allen. Casings discovered earlier on December 7, 1973, on the ground several feet from the tree were sent also to the crime lab on December 13,[19] in order to determine if there might be more bullets imbedded in the tree.[20]

On cross-examination, Detective Glynn acknowledged that during the investigation of the target shooting area, the police had found about four other shells that, in his estimation, were not .25-calibers. He also said that he found four .25-caliber shell casings on the ground. Glynn said that in the tree the gun owner identified as the one he used for target shooting, the police found and removed about five bullets. These were not all .25-caliber—only one was a .25-caliber, and that was removed and sent to the crime lab.[21]

By further investigation, police learned Wright bought a box of .25-caliber bullets from a local gun dealer in Scranton by the name of Bill Zingle, owner of Bill's Sporting Goods. From Zingle's records, Wright had purchased the .25-caliber bullets on October 4, 1973.

Detective Glynn testified to this information, recounting police investigation of gun stores in the region to determine if .25-caliber shells had been sold to William Wright. The police investigators had gone to Bill's Sporting Goods in Scranton and found the name William Wright listed in the store's ammunition sales record book. Glynn said that on November 12, the owner of Bill's came to police headquarters with his record book of ammunition sales, and that book contained a record of a purchase made by Wright on October 4 of one box of .25-caliber bullets. The record showed that Wright had listed his address as 1211 Pittston Avenue in Scranton, the address of the accused.

The prosecution then called Dale Allen, to testify to the receipt and identification of bullets removed from the boys' heads and from a tree into which bullets were fired by the same firearm.[22] Allen said in his testimony he examined a bullet lodged in a piece of wood coming from a section of a tree given him by the police and made a comparison of that spent projectile with the bullets coming from the boys' heads.

Allen then provided information on the type of examination he conducted to identify the caliber of a weapon based on the bullet fired by it. He recounted that he had received a plastic bag from Detective Glynn on December 13, 1973, containing a piece of wood with a discharged full-metal-jacketed bullet lodged into it. He also received another plastic bag with four discharged .25- caliber auto Remington Peters cartridge cases. Allen also said that on November 7 he received one plastic envelope with one discharged bullet, removed from the body of Edmund Keen, and another plastic envelope containing one discharged bullet, removed from the body of Paul Freach.

Allen explained at the hearing that he used a comparison microscope in making his opinion and described this instrument as made up of two compound microscopes connected together at the top with an optical bridge. This would enable the examiner to see both bullets at the same time, side by side.

Dale explained that a bullet, when discharged or fired from a gun, in the course of spiraling through the barrel of the gun, attains certain markings unique to that gun. He called it "lands and grooves." By analogy, I referred to a bullet's markings of lands and groves as a gun's fingerprints.

Using the comparison microscope, Allen compared the bullets removed from the murder victims' heads with the one bullet he received from Detective Glynn. He testified that on examination he found the bullet received from Glynn and the bullets removed from the heads of the boys matched and were discharged from the same gun. He explained he had come to this conclusion by comparing the striations in the lands and grooves and the markings of the two sets of bullets.[23] He also detailed the firing pin impressions analysis he performed to determine that the bullets were fired from the same weapon.[24] In spite of efforts on the part of the defense to interject an element of doubt as to the absolute fact of these findings, on the basis of some possibility two different guns might have fired the bullet, Allen remained steadfast in offering his expert opinion. He maintained, as a result of his testing, it was impossible for the bullets to have been fired by two different .25-caliber automatics. They were, he testified, all fired from the same weapon.[25]

Dale Allen concluded his opinion, and the magistrate accepted his testimony, with Allen being duly qualified to render such an opinion, that the slugs or bullets were fired from the same gun. At this moment in the hearing and by this testimony of Allen, the murder of the two boys had been clearly and definitively connected to William Wright, the defendant.

This was a most impressive feat of prosecution: the connection of the murders of the two boys to William J. Wright by the use of a .25-caliber pistol without having that weapon to produce in evidence at the trial. The manner in which this connection was made was the result of the efforts of the excellently trained and experienced work of the police. In particular, I give full faith and credit to the Scranton Police and the Pennsylvania State Police. I raise this as an aside only to inform the reader of this book that in most murder cases in which a firearm is used, and to connect the use of that firearm to the person accused, the very firearm needs to be produced at trial. To make the connection to Wright in this case, without the weapon, it was necessary to attain the testimony of witnesses in order to establish the chain of custody of the .25-caliber pistol by tracing the weapon and its use to William Wright at the time of the murders.

In closing the prosecution's case before the magistrate, I recalled Trooper Koscinski to play the recording made of William Wright on December 18, 1973, wherein Wright confessed to the murder of the two boys and described the manner in which he had perpetrated it and disposed of their bodies, as well as other crimes he committed.

The Confession of William Wright to the Murders of Paul Freach and Edmund Keen[26]

Q. [By Trooper Koscinski] Would you give me your full name, Bill?

A. William James Wright

Q. The date is December 18, 1973; the time is approximately 2:10 in the afternoon. Bill, would you tell us what happened on that night . . . that afternoon . . . in your own words?

A. I don't know exactly how to begin.

Q. From the beginning, Bill, that's all we can say.

A. I had worked all day at my job and come home, dropped the guy that worked off . . . worked with me . . . off at a local tavern, and I went home. I called a girl I was going with and asked her if I could come up for a while. We had been fighting, and she said no. I laid down.

Q. Bill, approximately what time was that when you got home?

A. About 4:15, something like that, I guess . . . quarter of. I don't know. Sometime after 3:30. Anyway. I got up, went out, and got my truck.

Q. What truck was it?

A. Yellow van. That blue truck was up in Tunkhannock. I went driving around. I don't know.

Q. Go on Bill, I understand, Bill, how it's hurting you, but go on, Bill, and explain what happened from there, Bill.

A. Isn't it enough that I said, "Look, I did it," and let it go at that?

PRELIMINARY HEARING 121

Q. No, Bill, we have to know exactly what happened. We have to know up to the point, Bill. . . . Tell us how you picked the boys up and where you took them, Bill. That's very important to us.

A. Driving around, I drove the truck up into that mining area you're talking about. I got out and looked around, I guess to see if it needed any poison, or anything, if there were any signs of rats.

Q. Is that on Cedar Ave., Bill, there?

A. Yes, that area you were describing, there's a big sign there. It says "Redevelopment Project" or something.

Q. Yes, the area of the old mine fire.

A. I parked the truck, and these two kids were coming up the road. I had this pistol . . . I had this pistol.

Q. Go ahead, Bill. Get it out, Bill. Get it out.

A. I don't know.

Q. Get it out, Bill. You've got to get it out of your system, Bill. You had the pistol, Bill. Did you force them into the yellow van?

A. Yes.

Q. Is that what you want to say?

A. Yes.

Q. Go from there. There's no problem there.

A. There sure as hell is.

Q. I understand.

A. I told you I did it, you know, and if you want, I'll go down and tell a judge I did it, but I don't want any . . . I . . . I . . .

Q. Then this other story that we had about the blue and white vehicle, and so on, that was in the paper, there was nothing to that, Bill?

A. Absolutely nothing.

Q. In other words, those boys were walking up, and you were over at the dump area. . . . Did you call them over, or did you . . .

A. Forced them into the truck.

Q. By gunpoint.

A. Yes.

Q. Did you kill them there, then, Bill?

A. Yes.

Q. Right there.

A. Yeah.

Q. Did you beat them before you shot them, or did . . .

A. No, I didn't.

Q. You shot them first.

A. I molested them, I guess, is what you call it . . . I guess.

Q. Before you shot them, Bill, or after?

A. Before.

Q. Did they holler?

A. No. Like I said, they were alive when the policeman stopped at the truck.

Q. They were still alive?

A. They were sitting in the back of the truck.

Q. Did you have the gun on them at that time?

A. No, they were scared. They were sitting in the back of the truck.

Q. Then what did you do, Bill, after that?

A. After I killed them?

Q. Yes.

A. I drove out of there, went down the avenue, Pittston I guess it is, until it went off, and I had to make that one-way street, went on out, and drove and drove sort of, like, in a circle. . . . I came to that place where I put them.

Q. Have you ever been out to that place before, Bill, in that area?

A. No, I was just looking for a place to put them.

Q. How did you pick that area?

A. It was still light.

Q. It was still light when you got out there?

A. Light enough that I could see it was a dumping area.

Q. Could you describe going up into there? Was there any big buildings there?

A. No, it was all fields. One big sign said "Camp Okee Chokee," or something like that.

Q. Was there a big white church there that you recall?

A. Not that I recall.

Q. But nobody else was with you then?

A. No.

Q. You were by yourself. Did you have . . . was there any carpet or anything involved with this? Or were the boys . . . was there a carpet in the van, or was there a carpet . . .

A. No.

Q. Nothing?

A. The stuff . . . it was on the dump. . . . I covered them with it.

Q. How did you cover them, Bill?

A. Threw it over them.

Q. Can you describe what was there?

A. It had gotten dark by then. . . . It was like dusky when I drove in. It was dark by the time . . .

Q. Did you clean the van out, then, after, or did you do anything to the van?

A. Yes.

Q. What did you do to it, Bill?

A. I emptied all the stuff out and washed it, I guess.

Q. There was a pair of glasses missing, Bill. Do you know where they are?

A. Well, that I remember. They were laying on the floor of the truck, and, as I come out of that area, I just threw them out the window, along the road.

Q. Along the dirt road or the macadam road?

A. It was a field alongside the road. It was on the right-hand side of the road as you come out.

Q. You threw them over in that field.

A. Kinda, I guess.

Q. Now, then, you went . . . where did you go from there, Bill?

A. I went back to Scranton. I didn't know where I was at first. I drove until I came, I think, it was what they call the Morgan Highway. It was, because I came out on Keyser-Oak Ave.

Q. What did you do with the gun, then, Bill? Where is the gun?

A. The gun is under the Elm Street pass over, where the Flood Company (or control) thing is.

Q. Elm Street pass over . . . is it buried there?

A. There's water there. I threw it in the river.

Q. You threw it in the river.

A. The creek or whatever the hell it is.

Q. That's Roaring Brook that comes down through there. When did you throw it there, Bill?

A. That night.

Q. That night?

A. That's what I said, yes.

Q. In other words, what ——— said?[27]

A. Was a lie.

Q. Was a lie?

A. You'll find the gun; you'll find that out.

Q. Now, this is one and the same gun that you bought?[28]

A. Yes. I took the clip out, threw the clip in one spot. They are all out in the same area. The shells are all laying there, and the gun itself is, like, under the bridge.

Q. Did you leave the shells in the box, or did you take them out loosely.

A. No, the shells that were in the gun are under there. The shells that were in my apartment I put in the rubbish, and I threw them out, you know.

Q. On the Monday, the 5th.

A. But, you know, that Monday, you check, it probably was a holiday, and the trash went out on Monday, but it wasn't picked up until Tuesday morning because, the garbage men weren't working Monday, and I didn't find that out until I read where they, you know, identified it as the gun.

Q. This was later on? That wasn't on a Monday night.

A. It was Monday night, you know. They picked up the garbage on Tuesday, because Monday was a holiday. Ordinarily it would have been a Monday pick-up.

Q. Monday night was the 5th.

A. Yes.

Q. The garbage was picked up on Tuesday instead of Monday. It was still dark when you were leaving?

A. Yes.

Q. Do you remember where you placed the books out there?

A. I just threw them over the edge, off the dump.

Q. Did you wear gloves or anything at this time, Bill?

A. No.

Q. Weren't you worried about prints?

A. No. I don't know what I was, at that time. You don't really know what it's like. It's . . . you're driven. . . . It's something you're doing, and you don't really brag about a thing like that.

Q. When these boys came walking up the street, were there any other boys near them or around them?

A. No, just the two of them.

Q. Just the two of them. Was it right after the policeman left, Bill, that you shot them?

A. Yes.

Q. You molested them first, is that correct?

A. Yes, I guess.

Q. Both boys?

A. Yes.

Q. Then as soon as you left there, you drove around, and you disposed of the bodies up in the dump. Is this when you went to the Northeastern Bank and made a withdrawal?

A. Yes.

Q. And then you talked to the guard from Farview there . . . this is after the shooting of the boys?

A. Yes, it was.

Q. So the shooting was just minutes after you picked the boys up, actually?

A. Less than five minutes after that policeman talked to me.

Q. Less than five minutes after he talked to you, you shot them?

A. Yes.

Q. And then you took them up and put them on that dump.

A. Yes.

Q. Then you came back, made your withdrawal, bought your clothes, and then went home?

A. Yes.

Q. That is basically correct?

A. Yeah.

Q. Did you ever pick these boys up at any other time, Bill?

A. No. First time I saw them.

Q. First time you ever saw them.

A. Yes. I didn't even . . . you know, you said something about seeing them every day. I didn't.

Q. You never saw them before.

A. I never saw them before. [Defendant mumbles.] It's like that kid on 81, you know. That happened.

Q. That actually happened?

A. Yes, and somehow, or another, I got a hold of myself.

Q. Or it might have happened again?

A. Yes. I hate even to tell you that. I don't know why the hell I did it . . . left him out. . . . Even then I figured maybe he'll tell them that'll be, you know . . . that'll stop me, or something, but I didn't care, you know.

Q. That's what I told you, Bill, when I first came in here, didn't I? You need help.

A. I knew it then. I tried to get it, you know, in my crazy way. I mean if I hadn't been, I don't think he'd have walked away neither.

Q. Do you feel better now, the little bit that you've told us?

A. I told you I don't feel better.

Q. I understand that part. Do you feel a little bit better now that you got this off your chest?

A. Yeah. It's just the beginning. Do you know that? It's just the beginning.

Q. Have we treated you all right?

A. Certainly. You fellows haven't done anything that you shouldn't have done or shouldn't be doing or, you know. I don't feel that you've...

Q. Violated your rights in any way?

A. I don't have any rights.

Q. You have as many rights as I have, William.

A. Well, all right. No, you haven't violated any of my rights.

[By Trooper Koscinski] I'm going to shut this off a minute, Bill.

Q. [By Detective Frank Glynn] We found the bodies of the Keen and Freach boys on the dump. Their clothes . . . their trousers and their shorts . . . were down around their ankles. Their jackets and shirts were up . . . had their arms bound on top. . . . Is this the way they were placed there?

A. Yes.

Q. What was the purpose of that? Is this the way you had . . . you were keeping them immobilized so they couldn't use their arms or their legs?

A. No, they were dead.

Q. They were dead. Had you had time to molest these boys prior . . . ?

A. I don't think, you know . . .

Q. On the Freach boy, can you tell us exactly, with the red and white plastic jacket . . . can you tell us what you did to him?

A. No.

Q. You can't?

PRELIMINARY HEARING 131

A. No. Can't? I won't.

Q. You won't. Okay. How about the Keen boy?

A. Same thing, Frank. I . . . no . . . no.

Q. We won't press that issue if you don't care to discuss it. For the record . . .

A. You got the record. I killed them, and, you know, you can do what you want.

Q. For the record, you had no accomplice?

A. No.

Q. There was nobody else involved. It was just you and the Keen boy and the Freach boy?

A. Yes.

Q. Okay. Would you say when the policeman came to the van the boys were alive, they were terrified, and they were sitting in the back of the truck.

A. Yes.

Q. Within five minutes after the time that the police officer left the scene . . . and you talked to him . . . you shot both boys. They were dead. Then you proceeded to take them to the dump, where you covered them over with whatever was available at the dump.

A. Yes.

Q. The rug was there?

A. Yes.

Q. Okay, and then you left. You didn't know exactly where you were, but you did find the Morgan Highway. You wound up at the mall.

A. Yes.

Q. Is that basically correct?

A. Yes.

[By Detective Glynn] Okay.

[End of Recording.]29

Those present at the hearing heard William Wright's account of his actions relative to the murders of Edmund Keen and Paul Freach. A number of elements of the confession are significant to note. When asked, for example, about the story that the young eyewitness had told police of seeing the boys take a ride in a blue and white Chevrolet driven by a man and a woman, Wright declared that there "was nothing" to this—"absolutely nothing."30 He recounted that "these two kids were coming up the road . . . [and he] forced them into the truck" by gunpoint and killed them then and there.31 But he affirmed when questioned that he molested them before he shot them but did not beat them; they were, he said, "scared" and "sitting in the back of the truck."32 After murdering them, he drove down Pittston Avenue and out of Scranton, looking for "a place to put them."33 This and further acts after the murders attest to Wright's efforts to cover up his crime and indicate careful, if not necessarily preplanned, thinking on his part. According to his statement, Wright located the dump by accident while it was still light enough to see. He said he was by himself throughout. He found the carpet on the dump and "covered them with it . . . [throwing] it over them."34 Later, he cleaned the van out, "emptied all the stuff out and washed it."35 He remembered that there was a pair of eyeglasses on the floor of the van, and as he drove out of the dumping area, he "just threw them out the window, along the road."36 After murdering the boys and disposing of their bodies, he returned to Scranton and withdrew some money from an ATM at the Viewmont Mall located on Route 6 and purchased some clothing at the mall and went home. That night he removed the clip from the gun and threw it and the gun in the water of the Lackawanna River under the Elm Street Bridge. The remaining shells that he had in his apartment, he said, he threw into the rubbish in front of his home on Monday evening, November 5.[37]

Wright slipped up in efforts to hide the crime when it came to the boys' schoolbooks. He threw the books over the edge of the dump, perhaps thinking no one would be around this late in the camping season, and the books would go unnoticed or that the remoteness of the dump's location was such that the books would never be found. Actually, some news accounts record that the dump's owner planned to plow over the dump on Monday, November 5.

The accused also revealed that after he put the boys in the van and molested them, a policeman had stopped by the van to inquire as to what Wright was doing there. According to Wright's account, he said that while this encounter took place, the two terrified boys were in the back of the vehicle. Less than five minutes after the policeman left, Wright said he shot both boys, an act that would later be used as part of the defense strategy in support of an impulse discontrol syndrome theory. Police and the district attorney, on the contrary, remained convinced that Wright molested and murdered the boys before he had the encounter with the policeman.

In an effort on the part of the investigators to confirm some of the stories that had circulated about Wright's earlier tracking the boys and driving around the area of South Scranton Junior High School, the trooper asked Wright it he had ever picked these two boys up at another time. Wright said the day he killed them was the first he had ever seen them. He said what happened that day was like what had happened a few days earlier with the hitchhiker on Interstate 81. There, however, he said he "got a hold of myself," or he would have killed him. He said, "I don't know why the hell I did it—left him out. . . . Even then I figured maybe he'll tell them that'll be, you know . . . that'll stop me, or something, but I didn't care, you know." He concluded by saying he hoped he would get some help.[38]

When questioned by Detective Frank Glynn, Wright also said he had placed the boys in the dump with their clothes—trousers and shorts—down around their ankles and their jackets and shirts up—effectively binding their limbs. Asked by the detective as to the purpose of leaving them thusly, was it his way of "keeping them immobilized so they couldn't use their arms, or their legs," Wright said he had no need to "keep" them immobilized, because they were dead. When asked at this point in his confession by Glynn what exactly he had done to the boys sexually, Wright said he would not tell this—he could not—and then he said, "I won't."[39]

Although Attorney Dunn renewed his motion to have the testimony introduced from the tape recording stricken from the record, as being "improper testimony presented at this time, and . . . contrary to my client's constitutional rights," the magistrate denied his request.[40] The defense attorney concluded with a motion for dismissal of the kidnapping charge because of insufficient evidence; dismissal of the involuntary deviate sexual intercourse charge, because it had not been proven; and dismissal of the murder charge, because they have not proven that Wright was the person who murdered either of the boys. The magistrate decided that the prosecution had provided sufficient evidence for a prima facie case on all six counts and ordered that Wright be bound over for county court action and recommitted to Chase Institution at Dallas without bail while awaiting trial.

In the days and weeks that followed, both prosecution and defense readied their cases and filed numerous motions.

8

PREPARING FOR THE TRIAL

Shortly after the beginning of the new year of 1974, on January 3, District Attorney (DA) Paul Mazzoni spoke with reporters from a local newspaper and told them there was no new news so far as William Wright and the Freach-Keen case was concerned. Wright's case was bound over to the next term of grand jury that was scheduled to convene during the week of January 7, and it was expected that the county grand jury would act on the charges against Wright. Saying he was going to meet with Scranton Detective Captain Frank Karam regarding the case, Mazzoni also stated he believed authorities had the right person in custody, responding to the continuing discussion in the community about the possibility Wright had not acted alone. He also echoed Mayor Peters's position on the need for ongoing investigation in the case, saying, "The investigation is continuing until all avenues of approach have been checked out."[1]

Meanwhile police involved in the investigation maintained they were confident that Wright acted alone, although officially police maintained the case was still open and they were still looking for another person and the blue and white car. To avoid confusion that might result from these seemingly contradictory positions, the paper reported that DA Mazzoni had "assumed command of all news releases since the case [went] to the grand jury."[2]

On January 10, 1974, Lackawanna County Court records show a hearing was held before Lackawanna County President Judge Otto Robinson for abatement of publicity on petition by the defendant, and the judge ordered that no statements could be provided to the news media that might interfere with the rights of the accused for a fair trial. These restrictions applied to attorneys and staff in the Public Defenders Office; attorneys and staff of the DA's Office; the Scranton Police; the mayor of Scranton; the director of public safety for Scranton; the State Police at the Dunmore, Wyoming, and Gibson Barracks; and potential witnesses for the defense and prosecution. The order requested that the news media comply and cooperate with these restrictions.[3] This was followed up four days later when the defense filed a motion for Abatement of Publicity Transcript.[4] The same day, January 14, the defense filed a petition for a Writ of Habeas Corpus Ad Prosequendum to the superintendent of the Dallas State Correctional Institution and to the sheriff of Lackawanna County in order to take Wright to a hearing on January 18, 1974, at 9:30 a.m. for arraignment. Wright's lawyer requested that civilian clothes be required for court appearance. This request was signed by Judge Otto Robinson, president judge of the Lackawanna County Court of Common Pleas.[5] A few days later, on petition of Attorney John Dunn, the judge appointed Dunn to serve as legal counsel for Wright.[6]

William Wright was arraigned on January 18, 1974, in Lackawanna County. On indictment No. 66-A, he was charged with "feloniously, willfully, deliberately, premeditatedly, and with malice aforethought kill[ing] and murder[ing] one Paul J. Freach, all of which is against the peace and dignity of the Commonwealth of Pennsylvania."[7] Later, at the trial in Bellefonte, Centre County, Judge R. Paul Campbell noted that at the arraignment Wright had entered a plea of not guilty—in fact, as Wright himself stated at this time, during the arraignment he had "stood mute," and the court "had entered a plea" for him.[8] Likewise, on indictment No. 66-B, in which he was charged with the "murder of one Edmund Keen," the court entered a plea of "not guilty" for Wright.[9]

As the prosecution continued to build its case, it requested a search warrant on January 22 for law enforcement officers with probable cause to search the premises or person of William J. Wright at Dallas Correctional Institution. The inventory of this search included a blood sample (two cubic centimeters), pubic hairs (six strands and roots), and hair from his scalp (with roots). This search was ordered to occur no later than January 24 during the daytime from 6 a.m. to 10 p.m. The order was signed by Judge Robinson.[10] Records indicated blood and other body samples were collected by Dr. George Hudock at the Chase dispensary on January 23 at 2:30 p.m., and the warrant was returned by Detective Frank Glynn.[11]

On January 25 the defense filed a motion for appointment of Robert L. Sadoff, MD, to serve as a medical examiner to assist in the preparation of the defense case. Judge James Walsh of the Lackawanna County Court of Common Pleas approved this motion.[12] On February 20, on petition from the defense, the court ordered that William Wright be taken by the Sheriff's Department to the office of Dr. Sadoff in Jenkinstown, Pennsylvania, for the purpose of examination and returned the same day to Dallas. Judge Edwin Kosik, also of the Lackawanna County Court of Common Pleas, signed this motion. Officials took Wright on Wednesday, February 27, for this examination.[13]

On January 21, a Sanity Commission was ordered by Judge Robinson on petition to determine the mental disability of Wright. Judge Robinson appointed the following people to serve on the commission: Dr. Henry Buxbaum, currently the chief psychiatrist at Clarks Summit State Hospital for the Insane; Dr. John Lesniak, a psychiatrist engaged in private practice in the region; and John J. Sirotnak, a retired judge. In April Judge Robinson signed an order to pay the three members for their work in accord with Section 408 of the Mental Health and Mental Retardation Act of 1966.[14] Their role was to examine the mental capacity of William Wright and determine "whether he [was currently] mentally disabled and commitment [was] necessary; was mentally disabled on the day of his arrest, December 19, 1973; was mentally disabled on the day of the alleged crime, November 1, 1973." The commission was also to "make recommendations to the Court so that the Court [could] issue an Order in accordance with act."[15] On February 22 the transcript of the Sanity Commission hearing was filed.

On April 15 the Sanity Commission filed its report with the court. The report included the statement that the purpose of the commission was to examine the defendant, William James Wright, "as to his mental capacity and physical ability to stand trial for the offenses for which he is indicted," and after conducting hearings, the commission submitted its report.[16] Surprisingly for some who had been engaged with this case, the commission concluded:

> [Wright] is in contact with reality; . . . he understands the nature and object of the proceedings against him and crimes for which he stands indicted; . . . he comprehends his own condition in reference to such proceedings; . . . he understands the nature of the punishment which might be inflicted upon him; . . . he is able to confer with his counsel with reference to such proceedings intelligently and make a rational defense; . . . he is physically and mentally capable to stand trial on the offenses for which he stands indicted.[17]

Based on the commission's report, the court stated, "[The court] approves of the same and it is ordered, adjudged and decreed that the Defendant William James Wright stand trial for the offenses for which he stands indicted"; Judge Robinson signed the order.[18]

John Appleton, interviewed on February 2, 2012, recalled this period. A local Scranton attorney, Appleton was engaged in private practice in 1973. He had been a law clerk for three judges in the Lackawanna County Courts and had only recently left that position to work in private practice for Attorney Harvey Gelb. He was also working with the Public Defenders Office, but, although he had read about the murders of the boys, he was not involved in the case. Then, Judge Otto Robinson, with whom Appleton had good relations, asked him to come to his chambers. Present in the room when he arrived were Judges Richard Conaboy and Edwin Kosik, the two other Lackawanna jurists for whom Appleton had clerked. Appleton recalls that Judge Robinson came right to the point of his summons of the young lawyer: he wanted him to be second chair for the defense of William J. Wright, the man who had been accused of the murders of Edmund Keen and Paul Freach. The impression Appleton had was that there had been other lawyers asked to do this before Appleton, and so, Appleton asked, "Why me?" Appleton never forgot Judge Robinson's reply: "Because you do not have any children."[19] Appleton said that, years later, when he had children, he fully grasped the meaning of Judge Robinson's response. Appleton accepted the assignment to assist John Dunn, the chief public defender, whom he knew, in the sanity stage of the case.

Having worked in the Public Defenders Office, Appleton knew the DA, Paul Mazzoni, who would prosecute the case. Appleton recalled that at first he did not realize the high level of anger that existed in the community—especially in the Minooka area—over the murders, but he was soon to experience this firsthand. He recalled that at the time of the preliminary hearing, he was shocked at the number of angry people who turned out and stood around as the parties in the case entered the magistrate court. As with earlier appearances of the accused, Scranton and State Police provided intense security, concerned that some attempt would be made on Wright's life. Things were at such an emotional level, said Attorney Appleton, that he and Dunn received death threats. State Police Trooper Gene Corbett—who was a chief detective in the prosecution—was assigned to protect Appleton and his wife. Appleton said the troopers stayed in their apartment on numerous occasions for protection.[20] However, then, as earlier, in spite of indications to the contrary, no violence or disorders occurred, and the prosecution and defense moved ahead to trial.

Appleton, who had met William Wright soon after he had taken on the assignment to assist Dunn with the sanity phase of the case, said he had a formal relationship with Wright aimed mainly at getting information from him as to what had happened. He found Wright to be cooperative and intelligent but at the same time wily and always looking to gain some information. Still, Appleton believed he had been able to develop some rapport with the accused. At this early stage in the defense, Attorneys Dunn and Appleton aimed at invoking the McNaughton Rule—which would involve determination of whether or not the defendant knew the difference between right and wrong in the trial. If this were the case, and Wright did not know this difference, then he was not legally guilty. However, according to Attorney Appleton, Wright still could have been incarcerated, perhaps for life. Of course, the Sanity Commission over which retired judge John Sirotnak presided ultimately found Wright sane.

The members of the commission interviewed Wright and decided he understood the difference between right and wrong and could assist in his defense. Appleton recalled the sanity hearing decision was a shocker to everyone involved in this case. Even Judge Robinson was shocked at the outcome. Clearly, said Appleton, the jurist thought there would be a sanity issue—especially considering the accused's incarceration at Farview State Hospital. Dunn and Appleton were just as shocked as anyone else and found it hard to comprehend the finding of the commission.

Notwithstanding the Sanity Commission report, the ultimate decision about the use of the McNaughton Rule as a viable defense would rest with the trial judge.

As a result of the commission's decision, the Wright case became a whole new case for the defense. Appleton said he thought, and still does think, whatever mental state Wright was in at the time of the Freach and Keen murders, he could not participate in his own trial. Appleton pointed out that Wright being unable to qualify under the very narrow standard of the insanity defense statute did not mean he was sane. In Appleton's view, Wright was not in his right mind.

During the attorney's involvement in the case he said there was an "eerie calm" about Wright—it was as if he was a witness and not a perpetrator. Going further, Appleton, speaking in 2012, said that he believed Wright should not have been released from Farview in the first place. Details that resulted in this happening came out in the subsequent trial and still later in a civil suit for the parents against Farview State Hospital and others over Wright's parole and placement with Vector Control in the greater Lackawanna County area.[21]

Recalling the murder, Appleton believed Wright's badge identifying him as a Vector Control officer was probably why the boys thought they had no reason to fear him. The badge could easily have been mistaken for a police badge, said Appleton. That, plus the Vector uniform and the gun, gave Wright a look of officialdom. Then, too, continued Appleton, Wright was physically an unassuming looking, slightly built person with an unthreatening appearance—all this served to trick the boys into believing that Wright was someone quite different from the murderer he really was. As to what actually happened, however, Appleton said William Wright never revealed to him how he got the boys into his van. Appleton said, as have others, the sad irony of the murders of these two boys was that five minutes either way, the murders might never have happened. From what we understand about the timeline of the case, if the boys had been five minutes earlier or later, and if Wright had been five minutes earlier or later, they would have missed each other. [22]

After the sanity hearing, Appleton's participation in the case ended. As he saw it, once the defendant has been found sane, the defense faced a number of problems with this case, including Wright's confession; the bullets recovered from the boys' bodies that matched bullets recovered by state police that ballistics experts proved had been fired from the same weapon, a weapon that Wright owned; and the boys' bodies and the various forensics recovered from them. In addition, the defense had to take into account the public's attitudes about the murder. There were numerous stories out there—in some cases propelled by media coverage of the case—that described the state of the boys' bodies when they were found. Wright had brutally assaulted the boys sexually. In addition, an earlier newspaper story had indicated the murderer had mutilated his victims, an idea that, although later refuted by medical and criminal experts and corrected in further newspaper accounts, was still out there. From the perspective of the defense in this case, it was hard to separate fact from rumor. In order to guarantee the constitutional rights of the accused and properly defend him, a change of venue was needed and was requested. This was subsequently granted. [23]

Appleton recalled the climate of anger and disbelief that prevailed in the region over the murders and called the case significant in a number of ways. He noted DA Paul Mazzoni, who, like everyone else, was angry about the murders of these two boys, was intent on making certain Wright was prosecuted to the full extent of the law. As Mazzoni has admitted, the case was personal, and as a parent of children around the same age as Edmund Keen and Paul Freach, he was fully invested emotionally, intellectually, and psychologically in it. Appleton said everyone in the case was affected by it—it was hard. It had to have been difficult for retired judge John Sirotnak, who presided over the sanity hearing. Appleton recalls the judge's demeanor during this period, and it was altered, in Appleton's opinion, by his responsibilities with the hearing.[24]

For people of this region, this case was different from anything that had gone on before, said Appleton. He could not recall any previous case that involved the level of anger this case caused, anger that was manifested in a number of threats to the defense and the crowds gathering outside the arraignment. He believes, as do others interviewed for this book, that this case changed the community in general, and especially the Minooka area, which was, said Appleton, akin to a "village" unto itself. Basically blue collar, this was an area that clung proudly to its history and to almost legendary people who had come from there, including famous baseball players, local "characters," and the like. Minookans were proud of their tight, strong, neighborly, and safe community. In Appleton's view, the murders of two of their own youths in the heart of Minooka changed the way people felt about their community. For many people, it was a revelation that this quiet, somewhat sleepy, and content little section of Scranton, located in a region known for its beauty, strong work ethic, commitment to multiple religious institutions, and conservative moral values and lifestyles, was not safe from predators and that sometimes responsible people in authority make very serious errors of judgment that affect the most innocent among us. On November 1 in Minooka, in broad daylight, two young boys on their way home from school met up with the realities of the evil and ugliness that exists in the world, and this community, Minooka and beyond, was never quite the same again.[25]

Appleton concluded his interview by calling the murders of the two boys by William Wright an instance of a "perfect storm of mistakes."[26] Voicing a view about this case that is held commonly in this region, Appleton clarified that there were mistakes in the sense that Wright should never have been out in the community under no real control and that Farview, as an institution for the criminally insane, had pursued a harmful policy in granting Wright parole. In spite of such common expressions, Farview, an institution that was protected under Pennsylvania's definition of sovereign immunity, and the officials of this institution, subsequently escaped guilt—at least legally—in a civil case involving Wright's murders of Paul Freach and Edmund Keen.[27] Publicly, however, that was another matter.

On March 13, 1974, Wright's attorneys, John Dunn and John Appleton, submitted an application for a change of venue for Wright's trial. A hearing on this application was ordered by Judge Edwin Kosik for April 15 at 2:30 p.m.[28] DA Mazzoni said in 2013 that he agreed with the change of venue request, because he felt he had a strong case that could be tried anywhere and wanted the case tried once and completed without danger of retrial on appeal.[29] Judge Robinson, in an order dated June 17, granted this application, and on July 2 the Pennsylvania Supreme Court ordered the change of venue—from Lackawanna County in the Forty-Fifth Judicial District of the Commonwealth to Centre County in the Forty-Ninth Judicial District. Judge B. R. Jones, chief justice of the Pennsylvania Supreme Court, signed the order.[30]

On August 26, with the change of venue granted, the trial of William Wright was scheduled to be held in Bellefonte, Centre County, Pennsylvania, before Judge R. Paul Campbell, president judge, with a pretrial conference set for August 27. Judge Robinson ordered that Wright be present at this conference and be temporarily released from Dallas into the custody of the Lackawanna County sheriff for transport to Centre County, during which time he would be held at Rockview State Prison in Bellefonte.[31] Following the pretrial hearing, Judge Campbell scheduled Wright's trial for Thursday, September 12, 1974.

Attorney Dunn-Defense Counsel-in Light Colored Suit, William Wright to Dunn's Left. Courtesy of the *Times-Tribune*, Scranton, PA

Prosecution Conference, DA Paul Mazzoni Bending Over Table on Right. Courtesy of the *Times-Tribune*, Scranton, PA

Preliminary Hearing, Scranton, PA, December 28, 1973. Courtesy of the *Times-Tribune*, Scranton, PA

Going to Trial, DA Paul Mazzoni on Right. Courtesy of the *Times-Tribune*, Scranton, PA

The Road to the How Kola Campground and Refuse Dump Where the Bodies of Paul and Edmund Were Found. Courtesy of the *Times-Tribune*, Scranton, PA

Mayor Eugene Peters. Courtesy of the *Times-Tribune*, Scranton, PA

Detective Frank Karam who Led the Investigation. Courtesy of the *Times-Tribune*, Scranton, PA

Farview State Hospital for the Criminally Insane, Circa 1950s. *Source:* Wayne County Historical Society, Honesdale, PA, Photo Archives

A View of Scranton from the Courthouse around the 1970s. Permission to use Granted by the Lackawanna Historical Society

Centre County Courthouse, Bellefonte, PA, Scene of the Trial. Courtesy of the Centre County Library and Historical Museum

9

THE TRIAL—SEPTEMBER 12, 1974

With William Wright's preliminary hearing concluded, the trial began months later. The following accounts of the trial days in italics are those of Paul Mazzoni.

After the preliminary hearing on January 18, 1974, and a true bill of indictment returned thereafter by the county grand jury, the defendant, William J. Wright, appeared in the Lackawanna County Court to be arraigned. The county court was located in Scranton, Pennsylvania, the county seat of Lackawanna. In Pennsylvania, every county has a municipality designated as its county seat, which by definition serves as the county's capital. Located in that municipality are the county courts, as well as other county government offices.

An arraignment was part of the criminal process then and remains so today. Defendants can waive their right to an arraignment. At an arraignment, the judge reads the charges to a defendant in open court, after which the judge asks the defendant how he or she intends to plead to the offenses—guilty or not guilty. In the case of William Wright, in answer to the charges, he stood mute, refusing to plead guilty or not guilty. When a defendant refuses to exercise either option, the judge, by law, must enter a not guilty plea for him and set the case for further proceedings, which may include a trial date. In the interim, after an arraignment but before the trial, counsel typically files motions challenging the sufficiency of the evidence or for a change of venue. Counsel of a high-profile case usually prefers the case be tried in another county than where the offenses occurred, because extensive publicity can impact the outcome of the verdict.

From the time the two boys were missing to the preliminary hearing and beyond, Wright's case had received daily publicity in northeastern Pennsylvania. Thus, for the sake of fairness, this publicity necessitated the trial be held in another part of Pennsylvania.

The defense counsel, John Dunn, Esq., filed the necessary legal papers seeking a change of venue. The local trial judge, Otto Robinson, granted the defense a change of venue. I, as the district attorney, did not object to the change. In the interest of justice and to avoid later appeals, I wanted this case to be tried only once, as quickly as possible, and without a reversal on appeal. I did not care where it was tried, because I was confident that I was going to attain a conviction on all counts.

In a case of first-degree murder, when the local county court grants a change of venue to a defendant, the site of the trial at that time was selected by the Pennsylvania Supreme Court. The Pennsylvania Supreme Court chose Bellefonte, Pennsylvania, which is the county seat of Centre County, located in the center of Pennsylvania, 150 miles from Scranton.

Known as the town of governors, because three Pennsylvania governors came from this small Pennsylvania town, Bellefonte is a beautiful community. Among its historic buildings is the Centre County Courthouse, the site of the Freach and Keen trial, a magnificent example of stately classic architecture, with a Greek Revival porch in front and topped by a cupola with Doric pilasters. The courthouse is located on a hill at the downtown square and park, through which a pristine brook winds.[1]

The judge assigned to preside over the trial was the Honorable R. Paul Campbell. I was allowed to use District Attorney Charles Brown's office at the courthouse.

The defense opted to have his client tried by a judge and not a jury panel of twelve people. I didn't object to this move, because it would facilitate the trial in my presentation of the evidence. Moreover, I only *had to convince one person of William Wright's guilt, not twelve. In a criminal trial by a jury of twelve people, the verdict had to be unanimous. After a meeting with Judge Campbell to inform him of our witnesses, our timetables, and the logistics of our processes, a trial date was set for September 12, 1974.*

At the opening of the trial on September 12, 1974, William Wright was asked a second time of his intentions of his plea as to the murder charges and other related charges of Paul Freach and Edmund Keen. This time he entered a plea of "guilty" to all the charges. It became apparent to me at this time that the defendant had it in mind to use a mental disorder as a defense or to mitigate his wrongdoing at sentencing if he were to be found guilty.

The judge went through the ordinary litany of questions posed to William Wright in order for him to accept his plea. There was no doubt in my mind that during the exchange of questions by the judge and answers by the defendant that Wright's counsel prepared him well for this part of the case.

I anticipated from the outset of this case after William Wright's arrest that a mental disorder of some sort would come into play by the defense, despite the Sanity Commission's finding that Wright was fit to stand trial.

Notwithstanding Wright's guilty plea, Judge Campbell made it clear he would wait until I had presented my case before accepting the plea. The judge wanted to be convinced there was sufficient evidence produced at trial by the prosecution to show Wright's culpable complicity in the criminal acts for which he was charged.

The trial of William J. Wright was conducted on three separate days in 1974: September 12, October 16, and December 12. Standing in front of President Judge R. Paul Campbell of the Centre County Court on the first day of the trial, Wright entered pleas of guilty to the two murders (indictments No. 66-A and B). He likewise changed his original pleas from not guilty to guilty in indictments No. 66-C and D, in which he was charged with engaging in deviate sexual intercourse with Paul Freach and Edmund Keen, and two indictments, Nos. 66-E and F, for kidnapping Paul

Freach and Edmund Keen.² Asked by Judge Campbell if Wright understood that he had the right to a trial by jury and that he was presumed innocent until he either pleaded guilty or was found guilty, Wright responded in the affirmative. The judge then asked Wright a number of questions, including if he understood the Commonwealth had the burden to prove the essential facts of a crime beyond a reasonable doubt; he had the right not to incriminate himself, if he desired; he had the right to demand the Commonwealth bring in witnesses who would accuse him of the crime; and he would have the opportunity to confront and cross-examine those witnesses in court. Judge Campbell asked Wright if he understood that if his pleas were accepted and "if the evidence warranted it," he could be found guilty of murder in the first degree. The judge also asked him if he understood first-degree murder was punishable by life imprisonment.³ Wright told the judge he understood and had made a voluntary, uncoerced confession. The judge asked Wright if his pleas in court that morning to the various indictments were not motivated by reason of his prior confession, and Wright said they were not. The judge asked him the reason for his plea now, saying, "[Do] you feel . . . you are indicating to the Court that you did, in fact, commit these offenses?" Lastly, Judge Campbell asked Wright if he understood fully everything going on "here and now" and that, based on his plea, he was "waiving the right of trial and . . . giving up that Constitutional right." Wright answered yes.⁴ And with that, the court session began.

The parents of the murdered boys saw Wright for the first time this day and later, according to reports, expressed annoyance with the way the judicial system, the trial proceedings, and those involved in the case seemed to defer to William Wright. To them it may have seemed that much time was being spent on details unnecessary to the major focus of the case: the brutal murders of their sons. Nonetheless, all four parents attended each day of the trial.⁵

With all the preliminary matters out of the way, I called Gail Freach, Paul's mother, to the witness stand as my first witness. Mrs. Freach testified that to the residence of the Freach family and other family par-

ticulars, including those of her son. She provided the court with detailed descriptions of the clothing worn by her son on the day of his murder and identified those items, shown in court, as belonging to P.J.

She then testified that Buddy's father, Edmund Keen, would often take the boys home from school after he got out of work. She explained that Edmund had called her the night before November 1 to say he couldn't pick the boys up the next day, because he had to take his car to a garage to have some work done on it. Mrs. Freach then said Paul took bus fare with him on November 1 in case of rain. Otherwise, she said, he would walk home, which, as it turned out, he and Buddy apparently did.

Continuing in her testimony, Mrs. Freach said when the boys walked home from school, some two miles away, P.J. would arrive home between 4:00 and 4:15 p.m. Paul usually walked home on Fridays, because he had an eighth-period study. When walking home, the boys walked along Cedar Avenue, a "direct line from their school, South Scranton Junior High School."[6]

Gail said suppertime at their home was 5:30 p.m. Although initially thinking that "maybe Mr. Keen had decided, as he had one other time, to take them to the garage with him," when P.J. wasn't home by 5:30 p.m., she "knew there was something wrong"—her exact words.[7] Little did Gail realize that he was never to return home from school again. When P.J.'s father, Paul Freach, returned home from work and learned that P.J. wasn't home, he called Edmund Keen; but no one answered, because Buddy's parents were at the garage and their four daughters at church, at the 5:30 Mass. As Catholics, the Keen and Freach families would be planning on attending church on November 1, All Saint's Day, a Holy Day observed by Catholics. At this point, Mr. and Mrs. Freach continued to assume that the boys were with Buddy's father at the garage to get the Keen's car. So they continued on with supper. At six o'clock Mr. Freach again called the Keens and one of the Keen daughters said "that they must be with Mr. Keen at the garage, that their mother and father weren't home yet."[8]

When the Keens realized Buddy wasn't home and Mr. Freach had not picked the boys up after school, the two fathers proceeded to drive *around South Scranton looking for the boys without success. According to Mrs. Freach's testimony, they also contacted other friends to inquire if they had seen the boys, but no one had. The police were called soon after.*

At this point of Gail Freach's testimony, I presented her with schoolbooks purporting to belong to P.J. for identification. She identified a book titled Spelling Time as a book P.J. brought home from school. There were also papers in the book written in P.J.'s handwriting, which she identified to be his writing. It was then that both the book and the papers found in the book were introduced in evidence to be made part of the official court record of the trial. This evidence was introduced again at the trial to connect Wright to the offenses from witnesses that were to follow.

Before completing her testimony, I asked Mrs. Freach if she had known her son to hitchhike to and from school or at any other time, to which she answered, "No way." [9]

Attorney John Dunn did not cross-examine Mrs. Freach, and she was asked to step down.

My next witness was Dorothy Keen, Edmund "Buddy" Keen's mother. She testified to where she lived and that she was a neighbor of the Freach family's on Colliery Avenue. She said the last time she saw her son was on November 1, 1973, asleep in bed. She worked at an electronics plant known as Weston, located in the town of Archbald, some eighteen miles northeast of her residence. Her hours of employment began at 7 a.m. Every morning she would leave for work before her son awoke. On November 1, 1973, she told the court she had laid out the clothes he was to wear to school as she had done every day.

Mrs. Keen described the clothing Edmund had worn on this day.[10] *At this point of her testimony, I presented the clothing Buddy had worn on November 1. She identified it as belonging to her son and as what she had laid out for him to wear. She also said that Buddy wore glasses. I then showed her a pair of glasses, which she identified as belonging to her son. Buddy's clothing and glasses were then introduced as evidence to be made part of the official court record of the trial.*

I showed Dorothy a book and school papers found inside to identify. Mrs. Keen clearly identified the handwriting on the papers as that of her son. She also recognized one of the schoolbooks as belonging to her son. The book and papers similarly were made part of the record and were used later in the trial to connect Wright to the offenses from witnesses who followed her.

In my examination of Mrs. Keen, she stated the next time she was to see her son was "in his casket."[11]

As Mrs. Freach had, Mrs. Keen testified to the routine regularly employed every day in taking the boys to school and their return home. Asked if he ever hitchhiked, she responded that he did not, saying it was because he "was very proud of the fact that . . . he could run home in seventeen-and-a-half minutes."[12]

The defense counsel had no questions for Mrs. Keen.

My next witness was Edmund Keen, Sr., Buddy's father. He testified he was unable to pick the boys up after school on November 1, and P.J.'s parents knew this.

Mr. Keen provided details concerning the reason he was unable to pick up the boys on November 1. He also said he had told his son on the morning of November 1 that if he was unable to pick the boys up, Buddy should take the bus. He told the court he assumed Buddy would walk home "like he always did when I wasn't there."[13] He said he usually picked the boys up at dismissal, at 3:25 to 3:30. He, his wife, and the Freach couple had coffee together, and he told them he had to "take the radiator out of the pickup truck, take it up to the garage, and have them put a transmission in the car." He added, "If there were any way possible that I could pick them up [from school on November 1], I would."[14]

Mr. Keen said he last saw his son at 8:20 a.m. on November 1. The next time was on November 5 at Tyler Memorial Hospital to identify his son's dead body prior to the commencement of the autopsy—four days after the boys had left for school.

Again, defense counsel had no questions of the witness.

I called the father of P.J., Paul Freach, who testified to the daily routine of taking the boys to school. On November 1, 1973, he dropped the boys off at school at about 8:35 a.m., which was the last time he saw his son alive. He further affirmed that the testimony of the Keen parents and his wife were correct.

Mr. Freach testified that he saw his son's dead body at Tyler Memorial Hospital on the evening of November 5, 1973, and identified the body as his son, P.J. Freach, to the authorities on hand, including the pathologist who was to conduct the autopsy. He and Mr. Keen went together to the hospital to make this identification of their respective sons. [15]

Defense Counsel Dunn had no questions of this witness.

The next witness I called was Edward J. Walsh, the principal of South Scranton Junior High School. His testimony was entered into record by stipulation. A stipulation of testimony is sometimes used at trial in lieu of live testimony of a witness when opposing counsel agrees with the evidence intended to be established by that witness.

Edward Walsh stipulated that the two boys had attended South Scranton Junior High School on November 1 and left school around 3:30 p.m. His testimony also confirmed the schoolbooks already entered into the record were in fact the boys' because of a corresponding number in the books that the school kept in their records indicating they had been issued to the boys.

Following this, statements of two schoolgirls, the last girls to see the boys alive as they set out for home after school, were read. According to this, the girls saw the boys together and alone walking, not in the process of hitchhiking, toward the boys' homes. This sighting happened at Biff's, a bar/restaurant about two blocks from the place of the boys' abduction on Cedar Avenue. Biff's, according to the girls, was in the 1700 block of Cedar Avenue. Attorney Dunn agreed to the stipulation of the girls' information. The court called on them for some identification information, specifically their names, ages (thirteen), and their addresses (South Scranton). The girls were then allowed to leave.

My next witness was perhaps the most important in this case. His name was Joseph McNamara of Scranton. He was the camper who found the schoolbooks with the boys' handwriting on papers at a remote dump site in Falls Township in neighboring Wyoming County on Sunday, November 4, 1973. He testified the books appeared in good shape. He put them in his vehicle, and on the way home to West Scranton had turned on his radio. He heard the names of the two missing boys and soon realized the books and papers belonged to the same boys.

He called the police, gave them this evidence, and took them to the dump site the next day to show police where he found the books. The camper's testimony was stipulated by opposing counsel and made part of the trial record.

I am convinced that without the camper finding the books and papers at the dump site, this case would never have been solved. I am also certain that anyone, especially on a complete reading of this book, would come to the same conclusion. First of all, the bodies of the two boys, and the evidence the bodies and location provided, would never have been discovered had it not been for the discovery of the books and papers. The bodies of the two boys contained the very bullet slugs needed to tie the shooting to William Wright, as the evidence from the following trial witnesses would prove.

My next witness was Scranton Police Detective Frank Glynn. Detective Glynn testified he received the phone call from Mr. McNamara, the camper, while on duty in the Detective Bureau on Sunday, November 4, 1973, about 2 p.m., informing the detective he found some books at the dump located in Falls Township after breaking camp near the How Kola Campgrounds. The camper, in his testimony, took Glynn and other po-

licemen to the dump site on Monday, November 5, 1973. Police then found a pair of glasses nearby, later identified by Edmund Keen's mother as belonging to her son. [16]

I presented the eyeglasses to Glynn to identify them as the glasses he found on November 5 near the dump site. They were then admitted into evidence and made part of the record.

The next witnesses I called were police officers from Wilkes-Barre, a city in Luzerne County some fifteen miles south of Scranton, who had police dogs as part of their force that were trained to sniff and detect evidence. Their testimony was similar to what I had presented at the preliminary hearing, indicating what led to the discovery of the two boys buried under debris in the dump, rolled up inside a large red carpet.

In addition, the district attorney (DA) called an FBI agent, Robert C. DeLoach, who was involved in the investigation; a photographer, Eugene Centi; a criminal investigator for the Pennsylvania State Police who had taken photos at the dump site; and Joseph Gorski, a criminalist from the Pennsylvania State Police who had recorded the circumstances relating to the uncovering of the bodies and their condition.[17] Both of the State Police officers came from the Wyoming Barracks in Luzerne County. Mr. Gorski conducted a preliminary investigation of the bodies of the two boys at the dump site and uncovered traces of semen on their bodies as well as evidence of sexual assault. Mr. Gorski's record was confirmed in the autopsy report prepared by Bryce Sheldon, Wyoming County coroner, and in the autopsy performed on the bodies of the boys by Drs. Hollis Russell and George Hudock, respectively.[18]

Mr. Gorski testified to his conduction of a full examination of the dump site with Corporal Centi, which began about 2:20 p.m. on November 5. After police uncovered the bodies, he began collecting evidence, taking notes on body temperature (to determine time of death), wounds, and other factors relative to the condition of the boys' bodies. Both boys were partially unclothed, their pants and underpants pulled down around their ankles and their other clothing pulled high up on their bodies (similar to the description given by William Wright in his confession). Both bodies had numerous cuts and bruises, and blood was visible on their heads and faces. Gorski further detailed evidence from the bodies of the sexual assault, testifying as to multiple signs of sexual abuse of the Keen boy.[19]

In my attempt to maintain a continuity of sequence in my presentation of the evidence to the trial judge, I called Bryce Sheldon, the Wyoming County coroner, as my next witness. He transferred the bodies to Tyler Memorial Hospital in Tunkhannock, Pennsylvania, in his official vehicle for the purpose of autopsies to be conducted to determine the cause of death. The defense stipulated to the facts related to Mr. Sheldon's presence at the dump site after the bodies were found and his transferral of the bodies from there to Tyler Memorial Hospital for autopsies.

In the course of doing an autopsy to determine the cause of death, oftentimes the pathologist will find evidence in the body that confirms cause of death. In this case, the pathologist had found a spent bullet, or slug, in the head of each boy. These slugs were turned over to the police present at the autopsy as evidence to be used at trial and to maintain the chain of custody of that evidence for use at trial. These slugs were also important to connect the weapon, a .25-caliber pistol, in the possession of William Wright on November 1, 1973.

Dr. Hollis Russell, a practicing physician for some eighteen years and a pathologist on the staff of Tyler Memorial Hospital, was called as my next witness. He testified he conducted an autopsy on the body of Edmund (Buddy) Keen on November 6 that began at 8:30 a.m. and was completed around 11 a.m.

Dr. Russell testified that in the course of the autopsy he removed a bullet from the base of the brain and skull of the Keen boy—from the left portion of the sphenoid sinus, the base of the brain and the base of the skull. He described the bullet as a spent projectile that was discharged from a firearm. He testified that the bullet had entered the boy's head at the mid-portion of the forehead and that there was an entry wound.[20] *Russell said he gave the bullet to Trooper William Koscinski of the Pennsylvania State Police, whom he identified in the courtroom.*

Dr. Russell found other injuries to the Keen boy's body such as cuts, lacerations, contusions, and abrasions that played no part in his death.[21] The doctor also testified death came almost instantaneously as a result of the bullet wound to the head, which caused "marked subarachnoid hemorrhage, hemorrhages along the course of the bullet," adding, "[That] amount of hemorrhage would cause pressure on the vital areas of the brain that control breathing."[22]

Dr. Russell testified that, in his opinion, this damage would have rendered the victim unconscious and would have "probably taken place immediately," and death moments after.[23]

The doctor also testified as to findings that could have indicated sexual abuse or sodomy.[24]

In addition to the doctor's testimony, I introduced a copy of his report into the record of trial.

I next called Pennsylvania State Trooper William Koscinski, a twenty-three-year officer with the State Police who had for the past ten years worked in criminal investigations at the Wyoming Barracks, to establish chain of custody of the bullets after removed at the autopsies.

Assigned to the case on November 5, the day the bodies were found, Koscinski went to the dump site and arrived sometime after 3 p.m. on that afternoon. He also went to Tyler Memorial Hospital that evening but had left prior to the identification of the boys by the two fathers. Returning to the hospital the next morning, he was present at the separate autopsies of Keen and Freach by Dr. Hollis Russell, who conducted the Keen autopsy, and Dr. George Hudock, who conducted the Freach autopsy.

The spent bullets removed from both boys—one from the Keen boy and one from the Freach boy—were given to Trooper Koscinski. Each was placed in separate sealed evidence bags appropriately marked and tagged by Trooper Joseph Gorski. Koscinski said the spent bullets appeared to have been fired from a .25-caliber firearm. Koscinski placed cards in the plastic bags with his name, initials, and the time of acceptance indicated. He further testified these were the same slugs doctors had given him at the hospital after the autopsies and that they had been in *his custody until the time he turned them over to Trooper Dale Allen at the crime lab the next morning.*

Trooper Allen, a ballistics expert, had an excellent reputation for determining not only the caliber of a spent projectile, or slug, but also for identifying the very firearm from which it was discharged. I had used Dale Allen in several criminal cases over the eight years I served as district attorney of Lackawanna County. He was very helpful to me as a witness in past homicide cases. In this case, I needed to tie the defendant to the gun used.

Following Trooper Koscinski's testimony, DA Mazzoni called Paul J. Farrell, who identified himself as Pennsylvania district supervisor of the Wilkes-Barre office of the Pennsylvania Board of Probation and Parole. Mr. Farrell testified that he had knowledge of William Wright and identified him seated in the courtroom. Mr. Farrell explained that Wright was on parole under Farrell's supervision at the time of the murders. He also detailed Wright's occupation with Vector Control.[25]

Farrell said his office "became aware" Wright had been released on a work program and was residing in Scranton around July 20, 1973. Prior to the murders of the boys, he had an interview with Wright, sometime in early September, which was the last time he talked with Wright before learning of the murders. After the murders on November 1, he spoke with the Scranton Police and the Pennsylvania State Police of the Wyoming Barracks (around November 6, 7, and 8) about various people under Probation and Parole's supervision who would be of interest. Once the bodies were found on November 5, and there was indication of sexual molestation, Farrell said that there were "numerous individuals" his office had under supervision "who had . . . [committed] aggressive acts or sexual offenses" whom he brought to the attention of law enforcement.[26] On November 8, because he had learned that Wright was living in South Scranton, Farrell brought Wright's "particular" case to the attention of Captain Karam of the Scranton Police.[27]

Farrell spoke with William Wright on November 14 in Wright's apartment to discuss Wright's activities around the date the boys had gone missing. Farrell said, "I obtained some information from Captain Karam that had me believe that, perhaps, he [Wright] could be involved in this."[28]

On my direct examination, Farrell said Wright initially was on parole under his office's supervision until he was placed in Farview's Alpha House program. In the spring of 1973, Wright was assigned to work for a company in Scranton under the auspices of the city government called Vector Control. It was an organization that operated under a government grant used to rid dump sites of pests and rats. The employees used chemicals to kill the rodents. Farrell testified Wright was given a van to use in going to the targeted dump sites to do his work.

In the very beginning, Wright was to return to the hospital at the end of each day's work. Then, in time, when Wright gave the authorities the impression of being trustworthy, they permitted him to take residence in the city. During the time Wright was in the Alpha program, Parole and Probation became less involved, leaving the management and control of Wright with the hospital. When the boys went missing, Paul Farrell, knowing Wright's past criminal history, the manner of the murders, and the opportunity for Wright to commit the crimes, suspected Wright. Farrell discussed the possibility of William Wright being the perpetrator with Captain Frank Karam of the Scranton Police Department.

It was Captain Karam who provided Farrell with the information police had garnered and the fact that Wright had come into possession of a gun. Karam asked Farrell to keep Wright's possession of this gun confidential and not to mention this to Wright. Karam knew at this time that Farrell had been talking to Wright. The police were on track of tying Wright's gun with the commission of the crimes.

Farrell testified Wright became upset when Farrell visited him a number of times after the murders of the boys, because Farrell wanted Farview to better supervise Wright. Farrell's feelings were understandable since Farview gave Wright more liberties than Parole and Probation. Wright, in essence, told Agent Farrell to back off, because he had been making progress with the people at Farview. He told Farrell he didn't see any reason for Farrell to be involved anymore.

When Farrell met with Wright, his conversation focused on questions about what Wright had been doing "up to that point [of the murder]." To Farrell, Wright looked like he had been "doing well." But Farrell conceded in his testimony that Wright's possession of a gun might have meant his appearance had been deceiving. Farrell tried to get specifics from Wright about his associates and activities. This was the objective of his meeting with Wright on November 14. According to Farrell, "We had a rather lengthy conversation during which I learned that he had been [at work] in the Tunkhannock area on the 1st." Wright was able to provide the timetable for his work in this region and for his return to Scranton that day, around 4 p.m., with a coworker. Farrell also found out that Wright had been dating a woman—something Farrell had not known about previously. Farrell made it clear he was conducting an investigation on Wright to determine whether he was involved in the murders of the two boys. Farrell acknowledged to the court that he thought Wright "had a pretty good story and it did check out at the time as far as where he was and what time he was back in Scranton."[29]

Continuing to check out Wright's alibi for the day of the murders, Farrell went to the homes of Wright's coworker and his alleged girlfriend. During his interview with the latter, Wright called her. "She spoke with him in my presence," said Farrell, "and then handed the phone over to me and I spoke with him briefly."[30] According to Farrell, Wright was upset he was meeting with this woman. Farrell told him to "cool down."[31]

On November 19, Farrell received a telephone call early in the day from Mr. Glacken, Wright's counselor and social worker at Farview. He told Farrell that Mr. Russell, Wright's immediate supervisor at Vector Control, had contacted him and that Wright had "taken off." Hearing this, Farrell, accompanied by Parole Agent Frank Walsh, talked with "a young man" who was living with Wright at his Pittston Avenue address. Given permission by the roommate, the officers checked out the apartment, and they found most of Wright's clothing and personal belongings still there.

Farrell then called the Harrisburg office of Probation and Parole and explained the situation to them, whereupon they authorized putting out a Wanted for Parole Violation Teletype. Farrell then informed the Scranton Police Department of the situation and police there issued the Teletype for Wright.

Wright was found in December (on the sixth or seventh) in Florida and returned to the Scranton area, confined first to the State Correctional Institution at Graterford and then changed to the Dallas facility around the thirteenth of December so that police would have more convenient access to him in their investigation of the murders of the two boys.

Attorney Dunn cross-examined Farrell, asking the witness a number of questions concerning his history with the accused. Farrell said that his first contact with Wright had been in 1967 and that Wright had been released from Farview in "May or June of 1973," a fact that only became known to Farrell one month later in July 1973. Farrell described for Attorney Dunn Wright's type of release in the Alpha House program. Farrell was unsure of the exact date of Wright's release but put it as "either sometime in the latter part or the last week of May or in June when he took up residence [on Pittston Avenue]." During this early participation in the Alpha program he was required to return to Farview. This aspect of the release program continued for Wright after terms of his release changed from a daily release to residence status, according to Farrell. This was part of his "release procedure" and would last "until that program . . . [was] terminated."[32] Farrell said, as far as he knew, the program was not terminated and still in effect.

Farrell said his office had been "carrying his [Wright's] case for some time at the Farview State Hospital . . . [but] . . . were not actively engaged in the supervision [of Wright] due to the fact that he was committed to Farview by the court." Farrell testified, "We were monitoring the progress of this case to determine when or if he would become available to the agency again. In this manner we made routine contacts with the hospital over the years."[33]

At this point in Farrell's testimony, Wright's history becomes murky as he moved through the combined systems of mental health hospitalization and corrections. Farrell said, "Around 1972 when this program was initiated . . . at that time the original commitment to Farview was terminated through a nol. pros.[34] in, I believe, Delaware County [where Wright had been accused of attempted rape and declared insane and thereby sent to Farview] hereby making him available to our agency."[35]

Continuing, Farrell testified, "[At that time] our Executive Board [Probation and Parole] took an action to return him to the state Correctional Institution and to ask for an up-to-date psychiatric evaluation to determine whether or not he should remain confined in the penal system or should be allowed to return to the streets."[36] Then, Farrell said, "[A person from Probation and Parole] . . . was approached by . . . the head of the social work department of the Farview State Hospital and informed us of the formalization of this new program; and [the Probation and Parole officer] apparently was asked by this person if Mr. Wright could be allowed to continue in this program as opposed to being brought back to the State Correctional Institution at that time."[37] Thus, as a result of Farview's request, the original action by Probation and Parole was rescinded, and the Executive Board of Probation and Parole said it had "no objection to the participation of Mr. Wright in this program, which would be a graduated release program to the community."[38] This release, as they understood it, however, did not include living in the community but required the inmate to return daily to the hospital.

Continuing on, Mr. Farrell testified that the Alpha program was established around this time (1972–1973), and a Probation and Parole agent continued to visit the hospital but made no contacts with Wright. The first phase of the program was not, reiterated Farrell, into the community but an "intensive counseling type of thing."[39] The parole officer assigned to Farview "carried the case statistically" and "made contacts with the various hospital staff to determine progress and in January 1973, Mr. Wright was still in the initial phase of that program."[40]

By March of 1973, around the twentieth, Farrell said, "Mr. Wright obtained employment with the Vector Control agency. This was while he was still in Farview; we knew at this point that he was leaving the institution to go to the community as a worker." His employment took him into the community as a daily worker while he still received active counseling at the hospital and was to return to the hospital each day. Probation and Parole, said Farrell, did not "interfere at that point."⁴¹

Asked by Attorney Dunn as to when Farview actually turned Wright over to Probation and Parole, Farrell said, "They didn't actually turn him over. We found he was in the community and, as such, we have a legal responsibility for him and we became actively involved in the supervision process at that time. This would be a duel type of supervision. He was still being counseled by Mr. Glaughlin [*sic*, Glacken]. He was living in the community. This was not what we had originally agreed to. We agreed to the plan; but we wanted to know when he would be out so that we could begin carrying his case actively."⁴²

Attorney Dunn asked Farrell if it were true that, at the time Probation and Parole assumed dual control of Wright (around August 1973), Wright was still under the control of Farview also. Farrell answered that Wright was under the Alpha House program—a program that was run only by Farview State Hospital and not connected to any program administered by the Pennsylvania Parole Board. Dunn asked if it were true that Wright participated in this program in May, June, July, and August of 1973 and that it was a "type of Farview State Hospital parole program."⁴³ Farrell said that it was. "In other words," said Farrell, "he was not recommitted by our board to the Correctional Institution but allowed to continue here [with Farview's Alpha program]."⁴⁴

Asked by Attorney Dunn as to when the Pennsylvania Parole Board came into the case in order to take control of Wright, Farrell said the board had charge of him in 1964, that "statistically he was classified as an unconvicted violator in a mental institution."⁴⁵

Asked further by Dunn if Wright was committed to a mental institution by court decree, Farrell answered affirmatively and said the decree had not been terminated. Mr. Farrell was unsure of the date of the decree's termination or the judge who had ordered it. Attorney Dunn asked, "Isn't it a fact that . . . [Wright's] commitment to Farview was never terminated by Court Decree?" Farrell responded that he could not recall if the court decree had been terminated or not, but he recalled the decree had come from Delaware County court in 1964, "pending disposition of some outstanding criminal charges that he had . . . he was committed there prior to trial."[46]

Dunn then asked, "Wasn't the commitment by the court [in Delaware] conditional upon his staying at Farview until the Court was advised of the betterment of his condition and authorize[d] his release?"[47] When questioned by the prosecution as to the relevancy of this line of questioning, Attorney Dunn stated he was attempting to show Wright was "under the control of Farview, that for absolutely no lawful purpose really, the Pennsylvania Parole Board agent took control . . . and as a result of that control, he was not turned over to them by any Court, he was not turned over to them by Farview . . . [that] as a matter of fact the decree of the judge committing him to Farview committed him there conditionally, that he not be released without returning to the court."[48]

When questioned by Judge Campbell about pursuing this line of questioning, Dunn responded, "[It has] relevancy . . . in laying the ground work for the testimony to be put on by the defense as to the position of the defendant at the time when he is accused of the acts of which he is accused."[49] Dunn was seeking a stipulation about the accused's commitment decree from the Delaware County Courts. At this point, Attorney Dunn read the order of commitment of William Wright, and it was put into the record. Issued on January 28, 1964, the order stated, "William J. Wright . . . is mentally ill and . . . he is of criminal tendencies. Accordingly the Court directs the said William J. Wright to be committed to the Farview State Hospital to be there detained and treated as a mentally ill person at the expense of the Commonwealth of Pennsylvania until further order of the court."[50] Dunn continued by saying the order was signed by Henry G. Sweeny, president judge, and was the Order to Term 165, March 1964, Delaware County.[51]

After objections from the prosecution over introduction of this order and the charges that were related to it, it was entered into the trial record.

Attorney Dunn asked if Wright had told Farrell of "any personal problems he had, any feelings or emotions he was experiencing."[52] Farrell answered only that Wright had "objected to [Probation and Parole] becoming involved in the supervision of his case."[53] Asked if Wright said why he felt this way, Farrell replied that the defendant had said he believed he was "making progress" and did not see the need for Probation and Parole to be involved.[54] Dunn asked, "In light of his request of your not becoming involved, did you still become involved in the case?"[55] Farrell answered, "We had been involved all along."[56]

Questioned further by Dunn if one of the conditions of his agency's involvement of Wright's activities in August, September, and October of 1973 included restriction of Wright's ability to travel, Farrell answered, yes. "Did this restriction preclude him from going to Farview on his own without pre-notice to his parole officer?" Dunn asked. Farrell said he did not know, that perhaps this might be the case. Mainly his office wanted to know where Wright was and if he was traveling and when and where he was traveling.[57] The assumption here was that the Farview inmate could return to Farview, that this was not considered "traveling," as such.

Completing his questioning, Attorney Dunn asked Farrell a cryptic question: "In the course of your meeting with Mr. Wright prior to November of 1973 and, during that portion of 1973, after August, whether or not Mr. Wright told you that one of the reasons why he did not want to have the parole board exercise any control over him was because he could not guarantee what he might do if the Pennsylvania Parole Board exercised control over him?"[58] Mr. Farrell acknowledged this was true; Wright had made this statement to him.

Following Farrell's testimony, I called my next witness, Captain Detective Frank Karam, a twenty-five-year veteran of the Scranton Police Department, with service that included four years as captain of the detective union. Captain Frank Karam and I worked very closely on this case to bring "Billy Wright" down. Of all the law enforcement personnel I had worked with over my eight years as district attorney, to me Frank Karam was the best. In the course of working with him to investigate and ultimately prosecute the man responsible for these heinous crimes, Frank Karam was key to the outcome. Frank and I both took the murders of the two Minooka boys very personally. The captain and I had boys at home about the same ages as P.J. and Buddy. We both knew those two boys could have been our sons. Frank had a good sense for converting information he discovered into evidence and tracing that evidence to the person(s) responsible for the crime(s). I was a lawyer. I had no training and little experience in police work as a district attorney at the time. I learned a lot about good police work from Captain Karam, for whom I still maintain a certain reverence and great esteem. In simple words, besides being a good cop, he was a good family man and a good friend to have in your corner in times of need and consolation. Sadly, Frank Karam will never be able to read the content of this book, as he died on Christmas Day 2013.[59]

In my direct examination of Captain Karam, he opened his testimony by telling how he had learned of information that made Wright a suspect in the case of the missing two boys on November 12, 1973. After talking to Agent Farrell on November 8, he called William Wright into his office at city hall.

Karam dispatched one of his detectives to bring William Wright to his office so he could talk to Wright. On his arrival, Wright was advised of his Miranda rights.[60] Present at this meeting were several other Scranton detectives, including Captain Frank Roche. Wright was told he was being questioned as a possible suspect in the murders of the two boys.

While two detectives questioned Wright in a separate room, Captain Karam said, Wright's boss told the police Wright had a .25-caliber gun. Karam said this fact made Wright "all the more interesting" to the police.[61] As this was unfolding, two police detectives, William Walsh and Eugene Genell, were scouring the city's gun shops to see who might have purchased a .25-caliber gun or .25-caliber bullets, eventually discovering that Wright had purchased some .25-caliber shells from Bill's Sporting Goods in North Scranton. Bill Zingle owned the store, and his ledger recorded Wright's purchase of .25-caliber bullets on October 4, 1973.

At first Wright denied having anything to do with the murders, but when confronted with information the police had about a .25-caliber firearm in his possession, he began to open up. Wright was shown a copy of a ledger from Bill's Sporting Goods. Bill Zingle was called by Captain

Karam to come to the Detective Bureau at city hall to identify Wright as purchasing the bullets from him. According to Karam, Zingle said, pointing to Wright, "That's the man who purchased the shells."[62] Initially, in this interview, Wright denied possessing a gun, because he didn't want any of his hospital supervisors or his parole officer to know this. A photographic copy of the logbook page containing Wrights signature for the bullets and the date of the purchase was entered into the trial record.

After Wright acknowledged having made the purchase of bullets, police told him they were looking for a gun involved in the murders. Wright denied having anything to do with the murders.[63] Captain Karam asked Wright to help them with this case, saying, "'Bill, if you help us get the gun, we can take this gun to ballistics and either prove your innocence or your guilt.'"[64]

Wright then disclosed to Karam, with other detectives present, he admitted buying the gun from an acquaintance. When asked by Karam as to where the gun was, Wright said he disposed of it by throwing it in his garbage at his house—garbage that was later picked up by the "garbage people."[65] Police "assumed that they threw it on the [DeNaples] dump up in Dunmore, Pennsylvania."[66] Captain Karam said that he then asked, "'Did you fire the gun? Could you help us get a slug so that we can get ballistics to make comparisons?'" Wright told police he had fired the gun "somewhere," saying, "I am not sure but I think it was around Greenbush Street."[67] Karam then asked him if he would accompany two of the detectives to the place where he had fired the gun to see if they could retrieve a slug or casing. Wright agreed, and this was done. Later, they returned with a casing from the general area where Wright had taken them. No bullet was found. Captain Karam made further attempts to locate the gun and spoke to Wright again later, on November 12; but Wright maintained that he did not have the gun, and the police could not find anything. Captain Karam said he then made preparations to make an extensive search of the DeNaples dump area in Dunmore on November 13. Police asked Wright to come back to headquarters on November 13. The search failed to uncover the gun. Wright returned to police headquarters as requested and asked police if they had found anything. Asked by the prosecution if police had tried to talk with him after this, Karam said police had tried to find him but to no avail.

Karam went on to testify about Wright's flight to Florida and subsequent apprehension for parole violation.

The defense counsel had a few questions of the captain, beginning with an inquiry as to whether or not Wright had offered Karam any reason for having a gun. Karam said he had, that the reason Wright gave was that he "used the gun on the dump . . . to shoot rats, or something."[68] Dunn then asked Karam if police had checked to find out if it was "unusual" for a Vector Control person to carry a weapon. Karam responded that he had and that it was not the usual thing to do. Pressed by Dunn on this further, Karam stated he had checked this out and found out that Wright "was not to carry a sidearm; neither was anyone else unless they got an okay from the chief of police."[69] Asked if any of Wright's coworkers carried a weapon, Karam stated he later discovered Wright's boss had a gun and carried it. Later, Dunn asked if Karam had made any determination about the boss carrying a gun, and Karam answered, "As a policeman and as deputy chief, we frown on that . . . [and] since then, we would not allow [him] to carry a gun."[70]

Moving on, Dunn questioned Captain Karam as to whether or not Wright had attempted to call Karam long distance between November 12 and December 6. Karam said he had a "hazy recollection" of someone telling him that there had been a long distance call from someone asking for him and that "it may have been from Florida," with the implication that Wright, after fleeing to Florida, had tried to call Karam.[71]

I called my next witness, William Wright's field supervisor at Vector Control. He explained the operation of Vector Control, saying it was a "program managed and financed by federal and state funds."[72] *He defined the word "Vector" as "any type of animal or insect that transmits communicable diseases in any way and rats most of all."*[73] *At the time of the murders of the boys, he said Vector had an office in the Scranton Municipal Building, more commonly referred to as city hall.*

Asked if he were still field supervisor, this witness told the court the program was no longer in Scranton, that it had become a mosquito control agency in a ten-county area. Asked if Wright was an employee of Vector, he said he was, and he was able to identify Wright for the court. He described Wright's duties as an employee of Vector. It was Wright's job to go out, survey the area assigned to him, determine the cause of the problem, and put out the bait. He had duties related to city garbage collection as well.

The Vector supervisor testified further that on November 1, in response to a call in late October from a Towanda Health Department representative, he had assigned Wright to an area in Towanda and Dushore, communities northwest of Scranton, just over one hour away by car. Wright was joined by another employee of Vector. The supervisor separately accompanied the two workers on that day. Vector had two vans for its use: a 1970 blue Dodge and a "newer" yellow Ford. Although it is unclear from this testimony to the driving arrangements made for this work day, Wright and the coworker drove the blue Dodge van. Before going to their first stop, they went to the supervisor's home in Tunkhannock.[74] It is unclear as to whether or not the supervisor drove the yellow van from the Scranton area to his home or if he was meeting the two workers at his home where the yellow van was located. In any case, the three men were at the supervisor's home, left the blue van there, and from there all went to Towanda together in the yellow van. They arrived in Towanda around 10:40 a.m. and left there about 12:30 to go to Dushore. After baiting three or four properties in Dushore, they returned to the supervisor's home, and Wright and the other worker left for Scranton in the yellow van.

According to the supervisor, Wright and the other worker left the supervisor's home sometime around three or after. The drive from Tunkhannock to Scranton might have taken anywhere from thirty to thirty-five minutes, perhaps longer due to afternoon traffic.

The supervisor testified Wright came to work on the morning of November 13 and was interrogated by police that day. Wright reported for work on November 14, but on November 15 called the supervisor saying he was sick and unable to come to work. In the days that followed, Wright did not report for work. The following Monday, November 19, the supervisor waited until ten o'clock for Wright to report, and when Wright didn't phone, the supervisor asked the coworker if he knew anything about Wright, since Wright often picked him up and took him home. That person told the supervisor Wright had not come to work the previous Friday as well, and the coworker had been unable to get in touch with him. At this point, the supervisor went down to police headquarters and told the chief of police that Wright was not at work.

The supervisor testified Wright parked the van across the street from his home on Pittston Avenue. After November 14, believing Wright had quit his job, the supervisor wanted the van moved, because Pittston Avenue was a "heavily traveled thoroughfare," and it would be safer to have it parked in front of the other worker's home.[75] This worker subsequently had his landlord drive the truck to his home and park it there.

The supervisor said that sometime after November 1, Gene Corbett, a Pennsylvania state trooper, came to his office and asked for permission to check the yellow van. The supervisor gave this permission, and the trooper and a colleague went to where the van was parked and went through it. After the search, the police told the supervisor that Vector could continue using the van. The supervisor said sometime between November 5 and 12, he noticed the van "had been washed and cleaned, inside and out and everything was stacked neatly." This was not how the van had looked on November 1 when Wright drove it to Scranton following his work in Dushore and Towanda.

Asked if there were any contents that had been moved from the yellow van to the blue van, he said at some point after November 1, he and the other worker had run out of bait when doing a job on the West Side of Scranton. Instead of picking up bait in its storage place (at Nay Aug Park), they went to the coworker's home, took the bait from the yellow van, and put it into the blue truck. They transferred about eight or ten fifty-pound bags of bait, a few boxes of bait block, a few cartons of bait stations, and, he thought, a chainsaw. They noticed underneath the last bag taken off the truck there was a big "red or pinkish spot."[76] He reported this finding to the police.[77]

On cross-examination, the Vector supervisor testified he knew of the gun, as Wright had shown him the pistol and asked him if he wanted to buy it. The supervisor said he didn't know of Wright's background at the time. He asked Wright from whom he bought the gun, but Wright wouldn't reveal the identity of the seller. The supervisor then told Wright he needed a permit to carry a gun. He recalled that the gun had no serial number.

The supervisor said he knew Wright had a .25-caliber pistol and related his knowledge of this to both Lieutenant Roche and Captain Karam on November 12, 1973. The last day Wright had reported for work was November 14, 1973.

Attorney Dunn asked the witness if, during the period Wright had worked for him at Vector, he knew Wright had been a patient at Farview. He responded that he had known this. Asked by Dunn if he knew Wright had a history of "mental imbalance," he said he had not known this.[78] Dunn then asked if Mr. Farrell or Mr. Walsh had consulted the witness prior to November 1 about Wright, and the witness said he did not recall any meetings with the two parole officers. Dunn asked further whether or not he had offered to supply Wright with a rifle to use while checking out the dumps, and he said he had not made such an offer. As for the .25-caliber gun that he said he knew Wright had, he testified that prior to November 1, he had not known Wright was carrying such a weapon. Rather, it was four to six weeks before the abduction of the boys that Wright showed him the pistol."[79] Dunn then asked if the supervisor had Wright "sworn as an additional patrolman to patrol the dumps."[80] He said he had, and the chief of Scranton Police, John McCrone, had performed the swearing.[81] Asked if he had mentioned Wright's pistol to any police officers in Scranton prior to November 1, he said he had not, adding, "I had not known what Bill's background was . . . when he showed me the pistol. I assumed that he brought it in because I am a collector of antique guns and when he showed me the gun, I had no interest in it because it was a modern gun."[82]

The supervisor said Wright had asked him what he thought the gun was worth, and he told Wright that if he were going to buy it, he would pay fifteen dollars for it, "because I would want to make a profit on it and I felt the gun was worth thirty dollars." He had asked Wright where the clip to the gun was, and Wright had told them that there "wasn't any."[83] In that case, he had told Wright he "wouldn't pay more than ten dollars for the gun."[84] When he asked Wright where he purchased the gun, Wright wouldn't tell him. According to this witness he told Wright it was illegal to carry a gun without a permit and that Wright should return it to its owner. Wright said he would do so immediately.

After this testimony, Dunn continued questioning the witness about the gun, its make (he didn't know, as there was nothing inscribed on it), the serial number (same answer), and the condition of the weapon ("[the] bluing was gone and it appeared old").[85] Asked if, as a gun collector, he knew all firearms had to be registered and that registration was by serial number, he said he knew this. Without a serial number, it would have been impossible to register this gun, and, as such, possession of the type of gun that Wright had was illegal. The witness acknowledged all this, and in addition, he said knowing this and that Wright had such a weapon, he still did not advise city police that "one of the employees who worked for the City of Scranton possessed a weapon which was not registered and which would be illegal."[86] In reply, the supervisor said he should have done so but didn't. Given that all this had happened four to six weeks prior to the murders of the boys on November 1, the implication was clear. If the Vector supervisor had given this information to the police, Wright might have been arrested for illegal possession of a firearm and at the very least returned to Farview, in which case the murders would not have happened. On redirect, Mazzoni asked the supervisor how he knew the gun was a .25-caliber, and the witness said he thought the caliber was on the gun and added that Wright may have shown him the gun three to five weeks before the murders.

I then called as my next witness, Bill Zingle, the owner of Bill's Sporting Goods, located on Providence Road in North Scranton. His testimony was stipulated to by the defense counsel. Zingle testified that Wright bought a box of .25-caliber bullets on October 4, 1973, and the record of this purchase was entered in the store ledger, which by law Zingle was required to keep and maintain. He also said that he was called to the Detective Bureau on November 12, 1973, to identify Wright as the person who bought the bullets. [87]

What followed next was a series of witnesses who turned out to be the centerpiece of our case, the so-called chain of ownership of the murder weapon.

It was necessary for me to prove in the presentation of my evidence not only that the bullets found in the bodies at the autopsy were .25-caliber but also that they were fired from the very firearm possessed by William Wright on November 1, 1973.

In Pennsylvania, a confession standing alone would not be sufficient evidence to warrant a conviction. A confession to be used as evidence for conviction had to be corroborated by other supporting evidence connecting the confessor to the crime. For this case, we had to connect the murder weapon to William Wright to support the confession, and we called several witnesses to do this.

First came the man who testified he knew Wright and sold Wright a gun on the same day Wright purchased shells from Bill's Sporting Goods—October 4, 1973. Wright paid twenty dollars for the gun. The witness said he had purchased the weapon sometime in August from another man. At the time of purchase, the gun was complete with a clip. The witness said he had not fired the gun while it was in his possession. [88]

Next I called the previous gun owner, who testified by stipulation he knew the man to whom he sold the weapon in question in the late August 1973. He said he had purchased the gun "sometime in the middle of the summer of 1973 from an individual named Bob or Bill from Mount Pocono at the Waco Diner."[89] He said before the sale to the previous witness he had fired shots into several trees in target practice in the area of East Lemon, Pennsylvania, not far from the town of Tunkhannock, in Wyoming

County. He later took police to the area and pointed to the exact tree into which the bullets were fired from the subject gun. Police took a section from the tree containing the bullet holes for analysis and comparison.

Next came Frank Glynn, a detective from the Scranton Police Department whose testimony had also been stipulated by defense counsel. Detective Glynn's testimony established the very part of the tree that was shot, pointed out to him by the gun owner. He said he and some other officers had gone with the gun owner to the East Lemon site. He said police chiseled a .25-caliber bullet out of the tree and then removed a section of the tree. Detective Glynn said he took this section to the crime lab in Harrisburg and gave it to the ballistics expert, Dale Allen. Glynn said further that police found four casings near the area of the tree containing the one .25-caliber slug.

These exhibits were taken from the tree site and turned over to Dale Allen on December 13, 1973, for him to remove the slugs and make a comparison with those removed from the boys' heads at the autopsies. The casings would be analyzed and compared with casings found at the 522 Greenbush Street site Wright had identified as a place where he had fired the pistol. This was the place Scranton Police took Wright on November 13 to show them where he had used the pistol for target practice.[90] On that day Wright had found one of the casings and handed it over to Glynn, while the other three were picked up by a Scranton detective.[91]

Then came the fourth witness, ballistics expert Dale Allen on the issue of the gun. He testified as to his credentials and experience and then provided the very evidence we needed to make our case convincing enough to Judge Campbell of William Wright's guilt to the standard of "beyond a reasonable doubt."

Allen said that around November or December of 1973 he had been at the Pennsylvania State Police Crime Laboratory in the ballistics section and that his job classification was "examiner of small arms and small arms ammunition."[92] As a ballistics expert, Allen was then asked about the four casings (exhibit C-26), four casings (exhibit C-27), and one slug (exhibit C-29) and how they compared with the slugs (exhibit C-24) taken *from the heads of the victims. He said he had received the two discharged four metal jackets, .25-caliber bullets from Trooper Koscinski on November 7—bullets taken from the heads of the boys—and the exhibits C-26, 27, 28, and 29 on December 13 from Detectives Glynn and Baggott. Following which, he conducted his analysis.*

Dale Allen said after removing the slugs from the tree, he used a comparison microscope, an instrument, to compare the striation or markings that appear as lines and groves on a bullet, made when a bullet travels down a barrel in its discharge. The striations or scratch markings, also known as "lands and grooves," on the bullet can be picked up by use of the comparison microscope in examining the striations. In this way a determination can be made as to whether it has been discharged from the same weapon. Using this method of analysis, Allen said that he could see both bullets, the ones removed from the boys' heads, and compare the "striations or markings" of these with the ones removed from the tree at the same time, side by side.[93]

Allen made a positive finding in his analysis and comparison of the bullets to have been fired from the same .25-caliber firearm. When asked for specifics as to similarities, Allen said he matched six lines and grooves of the bullets. He also said he matched the eight different casings—identifying them as discharged .25-caliber automatic Winchester western cartridge cases and four discharged .25-caliber automatic Remington Peters cartridge cases, using the comparison microscope for this analysis as well.

With the testimony of the fourth and final witness in the sequence of the .25-caliber pistol evidence and its use by William Wright in taking the lives of the two boys, we made out a convincing case of his guilt.

Joseph Gorski, a criminalist with the Pennsylvania State Police at the Wyoming Barracks, was recalled at this point to testify about forensic matter that he received or collected himself at the dump on the fifth of November 1973, as well as various items he collected at the hospital where the bodies of the boys were taken after discovery. These items included the boys' clothing, a rectal thermometer used to check for "acid phosphatase" in the body of Paul Freach, and some "black matter" found in his mouth. With particular reference to fibers and hair, he said he had collected these. He went on to state that he had found "numerous hair and fibers similar to that of the victim . . . and also one human hair that was dissimilar" on the jacket of Paul Freach.[94] *Gorski conducted a series of comparisons of the items and compared the dissimilar hair with that of William Wright. He found that the one dissimilar hair found on Paul Freach's jacket was similar to Wright's hair. He went on to say that he had received a sample of clothing taken from Wright's apartment and under the buckle of a right shoe had found a hair. He had also found a hair on the sole of the same shoe. He said that in testing these hairs they compared to the hair taken from Edmund Keen, hair that he had removed at the time of the boy's autopsy.*

Further, Trooper Gorski testified that he had processed for evidence the yellow Econoline Ford van owned by Vector Control and used by William Wright. In the course of this investigation he had found a small red fiber attached to the bottom of the spare tire. On analysis he found this fiber "similar or identical in all details to the fibers taken from the jacket of Paul Freach;. he also said that he found a hair attached to the bottom rim of the spare tire that was "similar in all details to the hair of Edmund Keen."[95]

Gorski continued with his testimony, saying he had found some red fiber and some blue matter on top of the armrest of the backseat of the yellow van. He tested the red fiber and found it to be "similar in all details to the jacket worn by Paul Freach" on the last day he was seen alive.[96] *Additional red fiber was also found under the backseat along with numerous hairs and other fibers. Gorski tested this red fiber and found it to be a match with the Freach boy's jacket. He also found human hair under the backseat of the van with a reddish stain on it that gave "preliminary positive tests for blood." However, he continued by saying there was "not enough of the reddish stain . . . to confirm whether . . . that substance was blood."*[97]

Additionally, Trooper Gorski said Scranton Police had given him some of Wright's clothing, which he tested as well, and on this clothing he found "several fibers, one of which was similar in all details tested to the fibers from the jacket . . . of Paul Freach."[98]

I next recalled Trooper Koscinski as a witness to establish a statement he attained from William Wright at Chase Correctional Institution located in Dallas, Pennsylvania, after Wright was brought back to Pennsylvania from Florida and was moved to Chase.

Trooper Koscinski visited Wright there on December 18, 1973—accompanied by State Police Corporal Gene Corbett and Detectives Glynn and Baggott. At this visit, the officers were able to get a statement from Wright in regard to the murders. Advised of his constitutional rights, Wright made his statement duly recorded on a tape recorder (exhibit C-30). After identifying William Wright as the person from whom he had obtained the recording on the eighteenth, Trooper Koscinski was asked to play the tape for the court.[99]

Wright had provided Trooper Koscinski with all the details of the killing of the two boys from the time he put them in his van at gunpoint in South Scranton to the disposition of their bodies in Falls. Koscinski said Wright had been Mirandized and was convinced what Wright told him was done of his own free will and was voluntary.

Following the playing of Wright's statement, the prosecutor asked Trooper Koscinski if he had an occasion to see the yellow van Wright drove on November 1. Answering in the affirmative, the trooper was then asked to describe the vehicle for the court. He did so, saying that it was a "paneled truck with doors on the side and rear."[100] Mazzoni then asked, "If you were sitting in the back seat, [behind] the driver's seat, would it have been entirely enclosed?" Koscinski said it would.[101] Defense Attorney Dunn did not cross-examine Trooper Koscinski, and with that the DA recalled Paul Farrell, the parole officer.

I recalled Paul Farrell, who testified to a conversation he had on January 8, 1974 with the defendant at Chase. At that time, in a lengthy conversation taking about four hours, Wright told Farrell the details of the murders, including "the manner in which the boys were abducted, how they were molested and eventually murdered."[102] *Wright told Farrell that on November 1, he "arrived back in Scranton around three thirty."*[103] *After he dropped his coworker off at his house after work (on November 1), he went home and called a girl he was seeing. He wanted her to go out but she refused. After lying down on his bed for a while, he got up and went out. The refusal is what precipitated his getting into the yellow van to drive around the block on Cedar Avenue and into the Cedar Avenue mine fire area near the boys' home. Then, Mr. Farrell recalled, Wright told him about meeting up with the boys at the location where he ended their lives.*[104] *According to Farrell, Wright said he "passed these two boys and stopped the truck and waited for them to approach. He forced them into the back of the truck at gun point."*[105] *Farrell said the rest is what Wright told other law enforcement people, with the only difference being where he disposed of the gun. Wright told Farrell he threw the gun and the clip into the Lackawanna River in Scranton.*

Before encountering the boys, Wright told Farrell he had observed a group of children in the area. Wright told Farrell that after forcing the boys into the back of the van at gunpoint, "he made one boy commit sodomy upon the other boy."[106] *At this point, Wright told Farrell he said he heard a vehicle coming, which, as it turned out, was a police car driven by a police officer. Wright said he "got from the back of the truck into the front driver's seat, put the gun in his pocket and the two boys remained in the back of the truck."*[107] *According to Farrell's understanding of Wright's story, the police officer and Wright talked to each other through the windows of each vehicle—something about Wright baiting the area.*[108] *When the policeman left, Wright said he "got into the back of the truck again and forced one boy to commit sodomy upon him."*[109] *Around this time, said Farrell, Wright took out his gun and shot "the one boy, not the one he was forcing at that time. . . . He [then] shot the other boy."*[110]

Wright refused to disclose details of the sexual assault in his taped confession. In this account, Wright said he had murdered the two boys about five minutes after the police officer left. However, this account is contrary to the belief of law enforcement authorities as to when exactly Wright murdered the boys. Police believe that when the policeman arrived at the mine fire site, the boys had already been murdered by Wright.

Farrell's testimony after this was key to the prosecution's argument that Wright was not a victim of discontrol syndrome when he murdered Paul Freach and Edmund Keen. Recounting for the court what Wright had told him of his actions following the murders, Farrell said Wright had told him he had driven the van with the bodies in the back "toward the Pittston area . . . turned right and went down into an area that he anticipated disposing of the bodies; but he felt that this was not a good place . . . [so] he continued on and subsequently ended up in the area where the bodies were found, in the dump area."[111]

Farrell said he had questioned Wright about the sexual assaults—if he had attacked the boys before or after he had murdered them, but Wright was "reluctant" to say anything. "Eventually, he did say that he . . . [in Minooka] . . . in the back of the truck . . . had raped one of the boys."[112] It is not clear from Farrell's testimony whether this occurred before or after the boy was killed.

Arriving at the dump site where the boys' bodies were subsequently discovered, Wright told Farrell he took the bodies of the boys out of the truck, "dragged them by the collars across the top and rolled them down over the bank [of the dump]. . . . He then went down to the bottom of the bank and climbed back up about half way down. He covered them with material there; and, according to him, he seemed to think that it was a piece of canvass. He wasn't sure what it was that he covered the boys with."[113]

Farrell said Wright told him that, after he had disposed of the boys' bodies, he drove back to Scranton via the Morgan Highway to Keyser Valley Road and turned left to go up to the Viewmont Mall.[114]

While at the mall, he told Farrell, he spoke with a person he had known as a guard at Farview, made a bank withdrawal with a "computerized card, and purchased some new clothes, went out, got back in the truck and drove."[115] Farrell said Wright said he was unsure where he had gone after this. It "seemed to be North Main Street [Scranton] . . . to

South Main [Scranton] and at the corner of one of the streets there . . . he pulled into a gas station, got gas . . . went into the men's room . . . and changed his clothes."[116] Afterward, he went home. Farrell did not recall whether Wright had told him of the disposing of his clothing, but he did tell Farrell that he had "disposed of the gun underneath the bridge along the [Lackawanna] River."[117] Wright said he "took the clip out, took the bullets from the clip and threw them separately into the water. Then he threw the gun back underneath the bridge."[118]

Mr. Farrell testified Wright told him that before he went home he went to a "dump site, an old dump site . . . where it is illegal to dump . . . in that area on Euclid Avenue."[119] There, Wright had said he "got rid of everything that was in the back of the truck; the poison and so forth and cleaned the truck out and then he proceeded home."[120]

Attorney Dunn did not cross-examine the witness.

Following Mr. Farrell's testimony, the prosecutor read a stipulated statement from Captain Frank Roche concerning the carpet found covering the boys' bodies. This statement indicated that, due to lighting conditions at the dump site, it was impossible to ascertain the makeup of the carpet, but it felt like canvass—which would concur with Wright's description of the material he had used to cover his victims.

I then recalled Captain Karam to introduce a letter he had received from William Wright while Wright was incarcerated at Chase after his arrest and awaiting trial. The date on the envelope was January 14, 1974; the date of the letter was Sunday, January 13. The letter was exhibit C-31. Captain Karam was asked to read the letter for the court.

This letter was introduced, and it read:

> *Sir: Since I last talked with you I have had two visitors. One, my brother, who indicated that you still feel that certain aspects of this case are still in doubt. He referred to the possibility of another being involved as one of the more important questions unsettled.*
>
> *Two, my parole agent, whom also expressed the same thoughts. In fact, he spent a few hours trying to get me to say that there was. There wasn't.*

> *It seems though that some sort of proof is required aside from just saying it. I am suggesting to you two possible methods. One, which I suggested to you before, a lie detector test, coupled with, perhaps, truth serum. I am not being dramatic in this suggestion, but sincere.*
>
> *The second method, a little more difficult perhaps for you to arrange, but if you feel it necessary, then I would say it could be, would be for me to go over the events of that day, as I remember them, where they happened. Quite possibly some things or someone might confirm what I have already told you.*
>
> *At this point I am concerned that someone might be unfairly accused and improperly subjected to harassment uncalled for.*
>
> *This letter then is both a request and a statement of willingness to do any or all of the things suggested; or, for that matter, whatever else is required to prevent the blame from falling on some innocent party. Respectfully, Bill Wright.*[121]

At this point, the trial was adjourned and would be continued, for more evidence to be introduced, on October 16, 1974.

Judge Campbell, prior to adjourning this court session, granted a defense motion for a delay in the proceedings in order to allow for opportunity for another psychiatric study of William Wright.

According to one reporter covering the trial, the families of the victims present for the day's court session found it difficult to accept this request. Both mothers were quoted as saying, "Wright had had plenty of time to prepare for court," and, "He's no more crazy than I am."[122] However, DA Mazzoni explained to the families that the state anticipated the introduction of psychiatric evidence by the defense. As such, the state was prepared to rebut defense psychiatric witnesses with "our own psychiatric experts."[123] The prosecution wanted no issues available to the defense on psychiatric matters, particularly since such issues could be used by defense on appeal. A new trial might be granted if such issues were present, and the state's mission in this case was to try William Wright one time—and one time only—and in so doing achieve the maximum verdict under the law for the accused murderer of the boys.

10

TRIAL—OCTOBER 16, 1974

Sections of this chapter composed by Paul Mazzoni are in italics.

On October 16, 1974, in Bellefonte, Pennsylvania, before the Honorable R. Paul Campbell, my presentation of the case of Commonwealth of Pennsylvania v. William J. Wright *resumed by my calling to the witness stand Dr. George Hudock, a pathologist and coroner of Luzerne County, Pennsylvania. He was my final witness, and he was to testify to the autopsy he conducted on Paul J. Freach.*

My questions of Dr. Hudock began with qualifying him as an expert witness in the field of pathology and in conducting autopsies. He said he was a coroner for a number of years, having performed some 2,500 autopsies over his career. The court accepted him as an expert in his field.

He then proceeded to testify to the autopsy he did of Paul J. (P.J.) Freach, first needing someone to identify the body. This was done by the father, Paul J. Freach, who arrived at Tyler Memorial Hospital moments before the autopsy began on November 6, 1973, at 11:20a.m.

Dr. Hudock had seen P.J.'s body at the dump site where he was discovered on November 5 and identified it to be the same body at the autopsy. The doctor, during his examination, found a gunshot wound of the head, with the entrance in the left parietal region above the left ear. [1]

Dr. Hudock told the court that the parietal region is often referred to in layman's terms as the temple region of the human head and that the path of the bullet was downward toward the front of the boy's body, through the left parietal lobe of the brain, through the corpus callosum (the white material in the middle portion of the brain), passing into the midportion of the brain, through the body of the sphenoid bone (the bone that supports the base of the skull), and coming to rest in the right posterior oropharynx (the area behind the throat on the right side).[2] The doctor said a bullet was found lodged in the region behind the throat on the right side in the right palatine tonsil (a collection of lymph tissues at the right rear of the mouth). The "bullet caused destruction of the brain" and subdural and subarachnoid hemorrhage.[3]

In addition to the brain damage caused by the bullet, the doctor said he found other injuries that indicated sexual abuse.[4] When asked whether or not he could give an opinion as to the cause of some bruises and abrasions he also found, the doctor replied that they were "caused as a result from blood [bruising], force and trauma being subjected to the skin and could be result of a fall at or near the time of death, or blows to the body."[5] The doctor provided specific detail of the sexual injuries.[6] He further stated that these findings on the boy's body occurred "immediately after or at the time of death . . . [and that] it did not occur [over] any extended period of time before the death of the boy."[7] Asked what might have been the cause of such injuries, the doctor acknowledged it was consistent with "an act of sodomy."[8]

These injuries did not cause Paul Freach's death. Dr. Hudock attributed the boy's death to the gunshot wound, with death being instantaneous— as was the case of Edmund Keen. Paul Freach's other injuries were consistent with a sexual assault.

The doctor, after removing the bullet from P.J.'s body, gave it to Trooper William Koscinski, who was present at the autopsy. I concluded my direct examination of Dr. Hudock at this point and rested my case.

On cross-examination, Defense Attorney John Dunn asked the doctor to describe the many contusions, abrasions, and the like the doctor had discovered on P.J.'s skin. The doctor did so, saying that on the thorax there were "reddish-purple discolorations"; "irregular black and blue marks and superficial abrasions on the right anterior Illiac spine . . . the right hip"; "abrasions . . . on the right lateral thigh . . . [upper part of the right leg], . . . the left anterior thigh [upper portion of the left leg], . . . [and the] left patella [left knee]."[9] Dunn asked the doctor if these could have been caused by pressure of garments, and the doctor said they could not but could have resulted from pressure from the clothing on the boy that had been pulled down around his ankles at the time of death, as opposed to "blows or . . . by falling." The discolorations in the thorax area, admitted the doctor, could have been the result of pressure of the weight of the carpet that covered the boys and, again, not by blows.

At this point, the trial took an unexpected turn. Wright informed the judge that he wanted to withdraw his plea of guilty. For the record, the Commonwealth objected, saying it had closed its case and now learned for the first time Wright's intention to make the change.[10] The judge responded that he was granting the defendant permission to withdraw his guilty plea "in view of the liberal feeling of our appellate courts with respect to the right of a defendant to withdraw a plea of guilty, and in view of Rule 320 of the Rules of Criminal Procedure, and in further view of the anticipated defense."[11] Defense Attorney Dunn noted for the record that the defendant had entered a plea of "not guilty" in the indictment, to which DA Mazzoni responded that this plea had been entered by the court at the time of the arraignment "because the defendant stood mute."[12] Speaking on behalf of his client, Attorney Dunn said the defendant would now plead not guilty, and this change of plea would apply to all six indictments against his client. Attorney Dunn then told the court they were waiving jury trial and would proceed with the trial being heard by a single judge. The judge, thereupon, went over the Constitutional rights of the accused for a second time as to his rights relative to a jury trial and to the testimony that had already been heard in the case, which would be taken into consideration by the court in determining his guilt or innocence.

Next the prosecution asked to reserve its rights to recall witnesses as needed in view of the change of plea. Wright's position on this request was that he believed the prosecution had put in all of the testimony necessary to establish the facts of the crimes and the degree of guilt. The defense said, "If it is merely going to be to add to that, then we would object to any further testimony. . . . If it is going to be to explain anything which would come up by way of rebuttal . . . we would not object. . . . We do feel that the District Attorney has presented all of his evidence to establish the degree of guilt."[13] The court responded that the Commonwealth had the "right to recall any witnesses to rebut any evidence presented by the defendant which you think is rebuttable."[14] However, DA Mazzoni explained that he was asking not only to rebut but also to "more fully develop something that had not been developed" in the case up to this point, "only because of the plea being entered."[15]

The change of plea did not indicate that Wright was now denying his guilt of the murders. Rather, this was the way the defense was now setting the stage for a claim that Wright was suffering from a brain disorder, which had been the reason for his actions—the so-called irresistible impulse doctrine.[16] The problem with this action was that Pennsylvania courts did not recognize irresistible impulse as a legitimate defense for murder. As one writer pointed out, irresistible impulse was perhaps best known from the book and motion picture *Anatomy of a Murder*.[17] In this case, the defense meant that Wright suffered from an uncontrollable impulse that had resulted in his murdering the two boys, and, although he knew that this was wrong, he could not stop himself. The irresistible impulse defense was not recognized under the McNaughton Rule, the test for insanity in Pennsylvania criminal cases since 1875, which provides that a person accused of a crime could not be held accountable for the crime if he or she were unable to distinguish the difference between right and wrong.

After changing his plea to not guilty, the defendant agreed to proceed with his trial without a jury and to allow the trial record of all testimony provided about the crime up to this point to stand.

My confidence in the case that I developed against the defendant did not wane because of the plea change. Knowing this could happen, I had not taken any chances with my presentation of the evidence I had given the court to consider. It was my firm belief from the very beginning of the trial that I was going to get William Wright and that he would never again be free to harm anyone. I wanted him to serve not one life sentence but two life sentences as well as consecutive sentences for the other criminal offenses. My mission from the very moment of the arrest was to attain the maximum length of incarceration, with no possibility for release on parole, effectively locking him away for the remainder of his natural life. There was no capital punishment law in Pennsylvania for first-degree murder at this time. The electric chair once used at Rockview Penitentiary was scrapped. The most I could expect to attain were life sentences, and I pursued two life sentences, one for each murdered boy.

I anticipated the defense would attempt to exploit Wright's history of mental illness as a defense or in mitigation of his sentence if the court found him guilty as charged. Whatever it was the defense had in mind, I was ready to attack it.

The first witness the defense called in its presentation of the evidence was Dr. Frank A. Elliott. Dr. Elliot was a neurologist and duly qualified by the defense to offer his testimony. He said his practice in neurology embraced "physical diseases of the brain and nervous system."[18]

The defense called the doctor as a witness to show from a medical standpoint that Wright suffered from a discontrolled syndrome that affected his ability to control his emotions. Dr. Elliott said, because of this diagnosis, the defendant, although knowing the difference between right and wrong [the McNaughton test], had no control over his impulses.

Dr. Elliott was an experienced physician who had been licensed to practice medicine and surgery in the state of Pennsylvania since 1959 and was licensed to practice in Great Britain and South Africa. He received his initial license in medicine in 1934 after graduating from medical school at the University of Capetown, South Africa—a medical school that was at that time accredited by the British Commonwealth government. After serving an internship in Capetown, Dr. Elliott went to England for a three-and-a-half-year residency, after which he was appointed as a consultant to the Emergency Medical Services of London during the first two years of World War II. According to his testimony, his "practice in this position included covering about six thousand beds."[19] After this, he transferred to the British Army and served there as a consultant neurologist, attaining the position of chief advisor to the British War Officer by the end of the war. Following the war, Dr. Elliott settled in London, where he worked at the University of London and was assigned to Charing Cross Hospital—identified by Elliott as "one of the old London teaching hospitals . . . well-known in the field of neurology for half a century."[20] He remained at this post from 1947 to 1959, when he was "invited to come to Philadelphia by the University of Pennsylvania to set up and head a new Department of Neurology at the Pennsylvania Hospital."[21] At the time of the trial, Elliott was a consultant neurologist at Pennsylvania Hospital, having retired from the directorship of the department one year earlier.[22] Asked about his medical specialty, Dr. Elliott said that as a neurologist he was involved with physical diseases of the brain and nervous system, an area of medicine for which he received training in "London at the National Hospital for Nervous Diseases, Queen's Square," and added that "subsequent training takes the rest of one's life."[23] As to his actual certification, he said he had been certified since 1938 in "General Internal Medicine, which includes Neurology."[24]

Elliott identified an impressive number of medial/professional associations both in England and the United States with which he was affiliated. Most recently he served as president of the Philadelphia Neurological Association. The doctor taught medicine since 1940 and held the rank of full professor at the University of Pennsylvania since 1964. Elliott had authored two textbooks on neurology, had written numerous articles, and contributed chapters to books and papers. In the course of his work, he said, he had written about "violence in brain-damaged individuals."[25] He had also served as a consultant to the National Institute of Neurology in Bethesda, Maryland. Dr. Elliott said he was currently a neurologist at the Pennsylvania Hospital and a consultant neurologist to the Children's Hospital of Philadelphia and Bryn Mawr Hospital. In this capacity, he usually met with over one hundred patients per month, according to his testimony. He acknowledged that very few of his patients suffered from recurring violence, but about twenty-three such patients were in his care at the present time.

At this point, the prosecution objected to this witness, saying, "His testimony [is] irrelevant as to the issue he intends to bring out and the purpose for which he is called to establish on behalf of the defense. . . . This has no relevancy at all to these proceedings under the law as established in Pennsylvania."[26] Attorney Dunn offered that Dr. Elliott was called because he had examined William Wright and that the purpose of the doctor's testimony was to establish Wright's mental illness and its affect on his actions.[27] Further, Attorney Dunn said the defense would "maintain that this inability to control his emotions, as a normal individual, has a bearing on the crimes with which he has been charged and would have a bearing on guilt, or at least on his degree of guilt."[28] This was not, said Dunn, an effort on the defense's part to impose an insanity defense.

The prosecution objected to this line of defense: "[This] has no legal import in the State of Pennsylvania insofar as it may relate to the McNaughton Rule . . . the only recognized principle of law in Pennsylvania," adding that to include anything else would "not be proper and not relevant."[29] The court accepted the prosecution's objection and said it would rule on it later. Dunn continued with his examination of Dr. Elliott.

Elliott began to tell the court that he had examined Wright on September 19, 1974, at the doctor's office at Pennsylvania Hospital, but the prosecution again objected on the basis that the witness had not been questioned by the Commonwealth on his qualifications, to which Attorney Dunn replied that he thought prosecution had waived this. Assistant

District Attorney ADA) Ernest Preate then asked the doctor several questions as to his qualifications in order to establish a "few points," including whether or not the doctor was a professor of psychiatry and a member of the American Institute of Psychiatrists.[30] The doctor responded no to both questions. Dr. Elliott also said he had never done any psychiatric or psychological consultations and was not certified by the American Board of Psychiatry, adding that his choice of medicine was neurology. He said he was certified "by these people," referring to neurological certification in Britain but not in the United States. Asked by Preate as to the type of examination he had conducted on the accused, Dr. Elliott said he interviewed Wright and conducted an EEG (electroencephalogram) examination, which the doctor said was a physiological examination.

Attorney Dunn objected to this line of questioning as beyond qualifications, but the court allowed the testimony. ADA Preate, for the prosecution, continued by asking if the doctor conducted "any psychiatric or psychological examination" on Wright, to which he answered no.[31] The doctor said he took a "history that is where the truth lies and confirmed it by the electroencephalogram."[32] This was the extent of Dr. Elliott's examination of the accused.

The prosecution objected to Dr. Elliott's testimony because of relevancy in that the examination the neurologist made of the defendant was a "physiological examination as opposed to one that would center upon the matters dealing with his mental capacity."[33] This objection was overruled by the court pending later evaluation of it "at the termination of the case."[34]

Dunn continued with his witness, asking Dr. Elliott about his examination of the defendant. Elliott said that the purpose of the examination he conducted was to "determine whether there could be any organic or structural reason for his behavioral disturbances in the past," adding later that he had been asked in the past by attorneys to examine patients "with a view to assessing physical incapacity."[35]

Dunn asked the doctor whether he had obtained a history during his examination of Wright, and the doctor said he had and that a neurological examination could not be made without a history. The purpose of the history was to establish a "pattern of abnormal behavior in the past."[36]

Dr. Elliott then recounted for the court Wright's history as told to him by the defendant.

Starting, as Elliott said was the standard, with "day one," his birth, in Elliott's words Wright told him that he had "a stormy first two weeks of life with cyanosis . . . lack of oxygen . . . and convulsions"—which he survived.[37] Skipping to "the next event of interest," the doctor said, according to the history, Wright, around the age of fourteen, at puberty, "had a series of convulsions at night in bed while asleep," but this stage passed.[38]

The prosecution again objected here as to the nature of this testimony, asking that the testimony be limited to what the defendant told the doctor for his case history and not to establish anything factual that might have occurred in this case. In other words, the doctor should not speculate on the truth of the defendant's history but rather only testify to what the defendant told him. The court agreed.

Attorney Dunn returned to his witness, and Dr. Elliott, continuing with the defendant's history, said that Wright told him he was examined in 1956 at Jefferson Hospital (in Philadelphia) for reasons not disclosed by Wright by a Dr. Kelley, a psychiatrist who administered an electroencephalogram that "showed no abnormality." However, Elliot said, the hospital "used an activating technique by an [sic] injections of something which will bring out latent abnormality and they found abnormalities of an epileptic character in his left temporal lobe."[39]

The prosecution objected, but the court overruled, saying the testimony was "purely case history," and Dr. Elliott continued. Wright told him he had "many attacks of rage . . . including events such as sudden and for no apparent reason, the killing of a cat; and a sudden sense of hating people and having to do something violent which culminated, according to his testimony to me [Elliott], in four homicidal attacks on people."[40] Wright told him further that all of these incidents were "unpremeditated and suddenly arose urging him that he had to do something violent . . . [acts that were] followed by exhaustion and remorse . . . were short-lived . . . lasted for a minute or perhaps a half hour at the most." Wright said he "could not understand why they happened."⁴¹

Continuing, Dr. Elliott told the court that Wright's history had revealed "poor impulse control in sexual matters, too, saying he had to ask about this because in his "knowledge of the discontrol syndrome . . . almost always the attack of violence have [sic] been accompanied by inappropriate and sometimes very horrid sexual attacks on people."⁴²

Explaining further, the doctor said the two go together—sexual attacks and lack of impulse control—and Wright admitted to this, telling the doctor that he could not understand it because "if individual 'A' would injure him, or he though [sic, thought] he had, he might attack individual 'B' as in the case of the disastrous attack on two boys."⁴³ Wright told Elliott he had "quarreled with a policeman that had passed by and this suddenly unloosed a rage attack against two boys physiologically."⁴⁴

Of course, Wright's story until this point was that he had forced Paul Freach and Edmund Keen into the back of the Vector van at gunpoint and molested them *before* the police officer came on the scene. Wright's intent in doing this was seemingly for the purpose of sexually molesting the boys and maybe included the intent of killing them afterward. Now, according to Dr. Elliott's testimony, Wright had told the doctor another version of the murders—one that was designed to support the discontrolled syndrome defense and that also, in effect, blamed his violent actions on the policeman who had stopped by the van on November 1.

Elliott continued with his testimony on Wright's history, saying such symptoms as recounted to him by the defendant are classically recorded as the discontrol, or discontrolled, syndrome, which is a physical disorder of the brain usually caused by brain damage in early life, especially at birth. In Elliott's view, "such people are often epileptic or had suffered temporary epilepsy, as well as he does . . . but such attacks are not strictly epileptic."⁴⁵ In reference to Wright, Elliott said, "[He] knows what he is doing; he knows that it is wrong and he can't prevent himself from doing it."⁴⁶

Asked by Attorney Dunn if Dr. Elliott had confirmed his conclusion by "scientific tests," the doctor said he had with an EEG, which allows the doctor to watch the brain waves of a patient. These brain waves have a "certain pattern for a brain that is normal and abnormal patterns sometimes when the brain is abnormal . . . abnormalities [that] are often hidden when the patient is awake, but . . . come out during sleep."[47] In Wright's case, when he went to sleep during the test, Elliott saw "very marked spike waves in the left temporal lobe"—the same as had been "discovered in 1956 by Dr. Kelley."[48]

Later, when asked to explain the abnormalities shown in the EEG, Elliott said there "was high voltage [large spikes] coming from the localized area of the left temporal lobe . . . [occurring] occasionally in the waking record . . . and much more obvious during sleep . . . an indication of damage to the epileptic focus in the temporal lobe. If such a person received, for example a tranquillizer such as 'elavil,' it would not reduce the size of the 'spikes,' and might actually aggravate the situation."[49]

Asked by Dunn as to why the temporal lobe of the brain is important in such cases, the doctor answered that this area of the brain contains the nerve centers that "are particularly concerned with aggression." In adults, these nerve centers are usually under the control of the "superior part of the brain. When there is damage to the temporal lobe, or elsewhere, the normal control that an adult practices on his impulses is broken down. He loses the capacity and will to control the impulses for aggression either in sex or aggression or driving, any form of aggression, on the road or anywhere else."[50] Since "these aggression centers are largely . . . in the temporal lobe, this seems to be why most people with this syndrome do have evidence of structural damage in the temporal lobe."[51]

Attorney Dunn inquired if this "damage [was] ameniable [sic, amenable] to psychiatric treatment, the doctor said it was not but could be 'partly' controlled by medication and surgical intervention, which is "required only in a very small minority of cases."[52] There are no guaranteed cures, for this illness, according to the doctor. Furthermore, medical treatment should be administered in confinement so that "if the subject forgot or refused his medication, something might occur."[53]

The doctor also said a person suffering from discontrolled [or discontrol] syndrome would not have normal control of his impulses. Asked again to explain the difference between a person who could distinguish between right and wrong and one not having control of his impulses, the doctor likened this to a child having a temper tantrum who knows he should not shout or scream but does it because he can't control it. According to the doctor, as the child "grows older the brain exercises control and the childish tantrums die down and are controlled.... [However,] in the case of a person with brain damage, the inability to control the emotional impulses especially aggressive sex or physical aggression is present and the impulses can't be controlled."[54]

Asked to explain to the court the result of his testing of the accused, Dr. Elliott said Wright was "eminently clear and concise in his statements" and was "obviously distressed looking back at his activities when he [was] not angry."[55] Continuing, Elliott said, Wright "clearly indicated without knowing what I knew was written about this motiveless murder, no gain to him, abrupt and for no reason at all. A minor irritation started and the whole thing exploded."[56] The doctor called this "characteristic," presumably of someone with this syndrome, and told the court that during such times "untold damage can be done" and afterward such a person feels "a sense of exhaustion which is like total exhaustion, sometimes sleep and then back to normal." According to this doctor, this is what happened, this "pattern," in "all four cases," referring to Wright's two previous murders: his great aunt, the young child, and the two Minooka boys.[57] Wright's actions were without reason, according to the doctor, in each instance.

ADA Ernest Preate then cross-examined Dr. Elliot. ADA Preate began by asking the doctor the meaning of temporal lobe epilepsy. Elliott answered that epileptic seizures have many forms, ranging from convulsions to periods of "bad behavior" that results from a scar, tumor, or some other type of lesion damage to the temporal lobe of the brain. Asked for further detail on this affliction, Elliott said seizures were the most common form of this type of epilepsy, with about 37 percent of those with it having some form of behavioral problems as well. He said he had treated many thousands of persons for this malady in the course of his practice. Asked if discontrolled syndrome was the same as psychomotor epilepsy or temporal lobe epilepsy, Dr. Elliott said they were quite different, but the two could "occur in the same people."[58] Preate then asked if "the act of aggression and sex involved here [in Wright's case] [were] due to an actual seizure phenomenon or brain disorder rather than just an emotional upheaval."[59] Dr. Elliott said they were not seizure disorders but that "everything you do or think is accompanied by electrical activity in the brain; and if you put an electrode into the brain during an episode of rage, you will find abnormal discharges; but these are not really epileptic discharges." "People," continued the doctor, "with discontrolled syndrome are perfectly well aware of what they are doing."[60] Elliott then stated that in comparison to this in a case of an epileptic seizure, confusion is the outcome, and people experiencing this are uncertain of what has happened as a result of diminished consciousness. According to Elliott, this difference is the basis for distinguishing between discontrolled syndrome and epileptic seizures.

The prosecution turned next to the causes of temporal lobe epilepsy. Elliott explained that the most common cause is damage to the temporal lobe at birth from a shortage of oxygen. Asked for symptoms that would make possible a diagnosis of temporal lobe epilepsy, Elliott said a patient would exhibit episodes of disturbed behavior, perhaps accompanied with generalized convulsion; perhaps a blank stare or brief lapse of consciousness. Such people might "suddenly run a hundred yards without knowing what they are doing or stopping; they might have simply a dream night experience of being far away and in another world; they might have a sense of bad smell . . . they might hear music or faces not there . . . brief [experiences after which the] patient feels exhausted and doesn't know quite what has happened and can not recall the events properly until the next time when it is repeated at irregular intervals."[61]

The doctor was then asked about further symptoms of temporal lobe epilepsy, including what might trigger an episode and whether during a seizure a person would have any control over his behavior. Elliott explained to the court that there were no known triggers for such seizures such as irritations or annoyances, though sometimes bright lights have been associated with onset of seizures. People under great emotional stress, said the doctor, experience an increase of attacks in a given period, but "irritation does not mean the triggering of a temporal lobe seizures whereas it does trigger these other discontrolled attacks."[62]

Turning now to questions about Dr. Elliott's examination of William Wright on September 19, 1974, the doctor explained he took all morning for this appointment but had actually talked with Wright for a period of about an hour and a half. During this session Wright discussed the deaths of the two boys with him. Asked whether or not Wright had amnesia about the murders, the doctor told the court Wright did not: "[He] knew everything he did; and he remembered it all."[63] Asked further if Wright had amnesia concerning any of Wright's past criminal actions, Elliott said Wright did not, that he remembered these as well. The doctor also said that prior to these events, Wright had experienced no accepted symptoms of onset of a seizure but that Wright had said he was exhausted and drowsy after committing the crimes. Such feelings, the prosecution noted for the court, were not a "significant factor" following the killing of the two boys, because they did not prohibit him from disposing of the bodies of the two boys, driving the van, and cleaning it out soon after the murders. The doctor responded that this was correct.

Asked once again to explain more specifically the meaning of discontrolled syndrome and if it was a "lack of impulse control for want of a better definition,"[64] Dr. Elliot said discontrolled syndrome was "associated with structural damage to the brain. It is not used in a psychiatric matter where a man full of tension and bitterness may act out his tension. This is something quite distinct."[65] The ADA then asked the doctor if it was his testimony that Wright's "lack of impulse control, this discontrolled syndrome," prevented Wright from "knowing and understanding the difference between right and wrong" when he murdered Paul Freach and Edmund Keen.[66] Elliott answered that Wright knew the difference when he murdered the boys. Asked further if Wright knew the "nature and quality of his acts," Dr. Elliott responded he did not know what Wright thought during the acts of murder but that he knew afterwards.[67] Then the doctor added there was a "yes and no answer" to understanding this matter. "It is," said Elliott, "difficult as a doctor. I have seen people in such attacks; they are not amenable to reason. You can't talk to them. They don't seem to understand what you are saying to them. I don't think they are in any frame of mind or mood to think of what they are doing. It is simply a tremendous urge, an animal urge to destroy."[68]

At this point in the proceedings, Dr. Elliott was asked to explain some of Wright's previous acts of violence, including his attempted rape of the girl in 1964 and the incident on October 26, 1973, when Wright attempted to sexually assault hitchhiker Thomas Nasser. The doctor responded that he had few facts about the attempted rape and did not know about the hitchhiker incident. Wright did not tell the doctor much about the attempted rape and nothing at all about the hitchhiker incident.

When defense objected to this line of questioning, the court told the prosecution to frame questions in an "if this occurred" form. The prosecution related the facts of the hitchhiker incident to the doctor and how the hitchhiker, held at gunpoint by Wright, attempted to talk Wright out of assaulting and killing him. At this time, according to ADA Preate, Wright "went through a reasoning process which was vocalized [to the victim]."[69] Then Preate asked the doctor if this scenario would be consistent with a person suffering from discontrolled syndrome. The doctor responded that it would not. Next Preate turned to Wright's attempted rape of a young girl in 1964 and asked the doctor if this incident would be a manifestation of discontrolled syndrome. Again, the doctor agreed that it would not be.

Next the prosecution turned to Wright's earlier murder of Wright's great-aunt in Pittsburgh in 1956. Dr. Elliott said Wright had talked with him about this. Wright, said the doctor, had also talked to him about the murder of the child in Delaware County. Preate asked, since it appeared that in Wright's case there seemed to be a "rather selective kind of situation . . . in which discontrolled syndrome operates sometimes and it operates again not at all," how could one know when Wright had it and when it didn't and "how else can he be judged except by his behavior."[70] Elliott responded, "Discontrolled syndrome is [a] profitless, motiveless, nonsensical thing . . . [with] no possibility of gain. It arises strong and abruptly. There is no thinking behind it; and it subsides as abruptly. . . . It is quite different from crimes committed for profit . . . as working out psychological problems."[71]

The ADA then asked the doctor two questions: Did Wright's attempt to burn down his great-aunt's house after murdering her to cover the evidence serve no useful purpose? Did the murder and disposal of the bodies of the two boys so they could not be witnesses against him serve no useful purpose? The doctor said they had not. Pressed further on this a second time, if this had in fact served a useful purpose, the doctor persisted and said it had not, adding, "You tell me."[72] The doctor maintained that Wright's actions with regard to his aunt's house was, "motiveless and profitless."[73] But, persisted the ADA, wasn't it true Wright murdered his aunt as she was on the telephone trying to call the police to report Wright, who had escaped from a juvenile institution? The doctor responded by saying that Wright had told him "he went suddenly berserk" because the aunt "kept bugging him with questions: 'Why did he go?' 'Why was he there?' 'What was he doing there?'"[74] The doctor said Wright told her he left the institution but did not tell him [Dr. Elliot] she was calling the police to report him.

Continuing to ask the doctor about instances in Wright's history he believed illustrated a lack of impulse control, the ADA asked Elliott if he had "any confirmation, other than the hearsay statement of William Wright that he suffered from convulsions and lack of oxygen in the first few weeks of his life."[75] Elliott said he had no confirmation of this but had recommended these things be checked out. He acknowledged the birth trauma incident was hearsay "from him to me."[76] The doctor was then asked if "the existence of [an] unpremeditated attack . . . does not establish, with a reasonable degree of medical certainty, the diagnosis of temporal lobe epilepsy?"[77] The doctor answered that it did not. Asked further "whether actions that serve no useful purpose . . . [do] not establish a diagnosis of temporal lobe epilepsy,"[78] the doctor stated, "That is a frequent symptom of temporal lobe epilepsy but not these malicious attacks on other people. Epileptics are not more dangerous . . . than other people. . . . If they are temporal lobe epileptics, then they are potentially more dangerous than other people."[79]

Responding to the state's questions concerning whether Wright's behavior might be symptomatic of someone who could be described as a "normal individual," the doctor reiterated no. He said all cases "so far documented of discontrolled syndrome have structural diseases of the brain [as opposed to a 'normal' person]. . . . Every documented case [of discontrolled syndrome] has been consistent, has been found to have damage of some sort early in life or late in life to either the temporal lobe or front lobe."[80]

Turning next to the electroencephalogram, ADA Preate asked the doctor if it wasn't true that about 15 percent of normal individuals show abnormal test changes. The doctor said, "Yes, but not this type."[81] He explained further, saying, "The single sided spikes to the temporal lobe [are] not normal and [are] not found in the population at large."[82] Preate then asked the doctor about a "normal electroencephalogram" and whether it was "not true that fifteen to twenty per cent of the people who do suffer from seizure disorders show a normal electroencephalogram."[83] When the doctor answered in the positive that this was so on "single readings," Preate asked how many readings Elliott had of Wright's test, and he said, "One."[84] Though Elliott had read the report of the earlier electroencephalogram of Dr. Kelley done on Wright when he was a youth, he had not actually seen the electroencephalogram, nor had he read the encephalogram that had been done of the accused at Farview State Hospital in 1967. Moreover, he had not read the May 22, 1974, encephalogram on Wright done at Wilkes-Barre General Hospital. In other words, Dr. Elliott was basing his diagnosis of William Wright on only one electroencephalogram and the history Wright gave had given him. He again acknowledged this to the court. The doctor said, "In clinical analysis, when you have seen a lot of cases, there is a feeling about it that is difficult to be scientific about. . . . The way this man, without any scientific knowledge . . . produced responses to non-suggested questions, he brought out consistent stories that I have heard in dozens of cases. . . . This is how you diagnose."[85]

The doctor was asked if he would agree the "release of inner tension to violent acts" does not by itself mean that temporal lobe epilepsy is present, and the doctor agreed.[86] Continuing with this line of questions, the doctor was asked if he would agree that such a release is a "common occurrence in everyday life with normal individuals," and the doctor said, "Very."[87] Then the ADA asked about so-called normal behavior and violent acts and if such actions were found in normal as well as abnormal person. The doctor agreed. Asked if it was normal for a person accused of a crime to refuse to confess in spite of feeling remorseful about it and if such a person would not necessarily be suffering from temporal lobe epilepsy, the doctor replied that such a refusal would signify sane behavior. Finally, ADA Preate asked, "[Isn't it true] all of the features found in William Wright's activities do not establish to a reasonable degree of medical certainty a diagnosis of temporal lobe epilepsy?" The doctor responded, "I never said he [Wright] had temporal lobe epilepsy. . . . He had discontrolled syndrome which is quite different."[88]

Seemingly, at this point, having excluded temporal lobe epilepsy as a factor in the murders of the boys, the doctor was asked for an answer that would state this clearly. However, Elliott said that, in his opinion, Wright's actions were related to discontrol seizure, a different condition and one that had status in the medical community but was at that point in no medical textbook except the text authored by the doctor himself. Explaining this lack of coverage of the condition, Dr. Elliott said that so far the medical community has been reluctant to say a great deal about this condition until more was known about it.

Asked if he was unsure of his diagnosis of Wright, Elliot replied that he was sure. The doctor went on to explain it was his understanding that his name had been given to Attorney Dunn by one of the "main proponents" of this illness and that in the United States there were several doctors who over a period of fifteen to twenty years had engaged in the study of discontrol syndrome. According to Elliott there was a good deal of literature and writing on the subject, but it was not yet included in student texts. As a fairly new area of medicine, the doctor said studies on animals had been performed for forty years and now the focus had begun to include humans. Asked by the prosecutor if this area needed more research, Elliott said this was true for therapy and treatment, presumably implying that more research was not necessary for diagnosis, because the syndrome was "well established and repeatable."[89]

As for the doctor drawing any conclusions so far as William Wright's actions and the murders of the two boys, Elliot said it was impossible to tell. Then the ADA asked, given "the fact that the killing of all witnesses to a crime severely hampers the detection of such a crime and the apprehension of the perpetrator," if Elliot could say "that the killing of those two boys serve[d] no useful purpose to William Wright?"[90] Elliott said he saw no useful purpose to the murders for Wright, and added that the sexual assault of the two youngsters by Wright was "what firms it up in my mind as a discontrolled syndrome. Rage followed by aggression with no meditation of activities. That is what makes it a discontrolled syndrome episode."[91]

Asked by the prosecution about the incident at the penitentiary where "Wright was padded" and how the doctor would characterize this,[92] Elliott said he believed this was "an illustration of a sense of outrage . . . to him . . . [an] appropriate action. . . . I wouldn't call it a real discontrolled syndrome."[93]

The doctor was then asked about William Wright's accounting to him of the murders and Wright telling the doctor he was "remorseful about these incidents." Elliott said this was a report of what he observed, because "when he [Wright] really got into the story he showed physical signs of emotion."[94] In response to this information, Elliott was asked whether or not it was possible that others who had examined the accused for "ten or twelve hours under stress conditions different from what you examined him would find that [his] remorse [was] not sincere."[95] The doctor said this would depend on circumstances and that an entirely different response might present depending on "all different situations."[96] The doctor said it would be a judgment if a different view existed of whether or not the defendant was sincere in his remorse.

Returning to whether or not Wright "lacked a substantial capacity to appreciate right from wrong"—the prosecution emphasized that the doctor's examination was fairly brief and based on one encephalogram—the doctor said Wright did understand the difference. The doctor was then asked if Wright had a "lack of substantial capacity to conform his conduct to the requirements of society."[97] The doctor answered that this was so, from his "story" plus the "record," adding that in addition to the known incidents, "there were probably others that we haven't heard about."[98] The doctor continued, saying, "There would be many episodes of behavior because these things occur regularly in a pattern in these people; and the major ones come to light in police court."[99]

Then the doctor was asked again about the hitchhiker incident on Interstate 81. He responded that this matter was not a discontrolled syndrome but a "foolhardy thing."[100] The prosecution persisted with this event, noting that it occurred only five days before the murders of the two boys, but the doctor said it is impossible to understand Wright's actions with certainty, as there are many aspects of personality. The doctor was then asked if Wright could have acted the same way a few days after the hitchhiker incident. Dr. Elliot said, "Ten minutes later."[101] Then asked how long discontrol lasts, the doctor responded that in his experience it "can last from five minutes to two or three hours" and occur "fifty or sixty times—once a week or once every six months. . . . It has no regularity."[102]

The doctor testified he had not found that the accused suffered from anything that indicated "progressive disease of the brain" or "motor sensory defects."[103] When asked about treatment for discontrol syndrome, the doctor said he was uncertain of the success of treatment for it, and the average ratio of success to failure among doctors treating it was "about a sixty-forty with the best results from surgery in very bad cases."[104] Surgery, he added, was not an option in Wright's case; the doctor said he would treat him with medication "for at least two years under close confinement."[105]

The ADA returned to questions about diagnosis of discontrolled syndrome at this point, what it is, and how it is manifested. The judge saw this line of questioning as repetitious, and ADA Preate completed the cross-examination with final questions to the doctor about causes of the syndrome. This ended with the doctor saying that, because injury to the brain is the common cause of temporal lobe diseases, he had been unable to make a diagnosis of this syndrome in Wright's case, because he only had Wright's story of brain damage.

On redirect examination by the defense, Dunn asked Dr. Elliott to restate his opinion as to the problem from which Wright suffered, and the doctor did so, stating it was his opinion that the accused suffered from discontrolled syndrome.[106] On concluding his testimony, Dr. Elliott reiterated that he had enough information about Wright to make a diagnosis and that there was evidence in his history of the discontrolled syndrome.

The second witness for the defense was a Dr. William H. Jeffreys, a certified neurologist who confirmed the medical findings in the electroencephalograms of William Wright.[107]

Similarly, as was done with Dr. Elliott, Dr. Jeffreys was duly qualified prior to offering his testimony on behalf of the defense.

Dr. Jeffreys stated for the court that he had specialized training in the field of neurology and was certified as a neurologist in 1961 by the American Board of Psychiatry and Neurology. He belonged to several medical groups, including the Pennsylvania State Medical Society, the Montour County Medical Society, the American Medical Association, the Philadelphia Neurological Society, and the American Academy of Neurology. He was a past president of the Montour Medical Society and had taught medicine at Geisinger Medical Center in Danville, Pennsylvania. Jeffreys held the rank of associate professor of medicine at Pennsylvania State University and was adjunct professor for bioelectronics there as well. He was well published in national journals but had not written any books.

On cross-examination by DA Mazzoni, Jeffreys acknowledged he had seen the original electroencephalogram taken of the accused in Wilkes-Barre while he was being held and following his confession. This is the study that Jeffreys had examined. He had never examined Wright personally and had not seen him until that day in the courtroom. Dr. Jeffreys said he had not seen the electroencephalogram Dr. Elliott had described in his testimony. The DA asked if that were the case, would it not be impossible for him to state these brain tests were "alike, identical, or even essentially alike?" The doctor answered that he could say they were "essentially alike."[108] Jeffreys added that he saw the same abnormalities on the electroencephalogram that Dr. Elliott had described seeing.[109]

Next, the defense called Dr. Robert L. Sadoff, a psychiatrist duly certified in that field of medical practice and duly qualified to offer testimony on behalf of the defendant.[110]

Dr. Sadoff said his profession was "physician" and that he was licensed to practice medicine in Pennsylvania in 1965.[111] He graduated from the University of Minnesota in 1959 and interned for one year at the Veterans Administration Hospital in Los Angeles for one year. He said his medical specialty was psychiatry and explained that psychiatry "is the study and treatment of people with diseases of the emotions and those who are mentally ill."[112] Sadoff had specialized training in this field and had received a master of science degree in Psychiatry in 1963. The doctor was a diplomat of the American Board of Psychiatry and certified in psychiatry since 1966. As was the case with the other doctors, Dr. Sadoff said he was a member of a number of medical associations, including the American Medical Association, the Pennsylvania Medical Society, and the Montgomery [County] Medical Society. He was a fellow of the American Psychiatric Association, the Pennsylvania Psychiatric Society, the American Academy of Forensic Sciences, and the American College of Legal Medicine. He was also a member of the Philadelphia Psychiatric Society and the American Academy of Psychiatry and Law. He was a past president of the American Academy of Psychiatry and Law and had taught medicine at Temple University from 1966 to 1972 and was then presently teaching at the University of Pennsylvania, where he held the rank of associate professor of clinical psychiatry. He also authored numerous papers for state and national medical journals and had written two books. He served in the armed forces as a psychiatrist at Fort Dix, New Jersey and held the rank of captain in the armed forces. All told, Dr. Sadoff had been in the field of psychiatry since 1960. Currently, while he was teaching, the doctor said he was still engaged in the practice of psychiatry and was treating and evaluating between eighty and one hundred patients a month. He acknowledged that he had testified "about a hundred times" as an expert witness in court prior to this date.[113] The doctor also said that he was a forensic psychiatrist and in that capacity had provided numerous opinions on mental questions related to persons appearing in court.

Dr. Sadoff said he examined Wright on February 27, 1974, in the doctor's office in Jenkintown, Pennsylvania, for the "purpose of evaluation and a trial," primarily to determine if the accused "was competent to stand trial and whether or not he was at the requisite state of mind at the time of the act for criminal insanity."[114]

Dr. Sadoff testified that he had taken a history of the defendant from the accused, which he used for the purpose of determining the accused's sanity. Asked to explain this history, the doctor said Wright had told him he was born with some difficulty, which Wright called "a physical thing."[115] Wright told the doctor he had "unidentified seizures at birth and there was some question about a calcium deficiency with tetnus [*sic.* tetanus] when he was born and that he had seizures in a hospital and remained there until they stopped or slowed. . . . [These] he thinks stopped completely at about age one."[116]

Wright, said the doctor, told him he had no further difficulty with seizures until puberty "when, in his own words he said he 'went into a change of life' at the age of thirteen."[117] At this age Wright told Sadoff he suffered convulsions while sleeping and "had loss of breath and had a feeling of being smothered."[118] The treatment he received for the convulsions was being put in a tub and, in Wright's words, "shocked out of it."[119] However, seizures, according to Wright, continued fairly regularly after this.

Wright recounted his history to Sadoff, including his difficulties with the law and his prior offenses up to the point of the murders of the two Minooka boys one year earlier:

Wright told the doctor that after having been given parole to work with the Vector agency in the greater Scranton region, there were times when he was almost like a policeman in the work he had to do to keep people away from the places he was treating for rodent control. He acquired a gun for this reason, because his supervisor had one, and because "he did not feel comfortable without one."[120]

Wright had also told the doctor that he "should never have been able to have one [a gun], but he did and he realized how badly he used it."[121] He recounted the story of pulling the gun on the nineteen-year-old hitchhiker, "threatening him and telling him that he wanted sex with him" and the boy's pleading with him.[122] Wright told Sadoff he let the boy go but didn't know why he did, because "the boy then did tell the police about the incident."[123]

Days after this, Wright said, his girlfriend told him she "didn't want him coming by anymore."[124] Sadoff testified that Wright said this made him feel "rejected . . . [and] he had to go out and find someone."[125] Wright then told Sadoff what happened next:

> [Wright said] he got into his truck with the gun in the glove compartment and began to look for someone. . . . He went up a dirt road near his home, saw the two boys walking around and made them get into the truck at gun point. . . . He then made them have oral sex with each other and then while they were in the back of the van, a police car drove up and he talked with the policeman for four or five minutes. After the policeman had left . . . he got back into the truck and had oral sex with the boys himself . . . after the police had come up [Wright said] he changed from *passive sexual relationships to aggressive sexual attack* [Sadoff's words] on the boys and then shot them in the truck.[126]

Wright told the doctor he "didn't understand why he shot them. He didn't need the sex. He did not need to shoot them. He didn't understand himself why he did so."[127]

After killing the two boys, Wright told Sadoff he "got back in the front of the truck and drove in a confused manner fourteen or fifteen miles looking for a place to put the bodies. He found a wooded area outside of

Scranton and said that after he had put the bodies in the woods he had intercourse with one of the boys. He then piled some dirt and branches over them and went back to Scranton."[128]

Wright told Dr. Sadoff that, returning to Scranton, the truck was "very bloody . . . [so] he dumped out all of the materials that were in [it] . . . went to a Mall . . . bought himself some new clothes and got rid of the others that had blood on them. He then went back to work and said he was arrested a short time afterwards."[129]

The doctor also told the court that during the earlier part of Wright's history to him, Wright had claimed he had killed a "little boy, aged five or six, after he was rejected by another female."[130] At the time of this murder, Wright was about sixteen. He told Sadoff he killed the child by shoving a "rifle down the little boy's throat choking him to death."[131] Wright said the police thought the child had died as a result of an accident and that he had not been arrested for this crime.

Defense Attorney Dunn asked Dr. Sadoff if he had observed Wright during the course of taking the accused's history, and the doctor said he had. In response to the attorney's next question about the doctor's observation and his thoughts on the sanity or insanity of the accused, the doctor clarified for the court that his "interpretation of the word 'sanity' . . . [was] a legal term which refers to a state of mind at a particular time with reference to a particular act."[132] As such, the doctor said he "would not use that term as an evaluation of a person's state of mind during an examination."[133] But, he continued, if he were to be asked if he thought that Wright was "psychotic at the time [of his examination he would say that he] did not think he was."[134] As for "insane," the doctor said he "reserved that for the word of criminal responsibility as a test in the State."[135] Attorney Dunn then asked his witness if the doctor had arrived at an opinion as to whether or not Wright could assist counsel in his trial. The doctor replied that, at the time of his examination of the defendant, he believed he was competent to do so.

Attorney Dunn then directed his questions to the EEG that had been conducted at Jefferson Hospital by Dr. Kelley in 1956 when Wright was a young person and his referring to it "as having indefinite readings."[136] He asked the doctor to elaborate on this position. Sadoff told the court that this was part of Wright's history and that this finding ("indefinite readings") was not his own, but that when he was describing the word "indefinite" the word came from the historical summary Wright had provided him. Wright had heard the test was "indefinite."[137]

Attorney Dunn asked Dr. Sadoff if he had checked the test himself, and Sadoff replied that, at the time when he was interviewing Wright, he had not. Asked if he had examined it since, the doctor said he had not, but he thought he had seen a copy of Dr. Kelley's report. The doctor then found the copy of the report and said he had examined it but never actually examined the EEG.

Dunn went next to Dr. Elliott's testimony about Wright suffering from discontrolled syndrome and asked the doctor if, based on his examination of Wright, he would agree with Dr. Elliott's diagnosis. Sadoff said he was in a position to comment on the diagnosis but wanted to clarify before offering a firm opinion. He said when he examined Wright he had "not thought about a discontrolled syndrome."[138] He had seen the EEG report and taken Wright's history and diagnosed him "as having a depressive reaction with sexual deviations and history of violent aggressive behavior."[139] Sadoff said his diagnosis did not go beyond that. He explained he was not a neurologist but did know about discontrolled syndrome. Having heard Dr. Elliott testify that morning, he felt "there was evidence to indicate that this is a great possibility and a plausible diagnosis."[140] Further, Sadoff said that, given the findings of the EEG, Wright's behavioral evidence, and the accused's history, he would concur with Dr. Elliott's diagnosis.

Thus, Dr. Sadoff corroborated the testimony of the doctors that preceded him in their testimony. The defendant knew the difference between right and wrong but was uncontrollably motivated in all that he did to the boys by a discontrolled syndrome impulse of emotions.

Attorney Dunn informed the court that he had no further questions of the doctor, beginning the cross-examination.

ADA Preate began by asking the doctor if he had reached any conclusion about the defendant's capacity to understand the difference between right and wrong on November 1, 1973, and the doctor replied that he had. Dr. Sadoff said in his examination of the accused, conducted in February 1974, he came to the conclusion that Wright did know the difference at the time of the murders of the two boys: "He did know that what he was doing was wrong."[141] Asked to explain the term "psychotic" as he had used in relation to the defendant, saying that Wright was not psychotic, Sadoff did so, including a standard explanation of a psychotic person as one who has a loss of contact with reality, accompanied with false beliefs about events; a person suffering from delusions and perhaps seeing or hearing things that are not there; a person given to mood swings. He added that very few people with psychosis are violent.

ADA Preate persisted by asking the doctor if Wright would have a lack of "substantial capacity to conform his conduct to the requirements of the laws of society."[142] The doctor responded by saying that in Wright's case there were "times when there is a decrease in the capacity to conform. . . . There may be times when it is substantial; but I don't think that there always are; I think there are relative degrees of his ability to conform his conduct as indicated by his previous behavior when he was able to control his behavior."[143] He continued, adding that there might be times, when Wright would be "so moved by the urge with aggression that he [would] have a lack of substantial capacity to conform his conduct." He added, "This is [not] necessarily true most of the time, although I think it is a possibility at some times."[144]

The ADA then asked, "If that is the case with the defendant, how could one tell when he has discontrolled syndrome?" Sadoff answered that he did not know, that, in his view, the best way to tell is to study the electroencephalogram for evidence showing Wright had some type of lesion on the temporal lobe. The doctor added such a presentment of brain damage would not in itself be a diagnosis of discontrolled syndrome but that there would have to be some form of "erratic behavior, usually of an aggressive sexual type" that would be manifested "over a period, but not necessarily a regular periodic basis, with the discontrolled syndrome."[145]

Alone, said the doctor, these factors would not be discontrolled syndrome, but, he added, "[with] the elements of the way they occurred and the suddenness of the attack and with the history of the positive EEG for the temporal lobe region, . . . they would be consistent [with discontrolled/discontrol syndrome]."[146]

Dr. Sadoff agreed with Dr. Elliott's explanation that there can be milder forms of discontrolled syndrome, saying that there are "variations or gradations of behavior," even those that are spontaneous may be indications of the syndrome.[147]

How would one relate discontrolled syndrome to the legal test for insanity? The doctor told the court that, in his opinion, they are not relevant; a person with discontrolled syndrome "knows the nature and quality of his act and knows what he is doing is wrong. There is no amnesia. There is no unconsciousness. There is no falling out . . . as there may be with temporal lobe seizure." As a result, discontrolled syndrome and the basis for the insanity defense in Pennsylvania, the McNaughton Rule, are two separate entities.[148]

The ADA then asked if discontrolled syndrome was a recognizable medical affliction with a reasonable degree of medical certainty or something still in the process of being studied and subject to some degree of uncertainty. Sadoff responded by explaining that this subject was still in the stages where medical professionals were arguing over its existence, "primarily because it doesn't have the observable feature that one can see in clinical form from temporal lobe seizures."[149] Some in the medical community believed, continued Sadoff, that it was "too easily produced by a person, or feigned by a person who wants it to look that way" with the result that there was doubt among experts; "They don't give it much credence."[150]

Sadoff said that he, however, did believe it happened in some people, but other medical authorities would argue the point.

In order to try to ascertain if Wright indicated to the doctor that he suffered any common symptoms of discontrol/discontrolled syndrome, the ADA returned now to questioning Sadoff about the day of the murders of the boys and his discussion of events on that day with Wright.

Asked if Wright seemed to be suffering any amnesia about the events of this day, the doctor said Wright had no amnesia about the details of that day and the murder. Furthermore, Sadoff said Wright had not described suffering any "aura or sensation" prior to the events, nor had he suffered any drowsiness after the murders. "His recollection," said Dr. Sadoff, "of the events of November 1 were very clear."[151]

ADA Preate concluded his questions of this witness, and the court asked the doctor if there was "little or no difference between the following three phrases: discontrolled syndrome, irresistible impulse, or lack of impulse control?"[152] Dr. Sadoff said there might be differences, and he went on to explain. According to him, the least serious of these was lack of impulse control. Many people, explained the doctor, lack control of their impulses, not as a result of a serious medical situation but due to deficiency of will. People who have irresistible impulse are "more likely to be closer to those with episodic discontrol where there would not be an unresisted impulse but an irresistible one beyond control"[153] ADA Preate then asked if that was the case, then would the worse scenario with regard to controlling one's impulses not be with someone who had discontrolled syndrome, whereas a lack of impulse control would be "just ordinary lack of will power."[154] The doctor answered in the affirmative.

Redirect for Dr. Sadoff was brief and confined to one question: Had William Wright said anything to the doctor about what should be done to him?

The doctor responded to Attorney Dunn's question by summing up what Wright had told him in his examination: that he "ought to be locked up because he was afraid of what he might do, that he does not have control over himself and until there is a treatment known to help him or cure the illness, he doesn't want to be on the streets."[155]

Defense Counsel at this time moved to have certain records of Wright's past introduced in evidence to be made part of the trial record of the case. These included those from Delaware County Courthouse, the Delaware County Prison; Juvenile Court, George Junior Republic (the juvenile reform school for frequent juvenile violators of the law, Pittsburgh); Farview State Hospital; and Chase Correctional Institution at Dallas.

The judge then ordered both prosecuting and defense counsels to review this evidence and be prepared to argue its admissibility at the outset of the next trial date, which Judge Campbell scheduled for December 11, 1974, but continued to December 12, 1974. The court then adjourned the trial to that date.

11

TRIAL—DECEMBER 12, 1974

Sections of this chapter composed by Paul Mazzoni are in italics.

At the beginning of the resumption of the trial on December 12, 1974, the defense counsel informed the judge on the record that his client did not want any of the institutional records introduced in evidence. Attorney John Dunn informed the court that, as a result of consultation with his client, Wright had directed him to state on his behalf that he "[did] not wish to have any more witnesses called in his defense at this time."[1] He then rested his case. The court accepted this and asked if there would be any rebuttal.

I, as the district attorney, had reserved in my case in chief, and during defense counsel's presentation of his case, my right to produce rebuttal evidence. I began with the state's first rebuttal witness. Rebuttal evidence is evidence that is presented at that stage of a trial to prove that the evidence presented by opposing counsel is not true nor accurate, and as such, should not be believed or accepted by the trier of facts, in this case Judge Campbell.

The prosecution first called Detective Edward Miller, a Lackawanna County detective attached to the District Attorney's (DA's) Office for some five years. The prosecutor asked Detective Miller if he had received any correspondence from William Wright that had been directed to the

DA's Office. Miller answered that he did receive a special delivery letter from Wright sent to the DA's office from the Dallas Correctional Institution in late August of 1974 (the letter was marked C-32 for identification). Attorney Dunn studied the letter and asked the prosecution for an offer as to the purpose of this letter. DA Mazzoni replied, "[We offer this] to show the frame of mind of the defendant which is rather consistent throughout his behavior, not only at all times since the arrest but during his stay at Farview State Hospital over a period of nine years (1964–1973); and that he does know the difference between right and wrong."[2]

Defense Attorney Dunn countered by saying that the question wasn't if Wright knew the difference between right and wrong on August 25, 1974, but if he knew the difference on November 1, 1973, in the act of murdering Paul Freach and Edmund Keen. Mazzoni responded, "It goes right to the very heart of the motive for his defense. . . . It does show a manipulative mind which we are going to show in our rebuttal witnesses."[3]

The court accepted the testimony, to which Attorney Dunn offered a further objection: that the "proper foundation" had not been laid. Further, Attorney Dunn said, "[There] has been no knowledge [of] where the letter came from [and] . . . nothing on [*sic*] testimony that the person who is testifying did . . . receive and receipted for this registered letter."[4]

At this point, the defendant, William Wright, said it was "okay" with him to allow Detective Miller to testify. Wright added, "He is right. I am, what is the word, 'manipulative,' but so would you be if you had done things that you don't approve of yourself and you had to find a way to defend yourself against."[5]

The prosecution explained to the court that it was its intention to lay the foundation for the letter sent by William Wright on August 28, 1974. It asked Detective Miller to identify the letter and examine the envelope and the contents of the letter. The detective identified the letter as being sent by William Wright from Dallas State Correctional Institution and the date, August 28, 1974. Attorney Dunn objected if the detective were to testify to the contents, but the prosecution told the court the detective was not going to do this; rather he was simply going to identify the contents contained in the envelope.

The detective did so, saying the letter contained several sheets taken out of a magazine with some words underlined plus a cover letter related to the article. Detective Miller stated the stationery used was from the State Correctional Institution at Dallas and the letter part of the contents and the envelope were typewritten with a signature at the end: "Sincerely, Bill."[6]

Asked what the detective had done with the letter on receipt of it in the DA's Office, Miller said he took the letter, unopened, directly to the district attorney, who read the letter immediately.

Attorney Dunn then cross-examined the witness. He asked Miller if he receipted the card for the letter. Miller said he had not, that the secretary had done so, but he had witnessed her receiving the letter and receipting it. Asked if he could verify that the signature, "Bill," was William Wright's signature, Miller said he couldn't say, adding he had seen other correspondence from the defendant. With this answer, Dunn agreed to stipulate to the admission of this correspondence if the DA's Office would also introduce into evidence every piece of mail that came from William Wright. The district attorney agreed to do this. With that, Attorney Dunn agreed to the letter being put into evidence.

My rebuttal witnesses started with medical professionals to attack the defense counsel's discontrolled syndrome defense. I began with Dr. John Lesniak, a local psychiatrist on staff at Clark Summit State Hospital for the care and treatment of patients with mental illnesses. He was also engaged in private practice in the Scranton area.

The prosecution first questioned the doctor about his background. The thirty-nine-year-old psychiatrist told the court he had attended the University of Scranton for undergraduate school and then Jefferson Medical College of Philadelphia. He interned at Misercordia Hospital in Philadelphia and took specialized training in psychiatry at Binghamton State Hospital in Binghamton, New York, and at the Upstate Medical Center in

Syracuse, New York. He said he had been engaged in the practice of psychiatry since 1969 and had seen numerous patients with mental disorders or mental illnesses. He further stated he had previously testified in court, in criminal as well as other cases, and offered opinions as an expert witness in his field. He had, he said, been appointed by the Lackawanna County Courts to serve on sanity hearings and evaluations of persons prior to court hearings on many occasions. Occasionally these cases involved mental illness in a criminal defense. Defense counsel stipulated to the qualifications of Dr. Lesniak.

Dr. Lesniak and the other two Sanity Commission members—Dr. Henry Buxbaum and Judge John Sirotnak—had the benefit in making the determination of Wright's past history of a very detailed psychiatric examination of Wright performed on two occasions while he was incarcerated at Chase Correctional Institution.

Beginning what would turn out to be a lengthy testimony, Dr. Lesniak told the court of his appointment to the Sanity Commission by Judge Otto Robinson in the fall of 1973[7] for determining whether the defendant could "participate in his own defense [and] whether he would understand the nature of the charges against him."[8]

In order to complete this determination, Dr. Lesniak said he had reviewed all available records concerning Wright's past history as well as Wright's record over the past nine years while a prisoner at Farview State Hospital. The hospital had records concerning his past history prior to his arrival there. Lesniak had also reviewed a "very detailed psychiatric examination of Mr. Wright performed on two occasions at the Dallas Correctional Institution."[9]

Saying that the majority of the records examined by the Sanity Commission had come from Farview, the doctor identified these records as "mostly . . . to do with Mr. Wright's condition, treatment and clinical course at the . . . hospital" during the period he was a patient there.[10]

Dr. Lesniak also reviewed ten reports and testimony at the previous trial of October 16, 1974, of the defense doctors. The doctor said he took issue with Dr. Elliott's testimony of Wright suffering from discontrolled syndrome. In essence, Dr. Elliott's testimonial opinion was that Wright knew what he did to the boys was wrong but couldn't prevent himself from doing it. Dr. Lesniak testified that this discontrolled syndrome was not a recognized medical clinical syndrome, and if it were, Wright did not fit its criteria. The doctor cited several of Wright's episodes in his past that supported his opinion, for example, the attempted rape of a twelve-year-old babysitter. Wright, said Lesniak, went to the house where this girl was babysitting, knowing she was there, attempted to rape her, and then abandoned the act and left the scene. In Lesniak's opinion, this failed attempt at rape did not support the discontrolled syndrome prognosis.

Before going on with this critique of Dr. Elliott's testimony, however, Dr. Lesniak was interrupted by Attorney Dunn, who questioned, "Where is Dr. Lesniak going, we are talking about two different things. One is an examination to determine whether or not a person is capable of assisting counsel in preparing for a defense; and another is an examination to determine the state or frame of mind as of the commission of an act. Those are two distinct matters that we seem to be drawing a relationship between them."[11]

The court intervened, saying that it was concerned over what it called "unprofessional," that is, for "one psychiatrist to be asked to criticize another psychiatrist."[12] The court said it thought it was "quite unfair to put this man in a position of criticizing his colleague . . . [and asked further] what is the relevancy? The competency of this man [Elliott] . . . is not what is involved in this case."[13] If, said the court, the doctor was going to offer an opinion, then he should continue to do that. The Assistant District Attorney (ADA) told the court Dr. Lesniak was also going to talk about discontrolled syndrome, and the line of questioning was leading to this. The court agreed, and Dr. Lesniak continued with his testimony.

Asked by the prosecution about the conclusions of the Sanity Commission, Dr. Lesniak said he concurred with its findings.

Next the prosectuion asked the doctor if he was familiar with "temporal lobe epilepsy." He responded that he was, because it was a "recognized clinical syndrome" which he "had occasion to study in the past and treat numerous people with this condition." He added, "I have a personal experience with this."[14] Asked about the symptoms of this condition, the doctor told the court that it was a "form of convulsive disorder or seizure disorder which is initiated by abnormal electrical impulses, usually in the temporal lobe of the brain, most especially in the dominant side." Lesniak went on to say it was manifested by such things as an aura or a strange feeling that something is going to happen, adding that loss of consciousness or amnesia often accompanied the condition. It can, said Lesniak, be further manifested by purposeless acts and some lethargy or tiredness after the onset "in conjunction with amnesia for the entire event."[15] Diagnosis can be made through a "thorough and complete medical history, not only from the patient but also from people around him who have observed such manifestations."[16] Further, the doctor said he would rely on his "own physical and neurological examination and . . . on a particular special examination such as brain wave tests, skull X-rays, brain scans, and perhaps even more specific, tests such as arteriography and pneumoencephalography which is injection of air into the brain spaces."[17] This latter test is different from the electroencephalogram (EEG) in that the EEG "specifically measures the electrical impulses as transcribed from the brain system through the boney structure of the head and onto a particular recording device."[18] Asked if he was familiar with the administration of an EEG, Lesniak said he was and that in this test the EEG "machine is merely an electrical apparatus that will multiply and measure the amplitude of electrical impulses given off from various areas of the brain substance. These are run through a series of wires from different areas of the head through a recording device and from that recording device they are put on a graph-type paper that can be read and interpreted."[19] In administering this test, Lesniak said the accepted method would be to give the patient a stimulus that would be some type of sedative prior to the test plus what is called a "flicker" photo stimulation, a bright light turning quickly on and off, to attempt to bring out or stimulate some "hidden underlying brain wave pattern."[20]

The prosecution next asked Dr. Lesniak if he was familiar with the 1956 report on Wright done by Dr. Kelly of Jefferson Medical School in which the doctor mentioned a drug called "Metrazol." The prosecution then asked the doctor to explain the nature of this medicine and its use. Dr. Lesniak responded that Metrazol was a "chemical compound that when administered can . . . cause a convulsive disorder even in normal people" and that earlier, in the 1930s, it had been used in conducting an encepholography in order to stimulate brain wave activity.[21] It was not used at the current time. Asked to comment on Dr. Kelly's report as to his agreement with its conclusion, Dr. Lesniak said the report indicated Dr. Kelly had believed the electroencephalogram he administered on Wright was normal but that, with the use of Metrazol stimulation, it showed some "latent abnormalities."[22] Lesniak stated he had questions about the quantity of the drug Dr. Kelly had used on Wright during the test, because it is now commonly known that giving it to someone during an electroencephalogram might cause an otherwise normal person to present with abnormal brain activity. Therefore, in light of incomplete information about the quantity of Metrazol used during Kelly's test of William Wright, Lesniak said he would question the results.

The prosecution next asked Dr. Lesniak if he had knowledge of other reports of electroencephalograms done on the accused, and he said he had and identified one such report of a test done at the Wilkes-Barre General Hospital on May 22, 1974. He acknowledged that this was the report Dr. Jeffreys had testified about on the previous day of the trial in October. Dr. Lesniak said he also had an electroencephalogram report done on Wright at Farview State Hospital in April of 1967. He said he was familiar with the report of the electroencephalogram that Dr. Elliott had testified to as well. While Dr. Lesniak had not had opportunity to actually study the results of these tests—three in all—he had read the doctors' reports. With respect to the Farview Hospital report, he said it appeared to be perfectly normal.

After some discussion about the Farview State Hospital report by the defense, ADA Preate continued, asking Dr. Lesniak about Dr. Jeffreys's testimony. According to Dr. Lesniak, the electroenceplogram performed on Wright at Wilkes-Barre General Hospital was sent to Geisinger Medical Center in Danville, Pennsylvania, because there was no one available at Wilkes-Barre General Hospital certified to read and interpret the test. As a result, Dr. Jeffreys, who was at Geisinger, became involved in the case. Jeffreys had not taken the test but had only been involved in reading the record of it—he had no "benefit of history or observation."[23] As to the findings of the EEG, Lesniak said it appeared to Doctor Jeffreys to be a "mildly abnormal EEG."[24]

Moving on now to the EEG administered under Dr. Elliott's supervision, ADA Preate asked Lesniak about the drug Elavil. Lesniak said Elliott mentioned this drug as a "tranquilizer."[25] Lesniak then took issue with this identification, saying Elavil was "just the opposite" of a tranquilizer; it was an "antidepressant given to people who are depressed."[26] Asked about the use of this drug and the administration of an EEG, the doctor said, "Many people who have been given this particular drug show abnormal electroencephalograms . . . because . . . of the drug."[27] It was, according to Lesniak, "one of the side effects mentioned in the literature from Merk, Sharp, and Dome, the company who manufactures it."[28]

Preate next asked the doctor reviewing all the EEGs what, in his opinion, they indicated. Lesniak answered, "They show a variance of findings, from completely normal electroencephalograms to one with mild abnormality."[29]

Lesniak was then asked about Dr. Elliott's testimony as to whether the defendant had temporal lobe epilepsy. Citing Dr. Elliott's testimony from page 54 of the court record from the October day of the trial, at which time Elliott had disclaimed that he had ever said Wright had temporal lobe epilepsy, Preate asked Lesniak's position on this. Lesniak answered that he agreed with the doctor.

Preate went on to ask Lesniak about Elliott's view that Wright suffered from discontrolled syndrome. Lesniak quoted what Elliott had earlier told the court, what this affliction was and that a person suffering from it "'knows that it is wrong and can't prevent himself from doing it.'"[30] Further, Lesniak said, referring to Dr. Elliott's testimony, that Elliott holds the view that discontrolled syndrome is, again referring to Dr.

Elliott, "a profitless act, a motiveless act, and a nonsensical thing with no possibility of gain. It arises strongly and abruptly. There is no thinking behind it and it subsides as abruptly."[31]

As to causes of discontrolled syndrome, according to Dr. Elliott, said Lesniak, there are many causes, but "he specifically seems to mention birth trauma and cyanosis at birth as one of the main causes."[32] However, Dr. Lesniak stated that a birth trauma would not necessarily be apparent on an EEG. Asked if he were familiar with William Wright's medical history from the records and from Wright's testimony, he said he was. Preate asked if, as such, there was anything in the records or in Wright's history to provide evidence that he had suffered a trauma or injury at birth. The doctor responded by pointing out he had been given the same information about Wright as Dr. Elliott had, and Elliott had said the information about birth injury was "hearsay from him [Wright] to me [Elliott]."[33] There was, said Lesniak, nothing that confirmed the defendant had suffered an injury to his brain at birth.

As for discontrolled, or discontrol syndrome, Lesniak testified he was not familiar with discontrolled syndrome so far as his practice of psychiatry was concerned. "[It] is not a recognized medical clinical syndrome," said Lesniak. "It is not mentioned in the accepted text books either of medicine, psychiatry or neurology."[34] He arrived at this opinion, he said, by consulting with medical texts, literature, conferring with certified neurologists and neurosurgeons in the Scranton area, and contacting specialists at Milton Hershey Medical Center and School in Hershey, Pennsylvania. The latter facility, in fact, conducted a "world search of the medical literature" in order to find information on discontrolled syndrome, said Lesniak.[35] All of these efforts were to no avail. The Hershey search was challenged by Attorney Dunn as information that came from another source and not from Lesniak; Lesniak had to clarify that Hershey had sent him a letter indicating it had found no information on the syndrome.

Moving on to the diagnosis of someone suffering from discontrolled syndrome, the ADA quoted Dr. Frank Elliot's testimony wherein he had said it was possible to diagnose based on a patient's history and an EEG, then later testifying it could be diagnosed with the "history alone."[36] Preate asked the doctor to comment on relying on a history and an EEG alone. Lesniak responded that he believed there were "dangers" to this type of diagnosis; in his opinion, with regard to discontrolled syndrome, "it could be easily mimicked by a person alleged to have performed a criminal act."[37]

Summing up what the doctor would require in order to arrive at a diagnosis, Preate asked the doctor if "a great deal of knowledge about how the EEG was administered and under what circumstances" would be necessary, to which the doctor said, "yes" and added that in this case that depth of information was not present.[38] Asked for a conclusion as to the doctor's review of everything concerning William Wright's medical history, including his own examination of the accused and Dr. Elliott's position that Wright suffers from discontrolled syndrome, the doctor said it was his professional opinion that "even if such a medical syndrome were to exist, I do not feel that Mr. Wright would fit the criteria stated by Dr. Elliott for this syndrome."[39]

Asked for his opinion as to whether or not Wright could control "his emotional impulses with respect to the matters which he told you and you examined him on," the defense objected on the basis that in order to answer, Lesniak would have to testify to something that was told to him by Wright. Dunn argued since Lesniak had not examined Wright for discontrolled syndrome, the doctor was therefore unable to determine "whether he had any physical or discontrolled syndrome at the time of the act [of murder]."[40] Lesniak, said Attorney Dunn, had examined Wright only to determine if Wright was sane according to Pennsylvania law and therefore could go to trial. The court overruled the objection.

We next asked about the hitchhiker on Interstate 81 north of Scranton who Wright picked up, threatened, but ultimately let go after the hitchhiker pleaded not to harm him. This incident was in conflict with Dr. Elliott's theory of William Wright having acted out as he had on November 1 because of discontrolled syndrome triggered by an emotional impulse.

Lesniak testified he had knowledge of the hitchhiker event and the attempted rape of the twelve-year-old girl—both incidents in which Wright was able to stop himself from completing the act or assault—from Wright, who told him of these assaults while undergoing examination for the Sanity Commission's investigation. Directing the doctor to the hitchhiker story, Preate asked Lesniak to tell the court about this as revealed to him by Wright. Lesniak said Wright had picked up a "young man on Route 81 and attempted to, at least threatened him with a revolver if fellatio was not performed," the "boy talked Mr. Wright out of it," nothing further happened, and the boy was released and not injured.[41] Preate asked Lesniak to comment on whether acts, such as with the hitchhiker, were "profitless" as related to one of the characteristics of discontrolled syndrome.

Mr. Dunn intervened with an objection to Dr. Lesniak's testimony about discontrolled syndrome because the doctor had not "stated any place that all of Mr. Wright's acts were profitless."[42] Asked to restate with more specificity, Preate directed questions to the witness about Wright's earlier acts of violence, starting with the murder of Wright's great-aunt and whether or not there was any profit or gain in it. Lesniak answered by reviewing the entire matter involved with the murder of Wright's great-aunt, beginning with the defendant's escaping from the juvenile detention facility in Pittsburgh and going to his great-aunt's home, where she began questioning him as to why he was there. She, said Lesniak, wanted an answer and was going to telephone Wright's family. This made Wright very angry, and he killed her, continuing to hit her even after she was dead. Then he ransacked the house, taking money and bonds. Before he left, he set fire to some clothes inside the house in an attempt to burn it down. In Lesniak's view, the attempt to burn the house down was "not a purposeless act, but an act of concealment."[43]

Attorney Dunn objected to the doctor's answer as not being responsive, whereupon the judge overruled the objection and told the ADA to refocus his question on whether Wright's action after the murder of the aunt had any profit or motive in it. Lesniak said in his opinion Wright's act (apparently referring to the murder and all that transpired afterward) "show[ed] motivation.... There was profit and it was not purposeless."[44] Furthermore, this act did not come on and go away quickly, as, said the doctor, it takes a fair amount of time to do all of the things that Wright did on this occasion (murder a person, ransack a house, take the bonds and money, assemble the clothing, and set the house afire). The crime was discovered shortly after it had taken place, but Wright was not connected to it. He returned to the juvenile facility and was there for about a month. During this period he did not "admit or talk about this murder" to the authorities.[45] Lesniak said he believed a series of events eventually tied the murder to Wright, starting with the Wright family reading about the murder in the newspaper and putting it together with William's being in the Pittsburgh area. Authorities subsequently questioned Wright, and he admitted murdering his aunt—but this was at least a month or so later, according to Lesniak's testimony.

As for the attempted rape of the young girl and the attempted sexual assault of the hitchhiker, Lesniak said these two events were also indicative of purposeful acts with no spontaneous elements. Regarding the attempted rape, Lesniak said Wright had told him he was at home on parole from prison in 1964 and living with some of his family. They invited him to go to a New Year's party, and he described the man checking on his daughter with decreasing frequency through the night.[46] This led Wright to leave the party and go to the house where the girl was babysitting. This is how the attempted rape happened.

In the case of the hitchhiker, Lesniak recounted the story Wright had told him about giving a ride to the college man who was hitchhiking on Route 81. When, said Wright, he had the hitchhiker in the car in a remote area, he threatened the man with his gun and told the man he wanted sex. According to the story Wright told Lesniak, the man talked Wright out of killing him, and no homosexual acts were committed. Wright then released the man.

Next Lesniak testified about the murders of the two boys and the possibility of gain or motive in these murders. He said he believed in this case "there were some precipitating factors that were brought out by Dr. Elliott," such as the act of the policeman stopping by the van and speaking with Wright for a time.[47] Lesniak recalled that in Elliott's testimony he had mentioned a quarrel of some sort had ensued between Wright and the policeman; afterward the policeman left. Lesniak said this incident with the policeman was, in his opinion, "a very traumatic situation that precipitated what happened later on."[48] Asked if there was any possible motive or purpose in killing the two boys, Lesniak said he believed the "purpose behind that was . . . to destroy some form of evidence after the policeman had observed some of the happenings and the quarrel that came about."[49] Asked if this reaction arose abruptly and subsided abruptly or was over a continuing period of time, Lesniak began to answer, but Attorney Dunn objected and the court sustained the objection, saying the point had been made.

The last question Preate asked his witness was with regard to the examination he performed on the accused and if it was limited in any way. Lesniak responded that this examination was not limited to any particular matter, "because in psychiatry and to give a more accurate feeling. . . . of a person's life, we dealt [sic] into the past person's record to a very extended degree."[50]

Consequently, said Lesniak, this examination "dealt with situations as best we could gather from day one until the time that Mr. Dunn would not allow us to question further. We did a very extensive examination."[51]

Cross-examination of Dr. Lesniak began with the defense asking the doctor about his medical training. The doctor repeated the details he had provided on this subject earlier in his testimony. Then, in an effort to undermine Lesniak's previous testimony about his knowledge of the stature of discontrolled syndrome with the medical community, Dunn questioned the survey of medical literature the doctor said he had undertaken with Hershey Medical Center on discontrolled syndrome. Dunn asked if the doctor had researched the syndrome at the University of Pennsylvania, Harvard University, Jefferson University, and Rutgers Medical School, the latter three medical schools Lesniak had just said he had attended. The doctor acknowledged he had not checked the literature from these schools and, when asked why he had not, he explained he used the Hershey medical facility for his research because it had a computerized program for medical research available to all physicians worldwide. This, he said, was a valuable research service for Pennsylvania doctors, and the fact that the research was on computers—on microfilm—suggested, according to Lesniak, this type of search could be implemented more easily and directly than it could at other institutions.

Dunn asked Lesniak to repeat that he had not found any medical literature on discontrolled syndrome in his search, including the articles Dr. Elliott said he had written about this condition. Dunn then asked if Dr. Lesniak had written to Elliott for information about his article. Lesniak said he had not done so, because Dr. Elliott had said his article on discontrolled syndrome was "being printed in a text book yet to be distributed."[52] Dunn probed further, asking Lesniak for more information on this matter, specifically if he, Lesniak, had asked Dr. Elliot for any information on the syndrome, noting that Elliott had testified that he had written more than one article on the condition. Lesniak repeated that he had not contacted Dr. Elliott. Then Dunn asked Lesniak if he had written to a "Dr. Mark" at Harvard University, who had, said Dunn, written an article in *Psychology Today* that presumably was concerned with discontrolled syndrome and had been included as part of the DA's exhibit in the trial. Lesniak replied he had read the article "last night" but was "not familiar with it."[53]

Attorney Dunn then turned his cross-examination to the doctor's service on the Sanity Commission to determine the sanity of Wright to go to trial and asked the doctor about the investigation he had done on the defendant. In particular, he returned to Dr. Lesniak's testimony that the investigation had conducted of Wright was not limited in any way, "that your examination dealt with information from day one."[54] Dunn then asked if Lesniak had checked on hospital records at the time of Wright's birth, records that might have supported Dr. Elliott's testimony that if Wright had suffered some birth injury, it could have resulted in scar tissue to his temporal lobe. Dr. Lesniak acknowledged he had not checked for these records. Dunn then asked if he had checked Western State Penitentiary, the facility to which Wright had been sent after conviction for the murder of his great-aunt in 1956, for records "to determine what type of medication he was receiving."⁵⁵ Again, the doctor answered that he had not. The attorney followed this with a question as to whether or not the doctor had read the letter from Dr. Kelly dated March 29, 1959, [sic] that Lesniak had testified about earlier that day. Lesniak answered that he did not recall whether he had read this letter before or after evaluating Wright. Asked next if Dr. Lesniak had evaluated the EEG report done at Jefferson Hospital "around 1953" and the "tape that shows various spikes . . . [the] result of electrodes coming about from the brain waves,"⁵⁶ the doctor identified the tape as "electroencephalographic tracing" but said he had not reviewed it.⁵⁷ Then asked if he had reviewed the tracing of the EEG done at Farview State hospital in 1967, Lesniak said he had not reviewed that either. Likewise, the doctor said he had not reviewed the tracings of the test performed on Wright at Wilkes-Barre General Hospital that Dr. Jeffreys testified about in October. Rather, Dr. Lesniak said he had "investigated the reports of these tracings by reputable encephalographers, such as Dr. Jeffreys."⁵⁸ Lesniak said he had also read the report dated September 19, 1974, that Dr. Elliott had read and that had been written by a Dr. Lewis Gromadski. Asked to tell the court Dr. Gromadski's conclusions on this report, Lesniak answered "many things for this type of EEG, mainly seen in a seizure disorder."⁵⁹ Asked to explain "many things," Lesniak said these were the doctor's words, not his, and then he responded to Attorney Dunn's request to read the entire conclusion of this report: "This is an abnormal EEG revealing focal sharp waves in the left mid-temporal and anterioral temporal region. This type of EEG may be seen in a seizure disorder."⁶⁰

Asked if the doctor knew why the EEG at Jefferson Hospital in the 1950s had been ordered for Wright, Lesniak said, "Some of the reports at that time were very nebulous from what Mr. Wright tells us they seem to be. He claimed some form of seizure disorder."⁶¹ Lesniak clarified this by saying he thought the reason for doing the EEG was because they were "nebulous."⁶² Dunn asked if Lesniak had examined the defendant's medical records from George Junior Republic, and Lesniak said, "no"; he said he had, however, examined the defendant's medical records from Farview State Hospital.⁶³ He clarified this answer as to the extent of his review of these records by telling the court this file contained many reports and had been reviewed over a period of time, some before seeing Wright and some after. He also said he personally had not read all of these records but focused only on those he felt were important to his work on the Sanity Commission.

Dunn turned his questions to the doctor's prior testimony in which he said, because "there is no documented proof of discontrolled syndrome in textbooks, there is no uniform acceptance" in the medical community.[64] Lesniak clarified that he did not recognize the existence of the syndrome "at this particular time" for this reason.[65] He was not saying it didn't exist.

As for the drug Metrazol, a drug that was said to stimulate seizures, Dr. Lesniak said he knew it was used in the conduction of the EEG test on Wright at Jefferson (in 1956), but there was no information on the record of the quantity used. As a result, it was impossible for Lesniak to make a statement as to the possible effects of this drug on Wright during the EEG as regarding inducing seizure as it would in normal people.

Attorney Dunn then turned to the doctor's testimony about the murder of the great-aunt and his previous testimony that it was not profitless with particular reference to "continually hitting his aunt after he killed her."[66] Attorney Dunn in pursuing this line of questioning was attempting to discredit the doctor's testimony and his conclusions of these acts being purposeful as to negate the supposition that Wright was driven by sudden, uncontrollable acts of impulse. If that were the case, then Wright's actions would fit into the discontrolled syndrome criteria; if not, Wright was not suffering the syndrome—at least not at the time of these acts of violence. Lesniak responded to the inquiry about the murder of Wright's great-aunt by saying one might guess that at the time of the murder Wright did not know that his aunt was dead and kept hitting her to make sure he had killed her. Asked to explain his prior testimony in which he had said this continuous hitting had occurred "'after he killed her'" and the obvious contradiction it implied, Lesniak said he could not, that his words were from the record.[67] Then Dunn asked several questions that would require the doctor to give precise times, such as how long it took to kill his aunt, ransack the house, and so forth, to which Lesniak replied that he didn't know. He said all information he had on this murder he had received from the murderer, William Wright, with some additional information that had been contained in Wright's Farview Hospital records, which he had read.

Moving on to the attempted rape of the babysitter again, Attorney Dunn asked the doctor questions that centered on the concept of purposeful acts by the defendant. With regard to the attempted rape, Attorney Dunn reminded the doctor he had testified this showed purpose. Then he asked how long it took from the onset of his attempt to rape to his fleeing the scene? Lesniak said he could only restate his prior testimony about the sequence of events, beginning with Wright at the New Year's party.[68] Lesniak said he did not know the length of time involved with this series of events. Nor, said the doctor when asked, did he know when Wright got the idea to rape the babysitter.

Dunn continued this line of questioning with reference to the hitchhiker incident on I-81 in October 1973. With this incident, as with the others, the doctor explained that his main source of information came from Wright as well as some other factual records—in this case actual charges that were pending against Wright for this attempted assault. Lesniak said he used all information he had at hand during his investigation for the Sanity Commission, but that for these purposes he believed he had "adequate information" from Wright alone.[69] He did not know if the charges involving the hitchhiker had been adjudicated at this point, and Dunn said this information might be hearsay. Lesniak stated he had some of this information from Wright. As such, Lesniak said he used this information in his investigation even though he did not know the outcome of the "charges" against Wright in the hitchhiker incident.[70]

Now Attorney Dunn moved to November 1, 1973, the murders of Edmund Keen and Paul Freach, beginning with the alleged argument Wright said he had with the Scranton policeman while the boys were still alive in the back of the Vector van. Lesniak said he learned about this quarrel from Dr. Elliott's report, from information the doctor had received from Wright.[71] This quarrel was said to have "suddenly unlocked a rage attack against [the] two boys, according to Dr. Elliott's conclusions."⁷² Lesniak said in reply to the question that he accepted Elliott's statement about the quarrel, "up to a point."⁷³ He then referred the defense attorney and the court to the October trial report, page 89, where Wright said he then "made them have oral sex with each other and then while they were in the back of the van, a police car drove up and he talked with the policeman for four or five minutes."⁷⁴ After this incident, according to Wright, "he got into the back of the van and had oral sex with the boys himself."⁷⁵ The doctor said these acts of sexual violence did not indicate a relationship with the "quarrel" with the policeman.⁷⁶

Dunn persisted in this line of questioning concerning whether or not there had been "profit" in Wright's killing the two boys. Dunn asked Lesniak what "profit" there was in killing the boys. Lesniak answered it was his "professional opinion" that after the murders, "profit" for Wright was gained in "hiding the particular evidence that may have . . . caused problems [for him] in the future."⁷⁷ Dunn asked why Wright did not kill the hitchhiker on Route 81 then, since doing so would have hidden "evidence" of his attempted sexual assault of that young man. Lesniak responded that he couldn't explain this seeming inconsistency in the defendant's behavior but added that he was basing his answer on the events surrounding the November 1 murder of the Keen and Freach boys as contained in Dr. Elliott's report.

The basis for Lesniak's response, he said, was limited, because the defense had not permitted the Sanity Commission members to examine Wright "completely and fully concerning this event."⁷⁸

Dunn turned to questions concerning whether or not Dr. Lesniak ever met or knew several doctors noted for studies in temporal lobe epilepsy and aggression—Drs. Vernon H. Mark and Frank R. Ervin. Lesniak said he had never met the doctors but was familiar with their work. With regard to Dr. Mark, Lesniak said, as far as he knew, Mark was more involved with temporal lobe epilepsy and aggression than with discontrolled syndrome, adding that Mark was a "very controversial figure in the medical world because of some of his surgical procedures" in cases involving temporal lobe epilepsy.⁷⁹

Dunn then asked if Lesniak's examination of Wright revealed anything that would indicate if Wright suffered from temporal lobe epilepsy, and Lesniak said, in his opinion, Wright did not suffer from this affliction. Asked what tests the doctor had used to make this determination, Lesniak said he had talked about this before—he used the EEG tests, but there was incomplete information available to make a thorough determination of whether Wright actually had this temporal lobe epilepsy. Dunn returned to the subject, saying in order to make a determination one would need a complete medical history, physical and neurological examinations, and evidence of the disease, a brain scan, and a pneumoencephalogram. Then he asked the doctor if he had conducted any of these tests on the accused. Lesniak said he had not. In an attempt to weaken Lesniak's conclusion that Wright did not suffer from this disease, Dunn noted that the doctor had arrived at this conclusion in spite of not performing these tests on the accused. The doctor was asked to clarify his conclusion and said Drs. Sadoff and Elliott agreed with this diagnosis and went on to say that this condition is well known in the medical field with well-documented symptoms. Dr. Lesniak then proceeded to describe systems of temporal lobe epilepsy in a patient as follows: "aura, strange feeling ... that something is going to happen."[80] Going on, the doctor said an attack is a purposeless action for someone with the condition, and there is amnesia of such acts followed by feelings of lethargy.[81]

Lesniak stated that in his examination of Wright he found none of these symptoms and that Wright did not have temporal lobe epilepsy. Dunn directed his last question to this point: that Lesniak maintained Wright did not suffer from this disease based on verbal evidence alone—a verbal examination of the accused—without benefit of an EEG or any other tests usually conducted to make this determination. Lesniak acknowledged this was the case, and Attorney Dunn concluded his cross-examination of the doctor.

In redirect examination, ADA Preate put questions to Dr. Lesniak that emphasized Lesniak's conclusions about Wright not suffering from temporal lobe epilepsy, which agreed with findings of Drs. Sadoff and Elliott, who had examined or studied the accused. Preate also asked the doctor to reiterate that he was familiar with the article written by Dr. Vernon Mark for *Psychology Today* on the subject of temporal lobe epilepsy, not discontrolled syndrome.[82] He also asked the doctor if he had the report written by Dr. Gromadski from the University of Pennsylvania that Dr. Elliott had used in making his conclusion about temporal lobe epilepsy and Wright. The doctor said he had the report, and, asked to comment on it, said Dr. Gromadski had stated in the report that Wright's EEG was abnormal, revealing "focal sharp waves in the left mid-temporal and anterior temporal region. This type of EEG may be seen in a seizure disorder." Asked to clarify, particularly as to if "seizure disorder" is the same as temporal lobe epilepsy, Lesniak said "seizure disorder" could mean a number of things, as it is a general term, and this report was "one part of a diagnostic study without the benefit of a clinical examination" of the accused.[83] Preate asked if this terminology meant the same as discontrolled syndrome, and Lesniak said no, that the doctor in this report was referring to something that was more "consistent" with temporal lobe epilepsy.[84]

Lastly, Preate asked Lesniak if the hitchhiker incident on I-81 that occurred five days before the murder of the two boys on November 1 was consistent with discontrolled syndrome. Lesniak said it was not, and re-cross-examination began.

Dunn, on recross, asked Lesniak if his conclusion on the report prepared by Dr. Gromadski and used by Dr. Elliott ruled out a temporal lobe epilepsy condition in the defendant, and Lesniak replied, "It doesn't rule [it] out, nor does it rule [it] in."[85] Dunn then asked Lesniak if it was possible Wright might have suffered from temporal lobe epilepsy. Lesniak said, "Not with the medical clinical history we have gotten from Mr. Wright."[86] In an attempt to qualify the doctor's conclusion here, Dunn asked if that conclusion had taken into account any prior medical or other information concerning the accused, including birth problems or defects, activity while at the juvenile facility, or problems while confined at Western Penitentiary. Lesniak said it had not, but pointed out that some "fifteen to twenty percent of people walking the streets without any neurological or abnormal cerebral pathology do show abnormal electroencephalograms."[87] Relying, continued the doctor, on a "particular isolated record is of no distinct clinical value" without an evaluation of the "entire person," that, added Lesniak, "in the words of Dr. Elliott, the essence of this is in the entire clinical findings."[88]

My next rebuttal witness was Dr. Henry Buxbaum. He initially told the court he was a practicing psychiatrist and currently serving as the superintendent of Clarks Summit State Hospital, an acute care psychiatric hospital located about eight miles north of Scranton. He was one of three appointed by the original trial judge, Lackawanna County Judge Otto Robinson, to serve on the panel of the Sanity Commission. Dr. Buxbaum, a graduate of the Vienna, Austria, Medical School, completed a three-year psychiatric residency at Danville State Hospital in Danville, Pennsylvania, and was certified by the American Board of Psychiatry in 1958. He had certifications in psychiatry and in medicine and had taken postgraduate courses at the University of Pennsylvania and Cornell University. He had been superintendent of Clarks Summit State Hospital since 1961, prior to which he had been clinical director of Danville State Hospital. He acknowledged he had testified prior to this case in courts in Pennsylvania and had been appointed to report to courts on people suffering mental disorders. After being duly qualified to offer his testimony as an expert witness, defense counsel stipulated his testimony would be substantially the same as given by Dr. Lesniak, including his medical conclusions and opinions.

By further rebuttal evidence, I offered the testimony of a lay witness who provided supporting facts to the rebuttal witnesses before him. He said he was a "therapy activity worker" or occupational therapist with outpatients at Farview State Hospital. He worked specifically as an occupational therapist (OT) for sixteen years and in some other capacity for four years, for a total of twenty years at the hospital. William Wright, he said, was assigned to him to undergo an occupational therapeutic program. He met with Wright on a daily basis. Wright was assigned to him from 1964 until 1968, assigned to OT in the craft shop, working there about five hours a day, five days a week, or twenty-five hours a week, doing different crafts, woodworking, ceramics, copper enameling, copper tooling, and artwork. He described Wright as being very good in craftsmanship, saying Wright was "very talented, very talented."[89]

When asked to describe for the court what kind of person Wright was based on his observation of him over the years, the therapist classified Wright as being a person who was "well-planned. He always had his facilities [sic, faculties], or whatever you call it. He was shrewd in the sense that. . . ."[90] DA Mazzzoni asked the witness again to describe what type of person Wright was, and he replied, "With respect to his shrewdness, I work with fifteen to seventeen people in my shop; and naturally, in this period of time, you meet them all and, in fact, I knew them very well; and Billy made it apparent that he was always helping others."[91] Continuing, he said, "[Wright] was always in the front, running everything. I couldn't say that he was manipulative; but I would say that he used every advantage that he could have;[92] he was, said this witness, like a "teacher's pet."[93]

When asked if there was any particular time when the defendant exhibited any behavior that might be described as being "uncontrollable," he replied, not as far as he knew. Asked further if the defendant ever exhibited in his presence any behavior he might describe as "uncontrollable rage," he again answered in the negative. Asked if Wright was in control of himself during the times the OT knew him, he responded, "yes." Asked if there had ever been any incidents with Wright during the time he had worked with Wright, the therapist said, "no." Not once, he offered, did Wright ever demonstrate any actions that one would describe as being uncontrollable. He described Wright as having a level temperament and never showing any intense mood changes or "vast changes of any nature. . . . [Wright] treated everybody well" and never gave him any trouble.[94]

This witness's testimony was very important to our rebuttal of the medical evidence offered by the defense of a discontrolled syndrome causing Wright's actions of November 1, 1973. Perhaps it was even more signifi-

cant by his testimony to point out to the court that William Wright was on a calculated mission to prove to he made a complete recovery and could be trusted to never again hurt anyone.

This is how the authorities and medical experts at Farview State Hospital for the criminal insane were fooled by Wright feigning a recovery. Only "Billy Boy" knew the truth. Believing he won over the trust of the hospital personnel, Wright was released from Farview on a daily basis to become employed with Vector Control. During the entire time, nine years at Farview, Wright remained the same person he was when he entered that facility for treatment in 1964. He hadn't changed. He only masqueraded a recovery, because, as the witness said, he was very "shrewd."[95] *During the trial, in my questioning of this witness, defense counsel objected to his description of Wright being a shrewd person. The basis of the defense counsel's objection was that the word "shrewd" connotes a criminal mind. The court overruled the objection, saying "I see it as complimentary."*

It has been said by many that hindsight is 20/20. Looking back there may have been some legal merit to the defense counsel's objection to the witness's use of the word "shrewd" as connoting a criminal mind in describing his client. The witness may have intended the use of that word as the defense counsel saw it.

In cross-examining the witness, Attorney Dunn asked if the OT had been aware during the time he worked with the defendant, or even during the period he was aware of Wright being at Farview, of Wright attempting suicide. The witness replied he had not known of anything of this sort—at least not during the time he worked with Wright in OT. Dunn clarified his question, asking if at any time that he was working at Farview he had known anything about a suicide attempt on Wright's part.

The witness said he had not and that, in his capacity as a therapist, he was only concerned with OT: "What he did elsewhere I have no knowledge of."[96]

Again, Dunn pressed the witness about this alleged incident, and the witness continued to respond that he knew nothing about an attempted suicide by Wright. Asked to explain, he reiterated for the court that his job and function at the hospital was confined to arts and crafts; he had never heard anything about Wright and suicide.

Dunn then asked the witness if, during the time Wright was working in OT, the defendant had ever been removed from the shop and placed in a different ward or shop. He responded yes to this. Asked if he contacted Wright after this removal, he said he had not, but Wright had written to him asking the OT to intercede for him; but, he said, he had no power to do so. That was, he said, a "security problem" and had nothing to do with "my occupation."[97]

According to this witness, Wright later returned to his shop. Asked to what ward Wright had been removed, the witness identified it as D ward, a disciplinary ward, a place of more security than his particular area. Why, asked Dunn, had Wright been sent to D ward? The OT said it had to do with "a spoon from the dining hall."[98] Spoons, he said, were collected as patients returned from dinner. This was a "security control and the patient drops it as he goes by." It was the witness's understanding that someone had taken a spoon, and when he spoke with Wright, the defendant told him that "he had the spoon and that he had turned it back in to security."[99] For this reason, Wright was transferred to the more secure ward. The witness offered his opinion of the incident for the court. He said he believed "Billy tried to get himself in a very good situation and when he was in A Ward, where there was this incident with the spoon, they were watching him . . . but that he took this spoon with the intention of turning it back to security with the intention of 'well, you don't have to watch me so close.'"[100]

Dunn asked if, during the hours when he did not observe Wright, the OT had any knowledge of the defendant showing "uncontrolled rage?"[101] The OT answered that he had no knowledge of this. Dunn then asked about the time guards returned Wright from D ward to the witness's work area. Did the guards tell him why they had put Wright in D ward? The witness said they had, but all he knew about this matter was they removed Wright to the more secure ward because Wright had written a note to him telling him about the spoon. Dunn asked if the OT had wanted to know the exact reason for this removal, and the witness said he had not, because that was "not [his] job."[102] He explained further, "We have security people at the Institution and my job involves occupational therapy. I have nothing to do with security."[103] Dunn then asked this witness what knowledge he had of this removal to D ward, but the witness maintained he knew nothing of the details or motivation for the hospital's decision to do so. Then Dunn asked if "anyone had told [the witness] that [Wright] attempted to take an overdose of pills."[104] The prosecutor objected to this question but was overruled. The witness responded he had never heard anything about this, adding, "We have a lot of rumors."[105]

Continuing with this line of questioning, Attorney Dunn asked the witness again, if he had not been told by a security officer or other source that Wright had attempted suicide. He continued to say he had not been told anything about a suicide. Then Dunn asked if the security people told the witness to "keep an eye on"[106] Wright when Wright was returned to the witness's area. He responded, "I knew Billy. They didn't have to tell me."[107] Asked for a specific yes or no, the witness said, "no."[108]

This testimony was followed in rebuttal by two employees of Farview who had daily contact with William "Billy" Wright in the course of their job assignments.[109] *The first worked there over a period of three years from 1968 to 1971 and had been employed in the maintenance and Vector Control area of Farview. In that role they had almost daily contact with the defendant. The second witness was a mechanic employed at the hospital for some fourteen years. During the month of October 1971, William Wright had been assigned to work under his supervision in the garage with vehicles and machinery. Wright's assignment was washing cars and changing tires.*

The testimony of these men came into the record of this trial by stipulation of counsel. They had provided stipulation evidence that Wright never exhibited unusual behavior nor any rage or passion and at all times appeared to be normal in all aspects of his makeup. They said they never noticed "any lack of control or uncontrollable rage or aggressive or sexual acts."[110]

My next witness in rebuttal was a social worker employed at Farview for just over five years beginning in 1969.[111] *We began by stipulating for the record that he had supervised Wright for about ten months and as such had "opportunity to observe and work with the accused who was a candidate upon recommendation of the staff for a work release program" that placed inmates into job placement programs called Alpha House.*[112] *He was the director of the Alpha House program. Officially he not only served as Wright's supervisor in entering the Alpha House program but also previously served as his counselor.*

Wright was under this witness's personal supervision during the time Wright became employed at Vector Control until August of 1973, when the witness took a leave of absence from Farview to attain a master's degree at Marywood University in Scranton, Pennsylvania. After this, Mr. Thomas Glacken took over directorship of this program and worked with Mr. Wright.

Continuing, in the very beginning of the Alpha program Wright was "given an option to stay at the institution under the Alpha House Program awaiting job placement or to be put out on the street under the supervision of the [Pennsylvania] Parole Board."[113] *Mr. Wright preferred being under the supervision of the personnel at Farview rather than the State Parole Board. Therefore he chose to stay at Farview, although he was still "under the auspices of the Parole Board."*[114] *The witness "was instrumental in getting [Wright] a job through the employment security office [with] Vector Control in . . . Scranton."*[115]

The social worker witness said he saw the defendant "every day in the last ten months before his release," and "from his observations, [Wright] appeared to be normal in all respects."[116]

Questioned by Attorney Dunn about "every day," this witness clarified this statement, saying there "may have been one or two days that I missed" and that it was more correct to say he "saw [Wright] consistently over that ten-month period . . . with the exception of his days off."[117] The social worker also said, even when he was not at work, Wright had "full coverage."[118] During this period the testimony indicated Wright had exhibited "no unusual behavior . . . that his behavior was normal, that he did not exhibit any rage, any extraordinary aggression, physical aggression nor abusive sexual exhibitions as well."[119]

About July 1973 Wright left the hospital and took up residence in Scranton in doing work for Vector. At that point in time, he became more directly a subject of control and supervision of the State Parole Board, although the social worker testified later during cross-examination that the defendant remained still under his personal supervision at Farview during the months of June, July, and August of that year. He testified that the manner in which the Alpha House prerelease program worked was from the moment an inmate went into the program, "the focus was on his future and not on his past."[120] When an inmate was allowed to enter this program, "he had already gone through the process with other hospital personnel."[121]

In cross-examination Mr. Dunn turned to the time frame during which the witness had supervised Wright—June, July, and August of 1973—when the defendant was allowed to leave Farview for work with Vector in Scranton. The witness said Wright left Farview in July but clarified that the program of release had been "set up in various stages" wherein Wright left the hospital and returned in the evening.[122] Uncertain, without his notes, of when exactly the defendant stopped returning to the hospital after work, Dunn asked was it possible that this release arrangement (returning after work) continued into August. The witness said it was.

Dunn then asked the social worker if he was familiar with any of Wright's "behavior problems" while at Farview, and the witness said he was not. Asked if, as Wright's counselor, he had not checked out Wright's previous history at Farview, the witness explained the program was a prerelease program, and when a person entered it, the focus was on his future rather than his past. Other than the occupational history of patients, the social work area at Farview, according to this testimony, focused on trying to "avoid going into an individual's past."[123] According to this witness's testimony, he knew nothing about any of Wright's earlier troubled history at the hospital, including attempted suicide, overdosing on pills, and the like.

Dunn asked the social worker for a brief history of his work at Farview, and the witness told the court he had started at Farview in 1969 as a ward counselor. It was in this capacity that he first met Wright. His earlier work had been under a federal grant, and when it expired he became a caseworker employed by the Commonwealth of Pennsylvania. He worked in this capacity for about a year and a half and then became a caseworker supervisor. After this, he became the director of the Alpha House program and remained at that position until he left to continue his education. He completed his master's and was at the time of the trial at the level of social worker II.

Dunn then went to Wright's previous history at Farview and showed the witness a copy of a "ward progress notes" report on Wright dated March 8, 1964, through March 17 1964, and asked the witness to read the report. The first report indicated that Wright had been transferred on March 8, 1964, from H to Q ward for "closer supervision."[124] Continuing, the report dated March 9, 1964, said Wright had been transferred from Q ward to R ward for "observation."[125] The report from March 10, 1964, said Wright was then in R ward and was described by the reporter as

> a white male who was involved in a series of patients being accused of mishandling of pills who, because of this, was changed to Q Ward (closer supervision). After his transfer, the patient, in immature judgment broke his glasses and is said to have swallowed the glass. Because of this he was removed to R ward (observation). His manner is cunning, shrewd, evasive, and suspicious whenever questioned and evasive in answering. A cunning white male well accustomed to prison life. He needs constant supervision, shows no remorse for any of his activities. Mental status remains stationary.[126]

After this, several other reports on Wright were read for the court having to do with Wright being transferred on March 12 from R to Q ward as "improved"; on March 16 transferred from Q back to R ward as "disturbed"; on March 17 transferred from R to H ward as "improved."[127]

Asked by the defense if, during the course of his work with Wright, he had ever heard about a "biography" of the defendant contained in Farview's official records, he responded that he had. Then asked to tell the court briefly what he knew of its contents, the social worker said he thought Attorney Dunn must be referring to the "incident involving the young child and the gun that William Wright was alleged to have injected into the child's throat."[128]

With that Attorney Dunn concluded his questioning of this witness, saying he would like to reserve the right to recall him at some point with the full biography of the accused.

My next witness was Thomas Glacken. He testified he became a Farview employee in December 1971, employed at this point as a social worker II classification. Glacken replaced the previous witness in August 1973 as the director of the Alpha House program. At the time Glacken took over the program, Wright was already out "in the community" and "on the street."[129] *The use of these phrases, "in the community" and "on the street," confirmed that Wright took up residence in Scranton and was no longer required to return to Farview every day after work. In essence, this made Wright more of a Scranton resident than an inmate of Farview, which made potential victims more accessible to him.*

William Wright, however, was not completely divorced from the director of the Alpha program and Farview in going out in the community and onto the street. Mr. Glacken knew where Wright was working (Vector Control) and testified that Wright came to the hospital about once every three weeks to talk about how he was doing with his job at Vector Control. Each time the defendant came for these meetings, he drove himself. Glacken said he personally saw Wright at the hospital about four times, perhaps five, during the months of August, September, October, and the very beginning of November 1973.[130] He also testified to a number of phone calls made to him by Wright to keep in contact with each other on his progress with the outside world.

According to this testimony, at the moment Wright took up residence in Scranton he technically came under the supervision of the State Parole Board.[131] During the times they met they "discussed his living situation in the community; if he had any problems; we discussed his work situation; . . . his parole situation; . . . his activities and so forth."[132] The purpose of these meetings, said Mr. Glacken, was to "provide support if he would need it."[133] Asked what impressions these meetings left with him, Glacken said he was left with the impression Wright was having "no substantial problems."[134] These visits, said Glacken, were "more or less a requirement" of Wright's status and were not related to any problems he might be having. From all appearances so far as Wright's appearances at these meetings were concerned, Glacken agreed with the prosecutor's characterization that everything seemed to be going "fine" with Wright during this period.[135]

Glacken said he did not see Wright in November; he spoke with him by phone—actually, he spoke with him on a number of times regarding "situations where we might not be able to get together and I contacted him by phone and checked how things were going."[136]

Mr. Glacken learned of the missing boys and said sometime after November 1, 1973, he contacted William Wright by telephone. Parole Officer Paul Farrell had contacted Glacken, informing Glacken he had given the Scranton Police a list of people his office was working with in this investigation and that Wright's name was on the list. The Alpha program director told the court he did not know what kind of problem Wright's name being on the list was going to create for Wright. In this phone conversation that ensued, Mr. Glacken learned Wright was aware of the situation and that police would likely pick him up for questioning. Wright denied any involvement in the murder of the two Minooka boys. The Scranton Police were looking for someone on parole with a background of sexual crimes and murder. Wright fit this profile on both fronts.

Mr. Glacken repeated for the court that Wright had told him "he was well aware that the police were going to pick him up and that he was waiting for them to come."[137] Wright also told Glacken he was not "uptight," and, as a matter of fact, he said "he was not in the City at the time [of the murders] but in the Tunkhannock area."[138] Wright, in effect, in this conversation was providing himself with an alibi: how could he have committed these crimes if he wasn't there to do them? This was a viewpoint originally accepted by the police, until the accused fled to Florida.

On cross-examination Defense Attorney John Dunn asked Mr. Glacken to state specifically how many times Wright reported to him while he was in the Alpha House program. Glackens said, due to the constraints of Wright's work responsibilities with the Vector agency, Farview left these meeting arrangements "somewhat loose."[139] Wright "came to the hospital when he had time to get to the hospital," and that averaged about every three weeks.[140] However, during this period, Glacken continued, Wright was under supervision of the State Parole Board and had to report to a parole officer as well.

Wright, testified Glacken, also contacted him by telephone in addition to meeting with him personally—contacts that occurred between the three-week meetings. These telephone calls were, said Glacken, for "more or less" specific reasons—nothing of very serious matter that this witness could recall.[141] He could not recall the purpose of these calls. These calls were in addition to the call in November made by Glacken to Wright. Some of the calls, said Mr. Glacken, had to do with meeting up with Wright in Scranton. Then there was something, recalled the witness, about Wright going "upstate"—he thought to New York—and that time he called to reschedule their appointment. Glacken said he knew this trip had been cleared with the parole board.

Dunn returned to questions about supervision of the accused, asking if Wright was under the supervision of the parole board prior to living in Scranton, during the time when he returned daily to Farview. Glacken said, as far as he knew, Wright was not at this point, but the witness also said he didn't "really know."[142] Then, asked if he recalled an incident when Wright came under the parole board's supervision, Glacken said he did but didn't recall the date; he thought it was sometime in August (1973). He then told the court of a conversation he had had with "[the psychologist] at the Alpha House Staff, and Paul Farrell at the hospital in regard to probation."[143] Dunn asked if this was after Wright had been sent to Scranton to work but not "totally released."[144] Asked later to say more about this meeting, Glacken said it was about Wright's "somewhat . . .

unusual situation in which the Parole Board had some interest [in Wright] and the hospital had some interest."[145] As that was the case, said Mr. Glacken, it was thought these interests should be coordinated so both areas—the hospital and the parole board—would be aware of what the other was doing, in order to avoid repetition. Dunn then asked if, as a result of this meeting, some type of coordinated plan was agreed to between Parole and the Alpha House program. Glacken said he did not think so: "It really wasn't because exactly whose responsibility it was at that point was kind of uncertain. I think the only thing resolved was that we would both continue [to supervise Wright]."[146] Asked further if he recalled speaking to Wright about this issue of dual supervision, Glacken said he could not, nor could he recall if he had discussed with Wright his earlier meeting with Paul Farrell of the State Parole Board.

Dunn asked the witness if he recalled a telephone call from Wright telling Glacken Wright had had a visit from the parole board just prior to his contacting Glacken. Glacken said he recalled this and he told the Court that Wright was "irritated" about this.[147] Asked if he kept notes of these calls, as director of the Alpha House program, Glacken said he did not. Dunn asked Glacken if he recalled that Wright had told him this visit from the parole officer had frightened him. Glacken said he couldn't recall this but admitted it was possible. The prosecution objected to this, and Glacken clarified, saying he didn't know for certain if Wright said he was afraid, but it was possible.

The director of social services at Farview was called as my witness in rebuttal.[148] *The testimony of this person was developed by stipulation. From August 1971 to 1973, the witness saw Wright many times, and, in his opinion, "Mr. Wright was a clear, normal, highly intelligent individual who exhibited no lack of control and exhibited no unusual behavioral pattern."*[149]

Our next rebuttal witness was a Vector employee.

Once again I reached an agreement by stipulation with defense counsel to put this witness's testimony on the trial record. This person was a Vector employee who worked with Wright on November 1, 1973, accom-

panying him to Towanda and Dushore, leaving the blue van in Tunkhannock at the Vector supervisor's house, and switching to the yellow van, with Wright driving, and returning to Scranton at the end of that working day at "approximately ten of four in the afternoon."[150] At this point the two workers went to Stelmac's Bar in West Scranton. The two had a "few beers," and then Wright left alone. That was the last that this worker saw Wright that day. His testimony was that on that day Wright exhibited "no unusual behavior; he was normal; he had complete control; no rage; no physical aggression; no aggressive sexual behavior on that particular day."[151] He characterized Wright's behavior throughout the several months preceding November that they worked together to be the same as that day.

His testimony as to the time of the return of William Wright to Scranton on November 1 destroyed the defendant's alibi that he was out of the area when the murders occurred. Wright was in fact in Scranton around 4 p.m. on the day of the murder, and, as he confessed, had the opportunity to drive to the area around Cedar Avenue, come across the boys on their way home from school, and assault and murder them.

At this point in the last day of the trial, I was awaiting the arrival at the courthouse of our next witness to testify. He was the chief psychologist at Farview.[152] He had seen the defendant several times over the years he had been at Farview. The defense counsel asked whether his testimony could be stipulated. We then began to relate to the court his testimony. His testimony would show over the years that Wright was of "superior intellect, with an IQ of 131, the top five or ten percent of the United States; that he was a shallow manipulative person; that he had a personality disorder but [was] not psychotic; he was emotionally shallow and immature, had a high level of physical and mental activity; that he never knew the patient to dysfunction or to be discontrolled or to perform bizarre acts."[153] If he were called, he would testify that "the defendant was not closely supervised toward the end of his stay at Farview and was allowed freedom of the grounds, had trustee status; and that the defendant had repressed sexual inversion, latent underlying homosexuality and that he practiced homosexuality and had talked about it with the staff at

Farview; and that upon release into the Alpha House Program, he was warned by him that this would be his last chance."[154]

Attorney Dunn asked for clarification of this arrangement. In particular, if Wright's arrangement at Alpha House did not succeed, would Wright be returned immediately to the regular hospital facilities? The prosecution responded that this was correct.

The prosecution next offered into the court record the testimony of a doctor who worked at Farview, telling the court that if he were called, he would testify about the EEG test he supervised in 1967 for William Wright and read that test and interpreted it as was testified to earlier that day by Dr. Lesniak.[155] With agreement to the stipulation from Attorney Dunn, the prosecution offered this evidence: Commonwealth Exhibit C033, the EEG as interpreted by the Farview doctor, dated April 24, 1967, and testified to by Dr. Lesniak that day. Defense Attorney Dunn said they would stipulate to the fact that the doctor had read the report that was testified to by Dr. Lesniak but not whether it was true or false. The court accepted this stipulation.

The last evidence I introduced into the record at the trial concerned the Sanity Commission report. This report contained the transcript of Wright's testimony. Among the matters he provided the Sanity Commission was the incident of the hitchhiker on I-81 five days before November 1. The defense agreed to stipulate to the hitchhiker incident as provided to the Sanity Commission by defendant William Wright. I then moved that the Sanity Commission report and the testimony by the Sanity Commission become part of the record. Attorney Dunn did not object, and the court agreed.

After a short recess, I informed Judge Campbell that we had no further rebuttal evidence to present, whereupon I rested the Commonwealth of Pennsylvania's case against William J. Wright.

Defense Attorney John Dunn addressed the court, saying that they had reserved the right to call "[an official] from the Chase Correctional Institution," but in the meantime they discovered that the information they would want to present could better be given by "[another Chase official]."[156] Dunn continued, saying if they were to call the latter person, he would testify that, after reviewing the correctional institution records (as opposed to records from Farview State Hospital) on William Wright from the 1950s onward, there were "many times when he [Wright] was placed in Administrative Segregation . . . a place where individuals are kept who can not control themselves."[157] Continuing with this same line, Attorney Dunn said, "There are two exhibits, one signed by the Medical Department Official, dated January 2, 1956 which indicates that he [Wright] was brought back into the hospital, into the dispensary because of cutting . . . a vein in his right arm and another dated December 26, 1958 which has to do with the eating and swallowing of glass remnants from a broken mirror."[158]

The prosecution had no objection to this information, and the court accepted the exhibits as 1 and 2 for the defendant to be admitted into evidence and attached to the notes of testimony.

Dunn said there was one additional matter he would like to present related to Mr. Glacken's testimony. Dunn explained to the court that this concerned the phone call Wright made to Glacken after Wright was visited in his home by the parole board official. Dunn said at the time of the telephone conversation, two people were present in Wright's home and stipulated that Wright was in a "highly emotional state, that he was very difficult to control and that in his conversation with Mr. Glacken, Wright said he was afraid, under the circumstances of being under the control of the Parole Board."[159] The court and Attorney Dunn agreed the call took place sometime in July, although Glacken did not recall the exact date. Wright joined in by saying the call was made to someone (name withheld) who might have told Mr. Glacken of it. Dunn said, "This is what the testimony would be." Dunn said further that Glacken said he did not recall the statement Wright made, but "it was possible . . . it could have been made."[160] Dunn concluded this matter by informing the court that he addressed this matter in order to support the fact that Wright had made this call to Mr. Glacken.

The defense did not present any rebuttal evidence to dispute the state's rebuttal evidence, and they rested their case. At this point the trial ended.

The following are copies of the official court record of Judge R. Paul Campbell's verdict on all the charges tried in his courtroom on September 12, October 16, and December 12, 1974.

THE COURT: As you know, this is the third time that we have taken testimony in this case, and the Court has reviewed the testimony prior to today from the prior sessions of court and the verdict of the Court is as follows:

As to No. 66-A, Indictment No. 66-A involving the death of Paul J. Freach, the Court finds the defendant guilty of murder in the first degree.

On Indictment 66-B, involving the death of one Edmund Keen, the Court finds the defendant guilty of murder in the first degree.

As to Indictment No. 66-C, 66-D, 66-E, and 66-F, the Court finds the defendant guilty as charged. A separate verdict will be filed in each case.

It is my duty now, Mr. Wright, to inform you of your appeal rights. They start with, since there has been a trial in this case, it starts with the filing of what is known as Post-Trial Motions. That is a motion for a new trial, or a motion in arrest of judgment and it is based on any possible defects or errors that may have been committed by the court or others in the conduct of the trial. Those motions must be filed within seven days; otherwise you will lose your right of filing such motions.

Following the filing of those motions, a time will be set at which those motions may be argued by the filing of Briefs of counsel.

The testimony will be transcribed and will be available for argument at the time of those post-trial motions.

Now, if those post-trial motions would be sustained in anyway, then you would either be discharged or a new trial granted; and if they were refused, at that time, the Court would impose sentence.

Following that, you would then have the right of appeal to the Supreme Court in two instances and Superior Court otherwise, I believe; but that must be taken within thirty days; and if you don't do it within thirty days, you will lose that right.

Now, during all of these proceedings, if you are unable to afford counsel, counsel will be provided for you without cost or without charge to you. It would be furnished by the County of Lackawanna.

We will, therefore, adjourn at this time and we will await the decision of you and your counsel with respect to whether or not you desire to file post-trial motions.

In either event, if you do, or if you do not, we will set a time for the hearing of the post-trial motions or coming back and receiving the sentence of the Court.

May I say to you, and this is for the benefit of all parties concerned in the courtroom that you have complete freedom, at this moment and from this moment on, to speak to police officers, to newspapermen or anyone that you want to talk to about this matter. The trial is now completed and, of course, it must be done in accordance with the rules and at the convenience and under the rules and regulations of the Correctional Institution in which you are detained; but there will be no, insofar as this Court is concerned, there will be no requirement or no restriction whatsoever on your speaking to anyone that you care to speak to.

Is there anything further from anybody?

THE DEFENDANT: One party has asked to talk to me and I want to talk to that party.

THE COURT: You are at liberty to talk to them.

MR. MAZZONI: I want to go on record and thank the Court for its patience and attention.

THE COURT: This court stands adjourned.[161]

On this, the last day of the trial, December 12, 1974, the prosecution focused primarily on presenting witnesses who would rebut the testimony of Dr. Elliott and his conclusions about Wright's suffering from discontrol or syndrome. Given the verdict, this was a successful strategy.

Now, in the stately courtroom in Bellefonte, Centre County, Pennsylvania, some 139 miles from Scranton, testimony before the Honorable Judge R. Paul Campbell in the case of the Commonwealth of Pennsylvania v. William J. Wright came to a conclusion. One writer noted this was "one year, one month and twelve days after the disappearance" of Paul Freach and Edmund Keen.[162] According to one reporter who attended the three days of trial, on this final day, with Wright now found "guilty" to the murders of the two boys, there was no "joy to the police and prosecuting attorneys," because "a key element of victory was missing. The parents of the victims—who had attended every court session—refused to comment on it [the proceedings], saying they still wanted to see what sentence Wright would get."[163] According to those present, the defendant, William J. Wright, showed no emotion.

Following his conviction, William Wright's lawyer filed a motion for a new trial, but Wright changed his mind before Judge Campbell was set to hear arguments on this appeal. Instead, Wright made a curious suggestion to the court that he would not pursue the new trial and would not pursue all his rights to further appeals, pardon, or probation if the court would order further testing on his brain. He based his argument in this request on his view that to date all testing done on him had been insufficiently detailed or in depth to show that he suffered some form of brain malfunction or injury that resulted in his history of violent crime. Judge Campbell answered Wright's request by saying it would not be granted by him in his court or in any other court.[164] *A reporter who interviewed Wright said the murderer based this theory of brain malfunctioning on what he believed was error in Pennsylvania's review of his past records. In Wright's view, his brain abnormality and dysfunction was discovered in 1956, after the murder of his great-aunt, but, to quote this reporter, "state officials negligently failed to have him properly cared for."*[165] *If he had received the proper care, Wright told this reporter, he would not, in his opinion, have committed the crimes he had, including the murders of the two boys from Minooka.*

Wright told a reporter following his trial that it was his intention to file a number of civil actions against Pennsylvania. He did file a lawsuit against the Lackawanna County Sanity Commission that had found him competent to stand trial. Wright's suit in federal court claimed the commission had negligently failed to determine the brain disorder that was the real cause of his murders of Paul Freach and Edmund Keen. This lawsuit was subsequently dismissed by the court.

After Wright had exhausted all of his posttrial motions and his appellate rights to no avail, he was sentenced by Judge Campbell on April 24, 1975. The sentence imposed on William J. Wright was consecutive life sentences for each victim, with additional time to be served on the remaining charges of ten to twenty years. The total time of imprisonment Wright was to serve, because of the consecutive nature of the sentence, was two lives, although he had only one to live out, after which an additional twenty to forty years was added. On the day of the sentencing before Judge Campbell, I argued that if he were to impose a life sentence on the death of the one victim with a concurrent sentence on the death of the other, he would be treating one of the boys' lives as less significant than the other's. Also, to ensure there would be no chance of Wright ever being released again into society, I pleaded for an additional sentence for the other crimes.

I pleaded relentlessly for the court to impose this sentence, because historically I have seen the Pennsylvania Parole Board release "lifers" before they died, only for those former prisoners to repeat the heinous crimes for which they were originally incarcerated. I was deeply concerned with Wright's sentence, because I had a feeling Judge Campbell was leaning toward the imposition of concurrent sentences on the boys' deaths.

Judge R. Paul Campbell ultimately agreed with my argument for the imposition of the maximum sentences under Pennsylvania law. At the time of the murders of the two boys, Pennsylvania's death penalty law had been declared unconstitutional, and, as a result, Pennsylvania had no capital punishment law in place. In 1974 a life sentence was the maximum penalty for murder in the Commonwealth.

Wright's harsh sentence served everyone well in the community of Lackawanna County and the entire region of Northeastern Pennsylvania. William Wright would never see freedom again. He died in prison on November 4, 2000. He was sixty-three years old. Most of Wright's life, from his first incarceration in the juvenile facility in Pittsburgh in his teens to his final incarceration for the murders of Paul Freach and Edmund Keen, had been spent in prison.

In closing my comments of this trial, I want to say that the scene at the dump when the boys' bodies were found will be imprinted in my mind to the last day of my life. Many people have inquired of me my feelings about the events of the crimes committed in this case. The truth is I still shed tears over these crimes, even more so in the writing of this book.

In addition to the lives of the two boys being snuffed out by a ruthless and senseless killer, I think of the survivors of both families: the parents of P.J., Paul and Gail Freach, and his four sisters, and Buddy's parents, Edmund and Dorothy Keen, and his four sisters. Dorothy Keen, at the time of Buddy's death, worked with my mother, Caroline Mazzoni, at the plant in Archbald known then as Weston Electronics. P.J.'s parents are still living, but Buddy's parents have died, with his mother, Dorothy passing away recently, in 2012.

12

THE AFTERMATH

Following the conclusion of the trial of William Wright on December 12, 1974, according to one reporter, the parents of the murdered boys—and many others in the community—remained convinced that, although Wright was the person who killed their boys, he could not have acted alone. This was not the position of Captain Frank Karam of the Scranton Police and other police services involved in the case, as well as the chief prosecutor, District Attorney Paul R. Mazzoni. Law enforcement officials were convinced William Wright had acted alone—as he had in previous acts of violence and murder. At the same time, they indicated they would continue to investigate any evidence to the contrary, despite William Wright's conviction. Mazzoni summed it up, saying, "But we can't go on rumors."[1]

Wright, according to one report continued to maintain that he should never have been released from Farview in the first place, that he was "not responsible for his actions and that the responsible parties were those who had mishandled his case over the years.[2]

According to the Timothy Thomas article, Wright's efforts to receive a new trial resulted in Judge Campbell's decision to dismiss his convictions on the kidnapping charges, "because fairly new case law [had] changed the definition of that crime . . . [and] Wright did not transport the victims when they were alive and did not hold them captives for any substantial period of time before they died."[3]

Wright, according to Thomas, continued to be in the news after his trial. He was interviewed in prison by a local television station. In this interview he reiterated his statement that he alone had murdered the boys. He also used this opportunity to tell the public he had had a brain malfunction for many years prior to the murders and should have been treated for this in prison or at Farview. He also told Thomas he had written a book, *Damn Billy*, presumably an autobiographic account of his life to that point in time. He said he was looking for a publisher. [4] If this book existed, it is not known what became of it.[5]

Wright's position on his mental condition and his accusation that the state of Pennsylvania, rather then himself, was, in effect, responsible for his crimes, provided the basis for another odd circumstance of this case. The Thomas article says Wright claimed to have spoken with the lawyer for the Freach and Keen families, who was preparing a lawsuit against a number of parties from the state on down—anyone who had been responsible for allowing Wright to be released from Farview State Hospital. Wright, in this instance, saw himself as a valuable support for this suit. It is not known to what degree this was true.[6]

Wright received further news coverage after his conviction. While still being held at Chase, he reacted violently after having his cell changed. According to this account, he made two homemade or "zip" guns and several .22-caliber shells and fired at a guard. The guns malfunctioned, and the guard was not injured. Wright tried to shoot himself as well, but the guns misfired again. Because of these acts, Wright was sent back to Farview for evaluation—a move that suggested to some that perhaps he would "become lost in the penal system again—possibly to be released on an unsuspecting public at some future date."[7]

After this, Wright pretty much disappeared into the correctional system of Pennsylvania. His death in 2000 was reported on the Pennsylvania corrections system's website. There were indications he had been moved around to various facilities within the prison system, and in time it appeared he was serving his sentences in state facilities nearer to his original home area outside Philadelphia, but details of this history were not available to the authors.

Farview State Hospital for the Criminally Insane was transformed into a state correctional institution (SCI) in 1995. Today it is a minimum-security prison and also houses a forensic treatment section for the mentally disabled. Prior to the transformation, the former state hospital and the corrections area were operated jointly by Pennsylvania's Departments of Public Welfare and Corrections—said to have been a one of a kind operational model in Pennsylvania. The conversion of the former mental hospital was the result of a number of circumstances, not the least of which was a series of exposé articles by Acel Moore and Wendell L. Rawls Jr. in the *Philadelphia Inquirer* in 1976 about the hospital that alleged brutal mistreatment of patients at the hands of guards and others in authority. The authors won a Pulitzer Prize in 1977 for their reporting. This resulted in an extensive investigation that ultimately affected the highest levels of state government.[8]

Although it is not in the purview of this book to discuss the lawsuits filed on behalf of the parents of the Freach and Keen boys, mention should be made that, according to news reports, even as the trial of William Wright was proceeding in the fall of 1974, the families filed lawsuits for sixteen million dollars against thirty-three defendants in federal court.[9] The suits named particular parties connected with Farview; the city of Scranton; officials in the Scranton Police Department; and others involved with Wright as a patient, an inmate, a worker for the Vector agency, and so on. Delaware County is also included for failing to prosecute William Wright for crimes in that area. An earlier newspaper account, dated October 25, 1974, reported a total of four lawsuits were filed against state and city officials and the state's insurance carrier. According to this account, two were filed with the Pennsylvania Commonwealth Court in Harrisburg, and two were filed with the Lackawanna County Court of Common Pleas in Scranton.[10] The Commonwealth Court action would result in that court's first jury trial since the court's creation in 1968.

The murders of the two boys had been a significant focus of widespread public attention from the time of their initial disappearance on November 1, 1973, to the trial of the accused murderer, William Wright, in the months of September, October, and December 1974. However, owing somewhat to the trial's location outside of Scranton, a noticeable decline in coverage can be noted, especially following the trial's conclusion. Even the coverage of the civil lawsuits by the families received relatively modest coverage. In essence, the high emotional level first generated by the murders—in particular the gruesome aspects of the killings—coupled with the frightening reality that two lives could have been taken away so easily by a killer who, in the collective mindset of the public, should not have been free, was almost impossible to sustain. The day Wright confessed marked a turning point in the public's interest in the case—even though a fairly large segment of the population thought (and some still do) Wright was not the only murderer in this case. After the confession and with the onset of the trial, a certain catharsis took place. People seem to have followed the trial, given the thorough news coverage of it locally, but, in reality, few doubted Wright would be found guilty and sentenced to a long prison term—which he was. People's interest simply moved on, as 1973–1974 and beyond were filled with big news items: the winding down of the Vietnam War, Watergate, President Nixon's resignation, President Ford's pardon of the former president, and the Patricia Hearst kidnapping. The leveling off of public interest in a traumatic event or experience is not unusual. Certainly those close to the boys—family and friends—continued to grieve. But for the larger community, the murders were displaced gradually by other life happenings.

In the years that have passed since the murders, however, the story of the two schoolboys and their vicious murderer has not been forgotten. Rather, the Freach and Keen murders have become internalized in the collective memory of this region of Pennsylvania. This tragic event has become part of the region's history. Evidence of this is inherent in a number of trends, such as in people's sense of concern about safety and the well-being of their children. Attitudes and behaviors about these were visibly altered as a result of the murders; many interviewed for this book say this is still the case today. After the murders, locals said there was never again the same sense of being secure in their communities and neighborhoods. Likewise, nothing speaks to the memory of this terrible event as the persistence of the recollection of the parties and events involved—if somewhat incorrectly as to details. The murders will never be truly forgotten. So many people of this region, indeed the authors of this book included, attest to this fact. Perhaps outside of the families of the boys, no group was more affected by the murders than the victims' peers, those who knew the boys or who heard about the murders—often from parents in an effort to warn them to be careful. A number of such people, now mature in age, have shared their feelings about this time, and a number have said the murders were not only a shocking learning experience for them but have become a cautionary tale they tell their own children. The murders remain a dark reminder of the dangers that lurk even in the light of day, in familiar areas where even the most benign-looking person can be a potential threat.[11]

NOTES

PROLOGUE

1. The hitchhiker, Thomas Nasser, interviewed by Kathleen Munley on July 18, 2011, provided details of this account.

1. MISSING BOYS

1. Robert Burke, "City Sorrows as Freach, Keen Couples Bury Only Sons," *Scranton Times*, November 9, 1973.
2. Paul J. Freach, interview by Kathleen Munley, August 11, 2011.
3. Timothy Thomas, "Fix My Brain or I'll Do It Again!" *Startling Detective*, May 1976, 7; Gene Coleman, "2 Missing City Boys Abducted?" *Scranton Times*, November 3, 1970, 1.
4. Freach, interview.
5. Ibid.
6. Ibid.
7. Gail Freach, testimony, Commonwealth v. William J. Wright, Court of Common Pleas of Centre County, Pennsylvania, September 12, 1974, 24.
8. Freach, interview.
9. Ibid.
10. Frank Karam, interview by Kathleen P. Munley, June 21, 2010. Other Munley interviews describe the boys this way as well: Michael Savitsky, Esq.,

January 31, 2012; Geraldine Ceccoli, October 30, 2010; Angela Scalzo, October 30, 2010; Anonymous, January 19, 2012; and Thomas May, November 7, 2010.

11. Ibid.

12. Coleman, "2 Missing City Boys Abducted?"

13. Detective Captain Frank Karam, interview by Kathleen P. Munley, June 21, 2010.

14. Coleman, "2 Missing City Boys Abducted?"

15. Comment made to Kathleen Munley by a resident of Minooka. Name withheld by request. Anonymous, interview, January 19, 2012.

2. INVESTIGATION AND A CAMPER'S DISCOVERY

1. Referred to as it was in 1973. The paper became the *Times-Tribune* on June 27, 2005. However, the *Times* purchased the *Tribune* back in the early 1990s and continued publishing the two papers until June 27, 2005.

2. Gene Coleman, "2 Missing City Boys Abducted?" *Scranton Times*, November 3, 1973, 3. In a later account, by Coleman in the *Times*, November 4, 1973, Paul Freach is listed as about five foot, four inches tall. Permission to use this quote received from the *Times-Tribune*, Scranton, Pennsylvania, October 19, 2014.

3. Paul R. Mazzoni, Esq., interview by Kathleen P. Munley, June 16 and 23, 2010. Mazzoni is the coauthor of this book.

4. Gene Coleman, "Leads Are Checked in Search for 2 Boys," *Scranton Times*, November 5, 1973, 1.

5. Ibid.

6. Ibid.

7. Timothy Thomas, "Fix My Brain or I'll Do It Again!" *Startling Detective*, May 1976, 8.

8. Coleman, "Leads Are Checked."

9. Frank Karam, interview by Kathleen P. Munley, June 21, 2010.

10. Frank Glynn, testimony, Commonwealth v. William J. Wright, Court of Common Pleas of Centre County, Pennsylvania, September 12, 1974, 43–45.

11. Karam, interview.

12. Gene Coleman et al., "Kidnap-Slaying Probe Pressed: 2 Minooka Area Schoolboys Sexually Assaulted and Shot to Death," *Scranton Times*, November 6, 1973, 1.

13. Paul Mazzoni, interview by Paige Costanzi, August 1, 2012.
14. Ibid.
15. Ibid.
16. Mazzoni; 2013; 2014.
17. "Rage, Sorrow Evident at Site," *Scranton Times*, November 6, 1973, 1.
18. Ibid.; Mazzoni, interview by Munley, June 23, 2010.
19. " Rage, Sorrow Evident at Site."
20. Ibid.
21. Paul J. Freach, interview by Kathleen P. Munley, August 11, 2011; ibid.
22. Coleman et al., "Kidnap-Slaying Probe Pressed," 1.
23. William Koscinski, testimony, Commonwealth v. William J. Wright, Court of Common Pleas of Centre County, Pennsylvania, September 12, 1974, 66–72.
24. Joseph J. Gorski, Testimony, Commonwealth v. William J. Wright, Court of Common Pleas of Centre County, Pennsylvania, September 12, 1974, 54–57.
25. Bryce Sheldon, quoted in Coleman et al., "Kidnap-Slaying Probe Pressed," 1.
26. Ibid.
27. Hollis Russell, MD, testimony, Commonwealth v. William J. Wright, Court of Common Pleas of Centre County, Pennsylvania, September 12, 1974, 60.
28. Ibid.
29. Ibid.
30. Ibid.
31. Ibid.
32. George E. Hudock Jr., MD, testimony, Commonwealth v. William J. Wright, Court of Common Pleas of Centre County, Pennsylvania, October 16, 1974, 3–6.
33. Ibid.
34. Ibid.
35. Ibid.
36. Ibid., 9.

3. WHO MURDERED PAUL FREACH AND EDMUND KEEN?

1. Gene Coleman, "Double-Slaying Probe Goes On, Rites Friday," *Scranton Times*, November 7, 1973, 3.
2. Ibid.
3. Robert Burke, "City Sorrows as Freach, Keen Couples Bury Only Sons," *Scranton Times*, November 9, 1973, 3.
4. Angela Scalzo, interview by Kathleen P. Munley, October 30, 2010.
5. Thomas Cummings, interview by Kathleen P. Munley, August 31, 2012.
6. Anonymous, interview by Kathleen P. Munley, January 19, 2012.
7. Burke, "City Sorrows," 3.
8. Ibid.
9. Ibid.
10. Rev. Thomas E. McCann's eulogy, quoted in Burke, "City Sorrows," 3.
11. Burke, "City Sorrows," 3.
12. Ibid.
13. William Halpin, "Police Busy Checking Tips, Seeking Clues," *Scranton Times*, November 9, 1973, 3.
14. Ibid.
15. Timothy Thomas, "Fix My Brain or I'll Do It Again!" *Startling Detective*, May 1976, 9.
16. Bill Halpin, "Tips in Murders Mounting: Bodies Weren't Mutilated," *Scranton Times*, November 10, 1973, 3.
17. "Rewards Now Top $11000," *Scranton Times*, November 7, 1973, 3.
18. The parent-teacher associations included the South Scranton Junior High School PTA, the Woodrow Wilson School PTA, and the Scranton Area Council PTA.
19. Mayor Eugene Peters, interview by Kathleen P. Munley, August 12, 2014. The former mayor recalls that the man who was later arrested and convicted of the murders attended this announcement.
20. According to the *Times-Tribune* of May 9, 2010, provisions for the scholarship also included that the scholarship recipient had to be a resident of Minooka or the son or daughter or descendant of an active member of Post 568, had to be accepted at an accredited two- or four-year college or technical institute, and had to be of good moral character (http://thetimes-tribune.com/news/veterans-news-5-9-2010-1,772897).

21. *Times-Tribune*, September 21, 2013, A2.

22. "Award to Honor Slain Youngsters," *Scranton Times*, November 15, 1973, 3.

23. Ibid.

24. Ibid.

25. Ibid.

26. Alfred M. Sporer, "President's Report to Scranton School Board and the Public, Time and Place-November 12, 1973, Prepared by the Secretary, November 14, 1973."

27. Dan Cusick, "Fearful Parents Pleas: Bus Rides for Children," *Scranton Times*, November 12, 1973, 3.

28. Ibid.

29. Ibid.

30. Robert Burke, "3 Named for Study of Busing Service," *Scranton Times*, November 13, 1973, 3.

31. Ibid.

32. Scranton School Board Resolution, July 1973, 1.

33. Scranton School Board Resolution to File of Solicitor, No. 23-1974, 1–2.

34. Ibid., 2.

35. Michael Bracey, *Minooka: The Story of My Hill* (Bloomington, IN: Xlibris, 2004), 123.

36. Ibid., 13; also, Philip V. Mattes, *Tales of Scranton* (privately published, 1973), 142.

37. The original ball field was located on Davis Street, but the land was sold; the new field is on Colliery Avenue.

38. Bracey, *Minooka*, 13.

39. Ibid, 15.

40. Ibid., 108–9.

41. Ibid.

42. Timothy Thomas, "Fix My Brain or I'll Do It Again!" *Startling Detective*, May, 1976, 8.

43. Ibid., 8–9.

44. Halpin, "Police Busy Checking Tips." November 9, 1973, 3.

45. "Murder Investigation Proves Slow, Tedious," *Scranton Times*, November 15, 1973, *Scanton Times* Freach and Keen archives.

46. Halpin, "Police Busy Checking Tips," 3.

47. Thomas, "Fix My Brain," 9–10.

48. Halpin, 3.

49. "Falls Area Focus of Murder Probe," *Scranton Times*, November 14, 1973, 33; also, Frank Karam, interview by Kathleen P. Munley, June 21, 2010.

50. "No Stone Unturned in Search for Killers," *Scranton Times*, November 24, 1973, 4.

51. Karam, interview.

52. Joseph X. Flannery, "Murder Leads Checked Including Crystal Ball," *Scranton Times*, November 25, 1973, A-3.

53. Ibid.

54. Ibid.

55. Ibid.

56. Ibid.

57. Ibid.

58. Jerry Gaetano, email interview by Kathleen P. Kathleen Munley, April 11, 2012; also, interview by Munley, September 28, 2010.

59. Gaetano, email interview.

60. Thomas Nasser, interview by Kathleen P. Munley, July 18, 2011.

61. Paul R. Mazzoni, interview by Paige Costanzi, August 1, 2012.

62. Ibid.

63. Jerry Gaetano, email interview.

64. Ibid.

4. THE MURDERER

1. Francis DeAndrea, "Man Awarded Half of Freach-Keen Case Reward Fund," *Scranton Times*, July 19, 1980, 3.

2. See William J. Wright, confession, Commonwealth v. William J. Wright, Court of Common Pleas of Centre County, Pennsylvania, September 12, 1974, 150–62.

3. Nasser, interview, by Kathleen P. Munley. July 18, 2011. Nasser recalls this as a new experience. Some parties he said felt that he didn't need the award. District Attorney Mazzoni thought he should get it. Final determination was made after a judicial hearing on the reward during which Nasser testified that he offered information in the case because he was afraid that Wright might come after him.

4. DeAndrea, "Man Awarded Half of Reward," 3. According to the *Times* account, Nasser testified that he offered information in the case because he was afraid of Wright and wished to cooperate with the police in Wright's apprehension regarding the indecent assault. He also acknowledged he was aware of the reward at the time of the State Police investigation but that the reward was not his reason for providing the information. See also, Nasser, interview.

5. In the court decision, Nasser was to collect monies from the following funds: $7,000 from the trustee of the Freach-Keen Reward Fund; $3,150 from the Northeastern Bank and Trust Co.; $2,500 from Lackawanna County; $1,500 from Weston Instruments; and $500 from Scranton Mayor Eugene J. Peters ("Man Awarded Half of Freach-Keen Case Reward Fund," *Scranton Times*, July 19, 1980, 3).

6. Robert Flanagan, "Minooka Woods Searched for Clues," *Scranton Times*, December 8, 1973, *Scranton Times* Freach and Keen archives.

7. Farview is now a Pennsylvania correctional facility under the jurisdiction of the Pennsylvania Department of Corrections.

8. In an interview with Paul Freach, father of one of the murdered boys, Mr. Freach recalled that Vector had serviced an area near his home and that it was entirely possible Wright had been involved in this work.

9. Timothy Thomas, "Fix My Brain or I'll Do It Again!" *Startling Detective*, May 1976, 10. Mayor Peters also covered this topic in an interview with the author on March 16, 2012.

10. The words "on leave" were sometimes used in news accounts of this period.

11. Paul J. Farrell, testimony, Commonwealth v. William J. Wright, Court of Common Pleas of Centre County, Pennsylvania, September 12, 1974, 72.

12. Ibid., 73–74, 75.

13. Ibid., 75.

14. Ibid.

15. Ibid.

16. Ibid., 76.

17. Ibid., 77.

18. Ibid., 77–78.

19. Ibid., 78.

20. It is likely that this name was misspelled and that the social worker at Farview was Thomas Glacken, who was in charge of the Alpha program.

21. Farrell, testimony, 80.

22. Ibid., 81.

23. Robert Flanagan, "Minooka Woods."

24. Ibid.

25. Robert Flanagan, "Officials Conferring on Course of Action," *Scranton Times*, December 19, 1973, *Scranton Times* Freach and Keen archives.

26. Thomas, "Fix My Brain," 10.

27. Ibid.

28. Wright, confession, 150–62. A complete copy of the confession was covered by the newspapers as well: Joseph X. Flannery, "Entire Recording of William Wright's Confession Heard at Murder Trial in Centre County," *Scranton Times*, September 15, 1974, *Scranton Times* Freach and Keen archives.

29. Wright told police that this area had a large sign saying it was a "Redevelopment Project" or something like this (Wright, confession, 150–62).

30. Flanagan, "Officials Conferring on Course of Action."

31. Ibid.

32. Ibid.

33. Ibid.

34. Ibid.

35. Gene Coleman, "Slaying of 2 Boys Charged to Wright," *Scranton Times*, December 20, 1973, *Scranton Times* Freach and Keen archives.

36. Ibid.

37. Dan Lacey, "Security Extremely Tight At Drama-Filled Hearing," *Scranton Times*, December 20, 1973, *Scranton Times* Freach and Keen archives.

38. Ibid.

39. Ibid.

40. Legally, the "obvious cause" known to lawyers is referred to as "probable cause".

5. WHO IS WILLIAM J. WRIGHT?

1. Timothy Thomas, "Fix My Brain or I'll Do It Again!" *Startling Detective*, May 1976, 10.

2. Ibid.

3. "Son Arrested for Slaying on Dad's Tip," *Gettysburg Times,* March 7, 1955, 6, http://news.google.com/newpapers?nid=2202&dat=19550307&id=wDAMAAAAIBAJ&sjid=LP4FAAAAIB&pg=3897,3674774.

4. "Aunt's Killer Gives Way to Tears," *Pittsburgh Press*, March 8, 1955. Article was part of a private collection on the Freach and Keen case.

5. Other accounts give his age at sixteen at the time of the murders.

6. "Aunt's Killer Gives Way to Tears."

7. John Lesniak, MD, testimony, Commonwealth v. William J. Wright, Court of Common Pleas of Centre County, Pennsylvania, December 12, 1974, 43.

8. "Son Arrested for Slaying on Dad's Tip," 6.

9. Alvin Rosensweet, "Background for Murder: Story of Billy Wright," *Pittsburgh Post Gazette*, March 7, 1955.

10. "'Brilliant Boy' Accused in Aunt's Brutal Killing," *Miami News*, March 3, 1955. Article is from a private collection on Freach and Keen case. IQ information was provided to police by school authorities. Without detailed information of the IQ, experts can challenge this information.

11. Rosensweet, "Background for Murder: Story of Billy Wright," 1.

12. Ibid.

13. Ibid., 2.

14. "Aunt Slayer Sentenced to 8 to 20 Year Term." *Pittsburgh Post Gazette*, June 17, 1955, 1.

15. The facility where Wright served his time is not known. Given his age and the location of his parents' home in eastern Pennsylvania, it is possible that he served in a facility near Philadelphia. The authors were unable to find correctional records for this.

16. Timothy Thomas, "Fix My Brain," 12. Thomas also interviewed Wright during the Freach and Keen murder trial period.

17. Donald Myers, MD, retired forensic psychologist, provided the authors with some comment on this analysis in interviews on June 20, 2012.

18. Specific information about the age of the babysitter and her relationship with the couple at the party vary. The tiral record of Wright's trial puts the girl at twelve and the daughter of the couple; multiple newspaper accounts put her age at eleven and a relative of the couple. See Thomas, "Fix My Brain," 12; and Lesniak, testimony, 46.

19. Lesniak, testimony, 46.

20. Thomas, "Fix My Brain," 12. In addition to this Dr. Lesniak's testimony on this crime; these facts were reported on by newspersons during the Freach and Keen trial.

21. His birthday was in August. In January of 1964, he would have still been officially twenty-six.

22. Quoted in Wendell Rawls Jr., *Cold Storage* (New York), Simon & Schuster, 1980), 13.

23. Rawls, *Cold Storage*, 13. Acel Moore and Rawls won a Pulitzer Prize for their investigative reporting of the Farview matter in 1977.

24. By some accounts, Wright had also attempted to sexually molest the child, and the child had reacted, whereupon Wright grabbed the pistol and jammed it down his throat. The name of the child has been withheld for privacy.

25. Thomas, "Fix My Brain,"13.

26. Description is taken from various areas in testimonies contained in the court record of the Wright trial.

27. Farview therapy activity worker, testimony, Commonwealth v. William J. Wright, Court of Common Pleas of Centre County, Pennsylvania, December 12, 1974, 78–80. Therapy worker's name has been withheld for privacy.

28. Ibid., 81.

29. Ibid., 82.

30. Ibid., 83–89.

31. Ibid., 86–89.

32. Farview maintenance and Vector Control area worker, testimony, Commonwealth v. William J. Wright, Court of Common Pleas of Centre County, Pennsylvania, December 12, 1974, 90. This witness's name has been withheld for privacy.

33. Farview mechanic employee, testimony, Commonwealth v. William J. Wright, Court of Common Pleas of Centre County, Pennsylvania, December 12, 1974, 90–91. This witness's name has been withheld for privacy.

34. Paul J. Farrell, testimony, Commonwealth v. William J. Wright, Court of Common Pleas of Centre County, Pennsylvania, September 12, 1974, 83–95.

35. Ibid.

36. Ibid., 85–86.

37. Ibid., 86.

38. Ibid., 86.

39. Ibid.

40. Joseph X. Flannery, "Vector Agency Knew Wright's Record," *Scranton Times*, June 1974, *Scranton Times* Freach and Keen archives. The other units of Vector included Lackawanna County, which provided services to that county and was under the supervision of Charles Harte, a former Republican county com-

missioner; Wilkes-Barre, directed by that city's health officer; Nanticoke; Hazleton and Luzerne County, which covered that city and all Luzerne County.

41. In 1973 the association received federal funding of $236,000 and state funding of $80,000 (Flannery, 'Vector Agency Knew Wright's Record").

42. Flannery, "Vector Agency Knew Wright's Record". Wright gained his position through the Bureau of Employment Security, which posted the opening. The name of the executive director has been withheld for privacy reasons.

43. Thomas, "Fix My Brain," 69.

44. Flannery, "Vector Agency Knew Wright's Record."

45. Ibid.

46. Ibid. Names of other Vector personnel have been withheld for privacy. Vector is no longer in service.

47. Ibid.

48. Ibid.

49. Farrell, testimony, 87.

50. Ibid., 87–88.

51. Ibid., 88.

52. Ibid., 89.

53. Ibid., 94.

54. Joseph X. Flannery, "Why Wright Was Freed," *Scranton Times*, March 7, 1974, *Scranton Times* Freach-Keen archives.

55. Ibid.

56. Farview social worker, testimony Commonwealth v William J. Wright, December 12, 1974, 91–92. This witness's identity has been withheld for privacy.

57. Ibid., 92.

58. Ibid.

59. Ibid., 92–93.

60. Ibid., 96.

61. Ibid., 96.

62. Ibid., 96–97.

63. Ibid., 98.

64. Ibid., 98–99.

65. Ibid., 98–99.

66. Ibid., 99. This "biography" seems to have disappeared. A number of people consulted or interviewed for this book recall having heard about it, but no one

knows what happened to it. It was supposed to have been kept in Wright's official records at Farview. It was not included in the trial.

67. Ibid., 99.
68. Thomas Glacken, interview by Kathleen Munley, August 9, 2011.
69. Glacken, interview.
70. Ibid.
71. The building that contained Alpha House was the Z building, the only separate building on the hospital grounds, except for the superintendent's home. Z building had security but at a lower level than the hospital proper. Alpha had its offices in a section of the first floor, with program participants housed in a separate section directly above. The building also separately housed twenty to twenty-five patients who were not part of the Alpha House program (Glacken, correspondence with Kathleen P. Munley, 2014).
72. Glacken, interview.
73. Farview chief psychologist, testimony, Commonwealth v. William J. Wright, Court of Common Pleas of Centre County, Pennsylvania, December 12, 1974, 112. The name of the chief psychologist has been withheld for privacy. Ibid., 112.
74. Ibid., 112. A 131 IQ, according to the psychologist's testimony, put Wright in the top 5 or ten 10 of the US population.
75. Ibid., 113.
76. Ibid., 112.
77. Ibid., 113.
78. Thomas Glacken consented to being interviewed by Kathleen Munley for this book.
79. Thomas Glacken, testimony, Commonwealth v. William J. Wright, Court of Common Pleas of Centre County, Pennsylvania, December 12, 1974, 101.
80. Ibid.
81. Ibid., 102.
82. Ibid., 103.
83. Glacken said that during the period from August to November 1973, he spoke with Wright several times by phone—conversations that were usually related to scheduling meetings. When they spoke he checked out how Wright was getting on.
84. Ibid., 104–5.
85. Ibid., 104.
86. Ibid., 106.

87. Ibid., 107.
88. Ibid., 107. The psychologist's name has been withheld for privacy.
89. Ibid., 108.
90. Ibid., 107–8.
91. Ibid., 109.
92. Ibid., 109–10.
93. Farview director of social work, testimony, Commonwealth v. William J. Wright, Court of Common Pleas of Centre County, Pennsylvania, December 12, 1974, 110–11. The director of social work's name has been withheld for privacy.

6. THE INVESTIGATION CONCLUDES

1. Referred to as it was in 1973. The paper became the *Times-Tribune* on June 27, 2005. However, the *Times* purchased the *Tribune* back in the early 1990s and continued publishing the two papers until June 27, 2005.
2. Gene Coleman, "Slaying of 2 Boys Charged to Wright," *Scranton Times*, December 20, 1973, *Scranton Times* Freach and Keen archives.
3. Robert Flanagan, "Officials Conferring on Course of Action," *Scranton Times*, December 19, 1973, *Scranton Times* Freach and Keen archives.
4. Attempts by the authors to obtain in-house reports of William J. Wright from the time of his conviction for the Freach and Keen murders to his death in November 2000 were unsuccessful. Access to prisoner files that might detail conversations Wright had during the twenty-six years of his incarceration for the boys' murders with prison authorities are confidential, sealed, and only available to law enforcement personnel by court order. The Pennsylvania Department of Corrections did report on its website that Wright died in prison in November 2000.
5. Robert Flanagan, "City Hall Soundings," December 30, 1973, *Scranton Times* Freach and Keen archives.
6. Frank Karam, interview by Kathleen Munley, June 21, 2010.
7. Flanagan, "City Hall Soundings."
8. Ibid.
9. Ibid.
10. Ibid.
11. Ibid.
12. Eugene K. Peters, interview by Kathleen P. Munley, March 16, 2012.

13. Robert Flanagan, "Murder of Two Youths Still Considered 'Open,'" *Scranton Times*, December 23, 1973, *Scranton Times* Freach and Keen archives. The words "close companion" were used in this account as a euphemism to suggest a homosexual relationship existed between the two men. In talking with people who worked at the hospital at this period, Wright was frequently described as a homosexual. From the beginning of this case, the theory was that the murders of the two boys were committed as part of a homosexual attack.

14. Ibid.

15. Bob Reese, "Wright's Lover Claims Second Man Involved in Twin Slaying," *Scranton Tribune*, March 31, 1978, 3. Name of the inmate is withheld for privacy.

16. Ibid.

17. Ibid. DA Preate succeeded two-term DA Paul Mazzoni in this office; Preate had been the assistant DA at the time of the Freach and Keen murders and during the Wright trial.

18. A number of people connected to Farview who were asked about this for this publication but were unwilling to be identified have attested to the known and close relationship the two men had in and outside Farview.

19. Reese, "Wright's Lover," 3.

20. Ibid.

21. Ibid.

22. Ibid.

23. Ibid.

24. Ibid.

25. Flanagan, "City Hall Soundings."

26. Ibid.

27. "Police Eye Additional Suspects," *Scranton Times,* December 31, 1973, *Scranton Times* Freach and Keen archives.

28. Ibid.

29. "Batsavage Denies Search Halt; Mayor Assumes News Control," *Scranton Times*, December 28, 1973, *Scranton Times* Freach and Keen archives.

30. Ibid.

31. Ibid.

32. Ibid. Quote is newspaper's account. It was revealed in this news account that three eyewitness had originally told the story about seeing the boys hitching toward home. One of these youths had provided the story of seeing them enter the blue and white automobile occupied by two people. The newspaper indicated

that one of the three had recanted his story around December 28. The stories of the other two eyewitnesses were seen as less credible and unsupported. According to newspaper accounts of the eyewitness's story, this youth had maintained this story even under hypnosis and said he had also been offered a ride but refused. See Bill Halpin, "Double Murder Laid to Wright Alone," *Scranton Times*, December 28, 1973, *Scranton Times* Freach and Keen archives.

33. "State Police Captain Says Evidence Points to '1 Man,'" *Scranton Times*, December 28, 1973, *Scranton Times* Freach and Keen archives.

34. Ibid.

35. Ibid.

36. Lance Evans, "Murder Case Confusion Raises Questions, Doubts," *Scranton Times*, December 30, 1973, *Scranton Times* Freach and Keen archives.

37. Ibid.

38. Ibid.

39. Ibid.

40. Eugene Peters, interview by Kathleen Munley, August 12, 2014.

41. "Batsavage Denies Search Halt: Mayor Assumes News Control," *Scranton Times*, December 28, 1973, *Scranton Times* Freach and Keen archives.

42. "Nothing New in Murder Case—DA," *Scranton Times*, January 3, 1974, *Scranton Times* Freach and Keen archives.

43. Joseph X. Flannery, "Court Limiting Statements to News Media about Wright," *Scranton Times*, January 10, 1974, *Scranton Times* Freach and Keen archives.

44. Judge Otto P. Robinson quoted in ibid.

45. Bill Halpin, "Lackawanna River Up; Gun Search Hampered," *Scranton Times*, December 21, 1973, *Scranton Times* Freach and Keen archives.

46. Ibid.

47. Frank Karam, testimony, Commonwealth v. William J. Wright, Court of Common Pleas of Centre County, Pennsylvania, September 12, 1974. Captain Karam's testimony begins on page 96 of the trial record. His testimony is summarized in this section. Previously captain of detectives, at the time of the Wright trial Karam's rank was deputy chief of police, having been promoted to this rank about three months prior to the trial. He retired at the rank of chief of police.

48. Name of previous owner withheld.

49. Dunmore, Pennsylvania, is a borough that adjoins Scranton. The dump referred to is the DeNaples dump in Dunmore, Pennsylvania.

50. Karam, testimony, 96–105.

51. Karam, interview.

52. Karam, testimony, 107.

53. At this point the Vector program was no longer in force within Scranton. It had become a mosquito control agency in a ten-county area (Vector Control supervisor, testimony, Commonwealth v. William J. Wright, Court of Common Pleas of Centre County, Pennsylvania, September 12, 1974, 110). The supervisor's name has been withheld. His testimony is summarized on pages 109–125 or the trial record.

54. The name of the coworker has been withheld.

55. Vector Control supervisor, testimony, 117.

56. Ibid., 121.

57. Apparent allusion to Scranton Chief John McCrone. Ibid., 122.

58. Ibid., 123.

59. Gun owner 1; gun owner 2, testimony, Commonwealth v. William J. Wright, September 12, 1974, 127–29.

7. PRELIMINARY HEARING

1. Preliminary hearing, Commonwealth of Pennsylvania v. William Wright, December 28, 1973.

2. Assistant District Attorney Ernest Preate, Esq., assisted DA Mazzoni in the preliminary hearing and in the later trial.

3. Preliminary hearing, Commonwealth of Pennsylvania v. William Wright, December 28, 1973.1–2.

4. Joseph Conlan, testimony, preliminary hearing, Commonwealth v. William Wright, December 28, 1973, 2–5.

5. The name of this person has been withheld for privacy.

6. Frank Roche, testimony, preliminary hearing, Commonwealth v. William Wright, December 28, 1974, 5–14.

7. The glasses were at first incorrectly identified as belonging to Paul Freach (preliminary hearing, 10). A corrected identification of the glasses was made by Mrs. Edmund Keen at the trial in September 1974 (Commonwealth v. William Wright, September 12, 1974, 30).

8. Roche, testimony, 12.

9. Ibid., 9. On cross-examination, Roche said there were two-by-fours on top of the carpet and below that a piece of tin, measuring about two by two. The

carpet was estimated to be about nine by twelve feet—the kind of carpet that was indoor or outdoor (ibid., 9–13).

10. Bryce Sheldon, testimony, preliminary hearing, Commonwealth v. William Wright, December 28, 1973, 14–24.

11. Ibid., 16.

12. Ibid., 17–22.

13. Ibid., 22.

14. William Koscinski, testimony, preliminary hearing, Commonwealth v. William Wright, December 28, 1973, 25–27, 65–78.

15. Dale Allen, testimony, preliminary hearing, Commonwealth v. William Wright, December 28, 1973, 50–65.

16. Gun owner 1, testimony, preliminary hearing, Commonwealth v. William Wright, December 28, 1973, 27–32. The name of the gun owner has been withheld for privacy.

17. Gun owner 2. testimony, preliminary hearing, Commonwealth v. William Wright, December 28, 1973, 32–37. The name of the gun owner has been withheld for privacy.

18. Frank Glynn, preliminary hearing, Commonwealth v. William Wright, December 28, 1974, 37–49.

19. Ibid., 40–41.

20. The bullets and casings were sent to the ballistics laboratory in Harrisburg on December 13, 1973; the officer did not know the date that the tree section was delivered there (ibid., 40).

21. Ibid., 42–43. The gun's owner testified that he had shot a clip and a half or two clips at the tree, but the police only found one .25-caliber bullet.

22. Dale Allen, testimony, preliminary hearing, Commonwealth v. William Wright, December 28, 1973, 50–65.

23. Ibid., 55–56.

24. Ibid., 57–58.

25. Ibid., 60–64.

26. William Wright, confession, preliminary hearing, Commonwealth v. William Wright, December 28, 1973, 67–76.

27. Name redacted. This is a reference to a statement made by Wright's roommate that he had once seen a gun in Wright's pocket.

28. Name redacted.

29. Joseph X. Flannery, "Entire Recording of William Wright's Confession Heard at Murder Trial in Centre County," *Scranton Times*, September 15, 1974,

Scranton Times Freach and Keen Archives. Reporter Flannery included an additional piece of information at the conclusion of his article on Wright's confession. He informed his readers that, in addition to this confession, Wright had made a confession to his parole officer, Paul Farrell, and Mr. Farrell provided this at the trial. This confession contained more explicit detail about the molestation of the boys by Wright. He told Farrell that he had sexually molested the bodies long after the killings occurred and just before he dumped the bodies.

30. Wright, confession, 69.
31. Ibid.
32. Ibid., 70.
33. Ibid.
34. Ibid., 71.
35. Ibid.
36. Ibid.
37. On cross-examination of Trooper Koscinski, Attorney Dunn asked for clarification of a statement Wright had made that in effect Wright's roommate in Scranton had lied about something. The trooper explained that Wright shared the apartment in Scranton with a boy about age eighteen. That person had told authorities he had seen a pistol in Mr. Wright's pants, suggesting Wright's story of disposing of the gun had been a lie (ibid., 72).
38. Ibid., 74–76.
39. Ibid., 75.
40. Ibid., 76–78.

8. PREPARING FOR THE TRIAL

1. Mazzoni quoted in "Nothing New in Murder Case—DA," *Scranton Times*, January 3, 1974, *Scranton Times* Freach and Keen archives.
2. Ibid.
3. Common Pleas Court, Criminal Division, Lackawanna County, Docket #12, January 10, 1974, 460.
4. Ibid., January 14, 1974, 460.
5. Ibid.
6. Ibid., 461.
7. Ibid., January 18, 1974, 461.

NOTES   275

8. Commonwealth v. William J. Wright, Court of Common Pleas of Centre County, Pennsylvania, September 12, 1974, 4.

9. Ibid.

10. Common Pleas Court, Criminal Division, Lackawanna County, January 22, 1974, 461.

11. Ibid., January 23, 1974, 461.

12. Ibid., January 25, 1974, 435.

13. Ibid., February 20, 1974, 383.

14. Ibid., April 9, 1974, 385.

15. Ibid., January 31, 1974, 435. The act is Act IV, Sec 408 (d) P.L. 96, 1966, Sp. Session No. 3, Act 20, 50 P.S. 4408(d).

16. Commonwealth v. William Wright, Court of Common Please of Centre County, Pennsylvania, April 15, 1974, 385.

17. Ibid.

18. Ibid.

19. John Appleton, Esq., interview by Kathleen P. Munley, February 2, 2012.

20. Ibid.

21. The civil suit is mentioned in the final chapter.

22. Appleton, interview.

23. Ibid.

24. Ibid. See also, Mazzoni interview, June 16 and 23, 2010.

25. Appleton, interview.

26. Ibid.

27. Ibid.

28. Preliminary hearing, order by Judge Edwin Kosik, March 13, 1974, 383.

29. Statement by Paul Mazzoni in conference, June 6, 2013.

30. Order by Judge Otto Robinson, July 2, 1974, 387.

31. Ibid., August 26, 1974, 388.

9. THE TRIAL—SEPTEMBER 12, 1974

1. Located on Bellefonte's downtown square, this lovely building has evolved over the years from a very basic structure built in 1805. Over the years various sections were added, including the porch, which was built in 1835. A major reconstruction and expansion took place in 1854–1855, and since this, the courthouse has remained virtually unchanged, except for an addition to the rear

of the building of a new cupola with a new clock. Much later, a modern section was added as well. For more information on this, see http://www.livingplaces.com/PA/CentreCounty/BellefonteBorough/CenterCounty. The courthouse was much in the news in the summer of 2012 as the scene of the trial of former Pennsylvania State University coach Jerry Sandusky.

2. In the Court of Common Pleas of Centre County, Pennsylvania, Criminal, Commonwealth v. William J. Wright, September 12, 1974, 4–5.

3. Pennsylvania did not have a death sentence for first-degree murder in 1973.

4. Criminal, Commonwealth v. William J. Wright, Court of Common Pleas of Centre County, Pennsylvania, September 12, 1974, 5–12. All testimony and details related to the trial proceedings, unless otherwise noted or direct quotes, are taken from the trial transcript for September 12, 1974, 4–174.

5. Timothy Thomas, "Fix My Brain or I'll Do It Again!" *Startling Detective*, May 1976, 75–76.

6. Gail Freach, testimony, Commonwealth v. William J. Wright, Court of Common Pleas of Centre County, Pennsylvania, September 12, 1974, 14–22.

7. Ibid., 21.

8. Ibid., 23.

9. Ibid., 27.

10. Dorothy Keen, testimony, Commonwealth v. William J. Wright, Court of Common Pleas of Centre County, Pennsylvania, September 12, 1974, 30.

11. Ibid., 33.

12. Ibid., 34.

13. Ibid., 35.

14. Edmund Keen, Sr., testimony, Commonwealth v. William J. Wright, Court of Common Pleas of Centre County, Pennsylvania, September 12, 1974, 35.

15. Paul Freach, Sr., testimony, Commonwealth v. William J. Wright, Court of Common Pleas of Centre County, Pennsylvania, September 12, 1974, 37–39.

16. The glasses were also identified by an optician who had fitted Edmund for them (Frank Glynn, testimony, Commonwealth v. William J. Wright, Court of Common Pleas of Centre County, Pennsylvania, September 12, 1974, 43–46).

17. Robert C. DeLoach, testimony, Commonwealth v. William J. Wright Court of Common Pleas of Centre County, Pennsylvania, September 12, 1974, 46–50; Eugene Centi, testimony, 51–52; Joseph Gorski, testimony, 52–57.

18. Ibid. More pronounced evidence of sexual assault and sodomy was evidenced on the body of Paul Freach, although these findings were not clearly determined (Gorski, testimony, 52–54).

19. Ibid., 56–57.

20. Ibid., 61.

21. Ibid., 61–62.

22. Ibid., 62.

23. Ibid., 63.

24. Ibid., 63–66.

25. Some of Mr. Farrell's testimony also appears in chapter 5.

26. Paul J. Farrell, testimony, Commonwealth v. William J. Wright, Court of Common Pleas of Centre County, Pennsylvania, September 12, 1974, 75.

27. Ibid., 76.

28. Ibid., 77.

29. Ibid., 78.

30. Ibid.

31. Testimony record erroneously used the work "cook" for the word "cool."

32. Farrell, testimony, 85.

33. Ibid.

34. Nolle prosse is a legal term for a decision not to prosecute.

35. Farrell, testimony, 85.

36. Ibid., 85.

37. Ibid., 85–86.

38. Ibid., 86.

39. Ibid.

40. Ibid.

41. Ibid.

42. Ibid., 87.

43. Ibid., 88.

44. Ibid., 87.

45. Ibid., 88. His use of the term "unconvicted" referred to the attempted rape that resulted in Delaware's decision to commit him to Farview.

46. Ibid., 88–89

47. Ibid., 89.

48. Ibid. 89.

49. Ibid., 90.

50. Ibid., 92.

51. Ibid., 93.

52. Ibid.,

53. Ibid.

54. Ibid.

55. Ibid.

56. Ibid.

57. Ibid., 94–95.

58. Ibid., 95.

59. I, Paul Mazzoni, am associated with Frank Karam's son in my law practice, the firm of Mazzoni, Karam, Petorak, and Valvano, located in Scranton, Pennsylvania.

60. The text of Miranda rights, the reading of which is any suspect's Constitutional right, is as follows: "You have the right to remain silent. Anything you say can and will be used against you in a court of law. You have a right to a lawyer, and if you can't afford one, the court will appoint one for you free of charge; and you may stop talking at any point in the questioning." The rights given Wright were read from a plastic card that I, as district attorney, provided to all law enforcement personnel before questioning a suspect.

61. Frank Karam, testimony, Commonwealth v. William J. Wright, Court of Common Pleas of Centre County, Pennsylvania, September 12, 1974, 98.

62. Ibid., 101. "Shells" is a word often used by gun owners in referring to bullets.

63. Ibid., 104.

64. Ibid.

65. Ibid., 102.

66. Ibid., 102.

67. Ibid.

68. Ibid., 106.

69. Ibid., 107.

70. Ibid., 108.

71. Ibid., 107. Captain Karam mentioned this matter in his interview with author Munley and said that regrettably he had just missed receiving the call. Recalling the incident, he said he felt that during the November 12 interview he had developed some rapport (a sort of "fatherly" connection) with Wright and that Wright might have wanted to talk about the murders with him at this point, perhaps to confess (Frank Karam, interview by Kathleen P. Munley, June 21, 2010).

72. Vector Control supervisor, testimony, Commonwealth v. William J. Wright, Court of Common Pleas of Centre County, Pennsylvania, September 12, 1974, 109. Name withheld for privacy.

73. Ibid., 109.

74. The court record incorrectly identified Tunkhannock as "Duncannon."

75. Vector Control supervisor, testimony, 117.

76. Ibid., 119.

77. Asked by the prosecution whether Wright had retained the keys to the blue truck after he had turned it over to him on November 1, the supervisor said Wright had kept the keys, and the blue truck was still "accessible to him in Scranton" after November 1 (ibid., 120).

78. Ibid., 121.

79. Ibid.

80. Ibid., 121–22.

81. However, he erroneously referred to McCrone as Crone.

82. Vector Control supervisor, testimony, 122.

83. Ibid., 122.

84. Ibid.

85. Ibid., 123.

86. Ibid., 124.

87. William Zwingle, testimony, Commonwealth v. William J. Wright, Court of Common Pleas of Centre County, Pennsylvania, September 12, 1974, 125.

88. Gun owner 2, testimony, Commonwealth v. William J. Wright, Court of Common Pleas of Centre County, Pennsylvania, September 12, 1974, 127–128.

89. Gun owner 1, testimony, Commonwealth v. William J. Wright, Court of Common Pleas of Centre County, Pennsylvania, September 12, 1974, 129.

90. Frank Glynn, Commonwealth v William J. Wright, court of Common Pleas of Centre County, Pennsylvania, September 12, 1974, 130–31.

91. Glynn, testimony, 129–34.

92. Dale E. Allen, Commonwealth v. William J. Wright, Court of Common Pleas of Centre County, Pennsylvania, September 12, 1974, 135.

93. Ibid., 136–38.

94. Gorski, testimony, 140.

95. Ibid., 141.

96. Ibid., 142.

97. Ibid.

98. Ibid.

99. William Koscinski, testimony, Commonwealth v. William J. Wright, Court of Common Pleas of Centre County, Pennsylvania, September 12, 1974, 145–62. According to the trial record, there were two tapes made of the confession. The text of this confession is given in chapter 7, "The Preliminary Hearing."

100. Koscinski, testimony, 163.

101. Ibid., 163.

102. Farrell, testimony, 164.

103. Ibid., 165.

104. Ibid.

105. Ibid.

106. Ibid.

107. Ibid., 165–66.

108. Ibid., 166.

109. Ibid.

110. Ibid.

111. Ibid.

112. Ibid.

113. Ibid., 166–67.

114. Ibid., 167. The name of the mall is incorrectly recorded in the trial record as New Mount Maill.

115. Ibid.

116. Ibid.

117. Ibid., 167–68.

118. Ibid., 168.

119. Ibid.

120. Ibid.

121. Ibid., 171–72. Captain Karam was asked to read from the top of the letter. It began: "Address all letters to William J. Wright, Number C-3808, State Correctional Institution at Dallas, Pennsylvania. Leonard JU Mack, Superintendent, Sunday the 13th to Captain Frank Karam, Scranton Detective Bureau, Scranton, Pennsylvania."

122. Thomas, "Fix My Brain," 78.

123. Paul R. Mazzoni, interview, June 6, 2013. **[AQ1]**

10. TRIAL—OCTOBER 16, 1974

1. Testimony and content in this chapter are taken directly from the trial record, Commonwealth v. William J. Wright, Court of Common Pleas of Centre County, Pennsylvania, October 16, 1974, 1–109, with exceptions noted in text and/or cited in endnotes.
2. George E. Hudock, Jr., MD, testimony, Commonwealth v. William J. Wright, Court of Common Pleas of Centre County, Pennsylvania, October 16, 1974, 5–6.
3. Ibid., 6.
4. Ibid.
5. Ibid.
6. Ibid., 6–7.
7. Ibid., 7.
8. Ibid.
9. Ibid., 8–9.
10. Court of Common Pleas of Centre County, Pennsylvania, October 16, 1974, 12.
11. Ibid., 12.
12. Ibid.
13. Ibid., 17.
14. Ibid., 18.
15. Ibid.
16. Timothy Thomas, "Fix My Brain or I'll Do It Again!" *Startling Detective*, May 1976, 76. This problem is referred to in the trial record as discontrol syndrome or discontrolled syndrome.
17. Ibid., 76.
18. Frank A. Elliott, MD, testimony, Commonwealth v. William J. Wright, Court of Common Pleas of Centre County, Pennsylvania, October 16, 1974, 22.
19. Elliot. 20.
20. Ibid., 21.
21. Ibid.
22. Ibid., 22.
23. Ibid.
24. Ibid.
25. Ibid., 23.

26. Ibid., 26.
27. Ibid.
28. Ibid.
29. Ibid., 27.
30. Ibid., 27–28.
31. Ibid., 29.
32. Ibid.
33. Ibid., 30.
34. Ibid.
35. Ibid., 31.
36. Ibid.
37. Ibid.
38. Ibid.
39. Ibid., 32.
40. Ibid., 33. The doctor did not articulate for the court if Wright identified the "four homicidal attacks on people," but it is likely Wright was referring to the murders of his great-aunt, the young child in his home area, and the Freach and Keen boys. However, he could have been referring to other instances of violence that, although "homicidal" in nature, did not result in actual murders. Access to Wright's records in the criminal justice system and at Farview might shed some light on this information and if any other such acts were known by authorities, but Wright's records are not available.
41. Ibid.
42. Ibid. Discontrol syndrome is also referred to as discontrolled syndrome in the trial testimony.
43. Ibid.
44. Ibid., 33–34.
45. Ibid., 34.
46. Ibid.
47. Ibid.
48. Ibid.
49. Ibid., 37–38.
50. Ibid., 35.
51. Ibid.
52. Ibid.
53. Ibid.
54. Ibid., 36.

NOTES

55. Ibid.
56. Ibid.
57. Ibid., 37.
58. Ibid., 39
59. Ibid.
60. Ibid.
61. Ibid., 40.
62. Ibid., 41.
63. Ibid., 42.
64. Ibid., 43.
65. Ibid., 43–44.
66. Ibid., 44.
67. Ibid.
68. Ibid.
69. Ibid., 46–47.
70. Ibid., 47.
71. Ibid., 47–48.
72. Ibid., 48.
73. Ibid.
74. Ibid.
75. Ibid., 50.
76. Ibid.
77. Ibid.
78. Ibid., 50–51.
79. Ibid., 51.
80. Ibid.
81. Ibid., 52.
82. Ibid.
83. Ibid.
84. Ibid.
85. Ibid., 53.
86. Ibid.
87. Ibid.
88. Ibid., 54.
89. Ibid., 56.
90. Ibid.
91. Ibid.

92. Ibid. The "incident" the prosecutor is referring to was not further explained at the trial, and no record of it is available.
93. Ibid., 57.
94. Ibid.
95. Ibid.
96. Ibid.
97. Ibid., 58.
98. Ibid.
99. Ibid.
100. Ibid.
101. Ibid., 59.
102. Ibid.
103. Ibid., 60.
104. Ibid.
105. Ibid.
106. Ibid., 71.
107. William H. Jeffreys, MD, testimony, Commonwealth v. William J. Wright, Court of Common Pleas of Centre County, Pennsylvania, October 16, 1974, 71.
108. Ibid., 78
109. Ibid., 71–79
110. Robert L. Sadoff, MD, testimony, Commonwealth v. William J. Wright, Court of Common Pleas of Centre County, Pennsylvania, October 16, 1974, 80–102.
111. Ibid., 80.
112. Ibid., 81.
113. Ibid., 84.
114. Ibid.
115. Ibid., 85.
116. Ibid.
117. Ibid.
118. Ibid.
119. Ibid.
120. Ibid., 89.
121. Ibid.
122. Ibid.
123. Ibid.

NOTES

124. Ibid.
125. Ibid.
126. Ibid., 89–90.
127. Ibid., 90. This account contradicts the view of law enforcement officials who believe the boys were already dead when the policeman arrived.
128. Ibid.
129. Ibid.
130. Ibid.
131. Ibid.
132. Ibid., 91.
133. Ibid.
134. Ibid.
135. Ibid.
136. Ibid.
137. Ibid., 91–92.
138. Ibid., 93.
139. Ibid.
140. Ibid.
141. Ibid., 94.
142. Ibid., 96.
143. Ibid.
144. Ibid.
145. Ibid., 98–99.
146. Ibid., 99.
147. Ibid.
148. Ibid.
149. Ibid., 100.
150. Ibid.
151. Ibid.
152. Ibid., 101.
153. Ibid.
154. Ibid.
155. Ibid., 102.

11. TRIAL—DECEMBER 12, 1974

1. Commonwealth v. William J. Wright, Court of Common Pleas of Centre County, Pennsylvania, December 12, 1974, 3. The specific information in this chapter is taken from the trial record of Commonwealth v. William J. Wright, December 12, 1974.
2. Ibid., 5.
3. Ibid.
4. Ibid., 6.
5. Ibid.
6. Detective Edward Miller. testimony, Commonwealth v. William J. Wright, Court of Common Pleas of Centre County, Pennsylvania, December 12, 1974, 8–9.
7. Court record gives the date as 1973, 17. The Sanity Commission was established January 21, 1974. The doctor was probably asked to serve on the commission earlier after the after the accused had been arrested.
8. John Lesniak, MD, testimony, Commonwealth v. William J. Wright, Court of Common Pleas of Centre County, Pennsylvania, December 12, 1974, 18.
9. Ibid.
10. Ibid., 19.
11. Ibid., 21.
12. Ibid.
13. Ibid., 21.
14. Ibid., 25.
15. Ibid.
16. Ibid.
17. Ibid., 26.
18. Ibid.
19. Ibid.
20. Ibid., 27.
21. Ibid.
22. Ibid., 28.
23. Ibid., 32.
24. Ibid.
25. Ibid., 33.

NOTES

26. Ibid.
27. Ibid.
28. Ibid.
29. Ibid.
30. Ibid., 34.
31. Ibid.
32. Ibid., 35.
33. Ibid.
34. Ibid., 36.
35. Ibid.
36. Ibid., 37. Referring to the trial record of October 16, 1974, 29, 61, 62.
37. Lesniak, testimony, 37.
38. Ibid., 38.
39. Ibid.
40. Ibid., 39.
41. Ibid., 42.
42. Ibid.
43. Ibid., 43.
44. Ibid., 44.
45. Ibid., 45.
46. The incident of the babysitter is told in two different ways: Dr. Lesniak refers to the babysitter as the daughter of the person at the party, whereas multiple news reports say that the couple at the party had employed the babysitter that evening to watch their child.
47. Lesniak, testimony, 47.
48. Ibid. Lesniak's testimony indicates he accepted Wright's story that the boys were murdered after the policeman left the scene.
49. Ibid.
50. Ibid., 48.
51. Ibid.
52. Ibid., 51.
53. Ibid., 52.
54. Ibid.
55. Ibid., 53.
56. Ibid., 54. Date of Dr. Kelly's examination is 1956, according to Dr. Elliott's testimony in October 16, 1974 trial, 34.
57. Ibid.

58. Ibid., 55.
59. Ibid.
60. Ibid., 56.
61. Ibid.
62. Ibid.
63. Ibid.
64. Ibid., 58.
65. Ibid.
66. Ibid., 60.
67. Ibid., 60–61.
68. Ibid., 62.
69. Ibid., 63.
70. Ibid., 63–64.
71. Dr. Elliott's testimony from the trial record, October 16, 1974, 33–34.
72. Lesniak, testimony, 64.
73. Ibid.
74. Ibid., 65.
75. Ibid. This testimony adds some clarity to the question of when the boys were sexually molested by Wright: prior to or after the arrival of the police officer. In this version of Wright's story, he forced the boys to engage in sex with each other before the officer arrived and, after the officer left, sexually molested them.
76. Ibid.
77. Ibid., 66.
78. Ibid.
79. Ibid., 67.
80. Ibid., 69.
81. Ibid.
82. *Psychology Today*, July 1974. No title or details were given of this in the trial record.
83. Lesniak, testimony, 71.
84. Ibid., 72.
85. Ibid.
86. Ibid., 73.
87. Ibid.
88. Ibid.

89. Farview occupational therapist, testimony, Commonwealth v. William J. Wright, Court of Common Pleas of Centre County, Pennsylvania, December 12, 1974, 80. Name withheld for privacy.

90. Ibid., 80.

91. Ibid., 81.

92. Ibid.

93. Ibid.

94. Ibid., 82–83.

95. Ibid., 80.

96. Ibid., 83.

97. Ibid., 85.

98. Ibid.

99. Ibid., 86.

100. Ibid.

101. Ibid., 87.

102. Ibid.

103. Ibid.

104. Ibid., 88.

105. Ibid.

106. Ibid., 89.

107. Ibid.

108. Ibid.

109. Farview maintenance and Vector Control worker, testimony, and Farview mechanic, testimony Commonwealth v. William J. Wright, Court of Common Pleas of Centre County, Pennsylvania, December 12, 1974, 89–91. Names withheld for privacy.

110. Farview maintenance and Vector Control worker, testimony, 90. The mechanic expressed the same sentiments, testimony, 91.

111. Farview social worker. testimony, Commonwealth v. William J. Wright, Court of Common Pleas of Centre County, Pennsylvania, December 12, 1974, 91–100. Name withheld for privacy.

112. Ibid., 92.

113. Ibid.

114. Ibid. This dual supervision of the accused was noted in the trial testimony of Mr. Paul Farrell of the Pennsylvania Parole Board. See Paul J. Farrell, testimony, Commonwealth v. Wright J. Wright, Court of Common Pleas of Centre County, Pennsylvania, September 12, 1974, 83–87.

115. Farview social worker. testimony, 92.
116. Ibid., 93.
117. Ibid.
118. Ibid.
119. Ibid., 93–94.
120. Ibid., 96.
121. Ibid., 97.
122. Ibid., 95.
123. Ibid., 97.
124. Ibid., 98.
125. Ibid.
126. Ibid., 98–99.
127. Ibid., 99.
128. Ibid.
129. Thomas Glacken, testimony, Commonwealth v. William J. Wright, Court of Common Pleas of Centre County, Pennsylvania, December 12, 1974, 101.
130. Ibid., 102–3.
131. Ibid., 101.
132. Ibid., 102.
133. Ibid.
134. Ibid., 103.
135. Ibid.
136. Ibid.
137. Ibid., 105.
138. Ibid.
139. Ibid., 106.
140. Ibid.
141. Ibid.
142. Ibid., 107.
143. Ibid. Name of psychologist withheld for privacy.
144. Ibid., 108.
145. Ibid., 109.
146. Ibid., 110.
147. Ibid., 108.
148. Farview director of social work, testimony, Commonwealth v. William J. Wright, Court of Common Pleas of Centre County, Pennsylvania, December 12, 1974, 110–11. Name withheld for privacy.

149. Ibid., 111.

150. Vector Control worker, testimony, Commonwealth v. William J. Wright, Court of Common Pleas of Centre County, Pennsylvania, December 12, 1974, 111. Name withheld for privacy.

151. Ibid., 111.

152. Farview chief psychologist, testimony, Commonwealth v. William J. Wright, Court of Common Pleas of Centre County, Pennsylvania, December 12, 1974, 112–13. Name withheld for privacy.

153. Ibid., 112.

154. Ibid., 112–13.

155. Farview doctor, testimony, Commonwealth v. William J. Wright, Court of Common Pleas of Centre County, Pennsylvania, December 12, 1974, 113–14. Name withheld for privacy.

156. Both Chase officials' names are withheld. 116.

157. Ibid, 116.

158. Medical Department Official, 116.

159. Defense counsel quoting statement made by two parties, 117. Both parties' names are withheld.

160. Ibid., 117.

161. Ibid., 118–20.

162. Timothy Thomas, "'Fix My Brain or I'll Do It Again!" *Startling Detective*, May 1976, 77.

163. Ibid.

164. Ibid., 79.

165. Ibid.

12. THE AFTERMATH

1. Timothy Thomas, "Fix My Brain or I'll Do It Again!" *Startling Detective*, May 1976, 77.

2. Ibid., 79.

3. Ibid.

4. Ibid.

5. Efforts to locate it have been unsuccessful. Pennsylvania Corrections does not provide access to prisoner files, papers, and the like, even after death.

6. Thomas, "Mix My Brain," 10.

7. Ibid., 79.

8. Wendell L. Rawls Jr. ultimately wrote a book on the subject, *Cold Storage*, published in 1980 by Simon & Schuster.

9. Joseph X. Flannery, "Slain Boys' Parents File $16 Million Federal Suit," *Scranton Times*, October 29, 1974. Another account has the number of defendants at thirty ("Jurors Selected for Liability Trial in Commonwealth Court," *Scranton Times*, October 25, 1977).

10. Joseph X. Flannery, "Mothers of Slain Youths File Four New Lawsuits," *Scranton Times*, October 25, 1974.

11. Kevin Ciccotti, interview by Kathleen P. Munley, September 5, 2013. Mr. Ciccotti, a close boyhood friend of Edmund Keen, recounted this circumstance to Munley and emphasized the reality of the murder of his friend by sending the authors a copy of a letter he had received by Edmund during the summer preceding his murder. The letter reveals a young boy who lived in a closely knit neighborhood and whose primary thought was on the prize he had won that summer for his baseball skills—a trip to see the New York Yankees play in New York City.

BIBLIOGRAPHY

Alinoski, Deborah. Interview by Kathleen P. Munley. September 16, 2011.
Allen, Dale E. Testimony. Commonwealth v. William J. Wright, Court of Common Pleas of Centre County, Pennsylvania, September 12, 1974, 134–38.
———. Testimony. Preliminary hearing. Commonwealth v. William J. Wright, December 8, 1974, 50–65.
Anonymous. Interview by Kathleen P. Munley. January 19, 2012.
Appleton, John, Esq. Interview by Kathleen P. Munley. February 2, 2012.
"Aunt's Killer Gives Way to Tears." *Pittsburgh Press*, March 8, 1955. Private collection.
"Award to Honor Slain Youngsters." *Scranton Times*, November 15, 1973, 3.
"Batsavage Denies Search Halt: Mayor Assumes News Control." *Scranton Times*, December 28, 1973. *Scranton Times* Freach and Keen archives.
Bracey, Michael. *Minooka: The Story of My Hill*. Indiana: Xlibris, 2004.
"Brilliant Boy Accused of Aunt's Brutal Killing." *Miami News*, March 3, 1955. Private Collection.
Burke, Robert. "City Sorrows as Freach, Keen Couples Bury Their Only Sons." *Scranton-Times*, November 9, 1973, 3.
Buxbaum, Henry, MD. Testimony. Commonwealth v. William J. Wright, Court of Common Pleas of Centre County, Pennsylvania, December 12, 1974, 74–78.
Ceccoli, Geraldine. Interview by Kathleen P. Munley. October 30, 2010.
Centri, Eugene. Testimony. Commonwealth v. William J. Wright, Court of Common Pleas of Centre County, Pennsylvania, September 12, 1974, 51–52.
Ciccotti, Kevin. Interview by Kathleen P. Munley. September 5, 2013.
Coleman, Gene. "2 Missing City Boys Abducted?" *Scranton Times*, November 3, 1973, 1, 3.
———. "Leads are Checked in Search for 2 Boys." *Scranton Times*, November 5, 1973, 1.
———. Untitled. *Scranton Times*, November 4, 1973. *Scranton Times* Freach and Keen archives
Coleman et al. "Double Slaying Probe Goes On, Rites Friday." *Scranton Times*, November 7, 1973, 3.
———. "Kidnap-Slaying Probe Pressed." *Scranton Times*, 1973. *Scranton Times* Freach and Keen archives.

———. "Slaying of 2 Boys Charged to Wright." *Scranton Times*, December 20, 1973. *Scranton Times* Freach and Keen archives.
Conlon, Joseph. Testimony. Preliminary hearing. Commonwealth v. William Wright, December 28, 1973, 2–5.
Commonwealth v. William J. Wright, Court of Common Pleas of Centre County, Pennsylvania, September 12, 1974, 1–174; October 16, 1–110; December 12, 1974, 120.
Commonwealth v. William Wright, Court of Common Pleas of Lackawanna County, Pennsylvania. Records 1974: February 22, 383; March 13, 383; March 20, 384; April 16, 386; July 2, 386, 388; August 26, 388; October 15, 388, 389; November 20, 389
———. Records 1975: January 3, 398; February 24, 389, April 1, 389.
Court of Common Pleas of Lackawanna County, Pennsylvania. Criminal Division. Docket 12. January 10, 1974, 460; January 14, 1974, 460, 461; January 16, 1974, 461; January 23, 1974, 461; January 25, 1974; 435, January 31, 1974, 435; February 20, 1974, 383; March 13, 1974, 383; April 9, 1974, 385; April 15, 1974, 385.
Cusick, Dan. "Fearful Parents Please: Bus Rides for Children." *Scranton Times*, November 12, 1973, 3.
DeAndrea, Francis. "Man Awarded Half of Freach-Keen Reward Fund." *Scranton Times*, July 19, 1980, 3.
DeLoache, Robert C., Jr. Testimony. Commonwealth v. William J. Wright, Court of Common Pleas of Centre County, Pennsylvania, September, 12, 1974, 46–50.
Elliott, Frank. Testimony. Commonwealth v. William J. Wright, Court of Common Pleas of Centre County, Pennsylvania, October 16, 1974, 19–71.
Evans, Lance. "Murder Case Confusion Raises Questions, Doubts." *Scranton Times*, December 30, 1973. *Scranton Times* Freach and Keen archives.
"Falls Area Focus of Murder Probe." *Scranton Times*, November 14, 1973, 33.
Farrell, Paul J., Testimony. Commonwealth v. William J. Wright, Court of Common Pleas of Centre County, Pennsylvania, September 12, 1974, 72–95, 164–68.
Farview chief psychologist. Testimony. Commonwealth v. William J. Wright, Court of Common Pleas of Centre County, Pennsylvania, December 12, 1974, 112–13.
Farview director of social work. Testimony. Commonwealth v. William J. Wright, Court of Common Pleas of Centre County, Pennsylvania, December 12, 1974, 110–11.
Farview doctor. Testimony. Commonwealth v. William J. Wright, Court of Common Pleas of Centre County, Pennsylvania, December 12, 1974, 113–14.
Farview maintenance and Vector Control worker. Testimony. Commonwealth v. William J. Wright, Court of Common Pleas of Centre County, Pennsylvania, 89–90.
Farview mechanic Testimony. Commonwealth v. William J. Wright, Court of Common Pleas of Centre County, Pennsylvania, December 12, 1974, 90–91
Farview occupational therapist. Testimony. Commonwealth v. William J. Wright, Court of Common Pleas of Centre County, Pennsylvania, December 12, 1974, 78–89.
Farview social worker. Testimony. Commonwealth v. William J. Wright, Court of Common Pleas of Centre County, Pennsylvania, December 12, 1974, 91–100.
Flanagan, Robert. "City Hall Soundings." *Scranton Times*, December 30, 1973. *Scranton Times* Freach and Keen archives.
———. "Minooka Woods Searched for Clues." *Scranton Times*, December 8, 1973. *Scranton Times* Freach and Keen archives.
———. "Murder of Two Youths Still Considered Open." *Scranton Times*, December 23, 1973. *Scranton Times* Freach and Keen archives.
———. "Officials Conferring on Course of Action." *Scranton Times*, December 19, 1973. *Scranton Times* Freach and Keen archives.

Flannery, Joseph X. "Court Limiting Statements to News Media About Wright." *Scranton Times*, January 10, 1974. *Scranton Times* Freach and Keen archives.

———. "Entire Recording of William Wright's Confession Heard at Murder Trial in Centre County." *Scranton Times.* September 15, 1974. *Scranton Times* Freach and Keen archives.

———. "Jurors Selected for Liability Trial in Commonwealth Court." *Scranton Times*, October 25, 1977. *Scranton Times* Freach and Keen archives.

———. "Mothers of Slain Youths File Four New Lawsuits," *Scranton Times*, October 25, 1974. *Scranton Times* Freach and Keen archives.

———. "Slain Boys' Parents File $16 Million Federal Suit." *Scranton Times*, October 29, 1974. *Scranton Times* Freach and Keen archives.

———. "Vector Agency Knew Wright's Record." *Scranton Times*, June 1974. *Scranton Times* Freach and Keen archives.

———. "Why Wright Was Freed." *Scranton Times*, March 7, 1974. *Scranton Times* Freach and Keen archives.

Freach, Gail. Testimony. Commonwealth v. William J. Wright, Court of Common Pleas of Centre County, Pennsylvania, September 12, 1974, 14–27.

Freach, Paul J., Sr. Interview by Kathleen P. Munley. August 11, 2011.

———. Testimony. Commonwealth v. William J. Wright, Court of Common Pleas of Centre County, Pennsylvania, September 12, 1974, 37–39.

"Freach-Keen Scholarship Winner." *Times-Tribune* (Scranton), May 9, 2010. http://the times-tribune.com/news/veterans-news-j9-2010-1.

"Freach-Keen Scholarship Winner." *Times-Tribune* (Scranton), September 21, 2013, A2.

Gaetano, Jerry. Interview by Kathleen P. Munley. April 11, 2012.

———. Correspondence with Kathleen P. Munley. September 28, 2010; April 11, 24, 2012. September 23, 2014.

Girlfriend of defendant. Testimony. Commonwealth v. William J. Wright, Court of Common Pleas of Centre County, Pennsylvania, September 12, 1974, 143.

Glacken, Thomas. Correspondence with Kathleen P. Munley. August, 20. 2014.

———. Interview by Kathleen P. Munley. August 9, 2011.

———. Testimony. Commonwealth v. William J. Wright, Court of Common Pleas of Centre County, Pennsylvania, December 12, 1974, 100–110.

Gorski, Joseph J. Testimony. Commonwealth v. William J. Wright, Court of Common Pleas of Centre County, Pennsylvania, September 12, 1974, 52–57, 138–43.

Glynn, Frank. Testimony. Commonwealth v. William J. Wright, Court of Common Pleas of Centre County, Pennsylvania, September 12, 1974, 43–46, 129–34.

———. Tesimony. Preliminary hearing. Commonwealth v. William Wright, December 28, 1973, 37–49.

Gun owner 1. Testimony. Commonwealth v. William J. Wright, Court of Common Pleas of Centre County, Pennsylvania, September 12, 1974, 127–28.

Gun owner 2. Testimony. Commonwealth v. William J. Wright, Court of Common Pleas of Centre County, Pennsylvania, September 12, 1974, 129.

Halpin, Bill. "Double Murder Laid to Wright Alone." *Scranton Times*, December 28, 1973. *Scranton Times* Freach and Keen archives.

———. "Lackawanna River Up. Guns Search Hampered." *Scranton Times*, December 21, 1973. *Scranton Times* Freach and Keen archives.

———. "Police Busy Checking Tips, Seeking Clues." *Scranton Times*, November 9, 1973, 3, 8–9.

———. "Tips in Murder Mounting: Bodies Weren't Mutilated." *Scranton Times*, November 10, 1973, 3.

Hudock, George E., Jr. MD. Testimony. Commonwealth v. William J. Wright, Court of Common Pleas of Centre County, Pennsylvania, October 16, 1974, 3–11.

Jeffreys, William H., MD. Testimony. Commonwealth v. William J. Wright, Court of Common Pleas of Centre County, Pennsylvania, October 16, 1974, 71–79.

Karam, Frank. Interview by Kathleen P. Munley. June 21, 2010

———. Testimony. Commonwealth v. William J. Wright, Court of Common Pleas of Centre County, Pennsylvania, September 12, 1974, 96–108, 169–73.

Keen, Dorothy. Testimony. Commonwealth v. William J. Wright, Court of Common Pleas of Centre County, Pennsylvania, September 12, 1974, 28–34.

Keen, Edmund. Testimony. Commonwealth v. William J. Wright, Court of Common Pleas of Centre County, Pennsylvania, September 12, 1974, 37.

"Kidnap-Slaying Probe Pressed: 2 Minooka Area Schoolboys Sexually Assaulted and Shot to Death." *Scranton Times*, November 6, 1973, 1.

Koscinski, William. Testimony. Testimony. Commonwealth v. William J. Wright, Court of Common Pleas of Centre County, Pennsylvania, September 12, 1974, 66– 72, 145–64.

———. Testimony. Preliminary hearing. Commonwealth v. William Wright, December 28, 1973, 25–27, 65–78.

Lacey, D. "Security Extremely Tight at Drama-Filled Hearing." *Scranton Times*, December 20, 1973. *Scranton Times* Freach and Keen archives.

Lesniak, John, MD. Testimony. Commonwealth v. William J. Wright, Court of Common Pleas of Centre County, Pennsylvania, December 12, 1974, 13–74.

Mattes, Philip V. *Tales of Scranton*. Privately Published, 1973.

Mazzoni, Paul R., Esq. Interviews by Kathleen P. Munley, November 7, 16, 23, 2010; 2013; 2014.

———. Interview by Paige Costanzi. August 1, 2012.

May, Thomas. Interview by Kathleen P. Munley. November 7, 2010.

McNamara, Joseph. Testimony. Commonwealth v. William J. Wright, Court of Common Pleas of Centre County, Pennsylvania, September 12, 1974, 42–43.

Meyers, Donald. Interview by Kathleen P. Munley, June 20, 2012.

Miller, Edward. Testimony. Commonwealth v. William J. Wright, Court of Common Pleas of Centre County, Pennsylvania, December 12, 1974, 3–10.

"Murder Investigation Proves Slow, Tedious." *Scranton Times*, September 15, 1973. *Scranton Times* Freach and Keen archives.

Nasser, Thomas. Interview by Kathleen P. Munley. July 18, 2011.

"No Stone Unturned in Search for Killers." *Scranton Times*, November 25, 1973, A-3.

"Nothing New in Murder Case." *Scranton Times*, January 3, 1974. *Scranton Times* Freach and Keen archives.

Peters, Eugene K. Interview by Kathleen P. Munley, March 16, 2010; additional comments, August 12, 2014.

"Police Eye Additional Suspects." *Scranton Times*, December 31, 1973. *Scranton Times* Freach and Keen archives.

Preliminary hearing. Commonwealth v. William Wright, December 28, 1973, 1–70.

"Rage, Sorrow Evident at Site." *Scranton Times*, n.d. *Scranton Times* Freach and Keen archives.

Rawls, Wendell. *Cold Storage*. NY: Simon and Schuster, 1980.

Reese, Robert. "Wright's Lover Claims Second Man Involved In Twin Slaying." *Scranton Tribune*, March 31, 1978, 3.

"Rewards Now Top $110,000." *Scranton Times*, November 7, 1973, 3.

Rosensweet, Alvin. "Background for Murder: Story of Billy Wright." *Pittsburgh Post Gazette*, March 7, 1955, 1, 2.
Russell, Hollis, MD. Testimony. Commonwealth v. William J. Wright, Court of Common Pleas of Centre County, Pennsylvania, September 12, 1974, 58–66.
Sadoff, Robert L., MD. Testimony. Commonwealth v. William J. Wright, Court of Common Pleas of Centre County, Pennsylvania, December 12, 1974, 80–102.
Savitsky, Michael, Esq. Interview by Kathleen P. Munley. June 21, 2010.
Scalzo, Angela. Interview by Kathleen P. Munley. October 30, 2010.
Scranton School Board. Resolution. July 1973.
———. Resolution to File of Solicitor, No. 23. July 1974.
Sheldon, Bryce. Testimony. Preliminary hearing. Commonwealth v. William Wright, December 28, 1973, 14–24.
Snyder, Agnes. Testimony. Commonwealth v. William J. Wright, Court of Common Pleas of Centre County, Pennsylvania, September 12, 1974, 46.
———. "Son Arrested For Slaying on Dad's Tip." *Gettysburg Times*, March 7, 1955, 6. http://news.google.com/newspapers?/nid=2202+dat=19550307&id- wDAMAAAAIBAJ.
Sporer, Afred M. "President's Report to Scranton School Board and the Public, Time and Place-November 12, 1973, Prepared by the Secretary, November 14, 1973."
"State Police Captain Says Evidence Points to 1 Man." *Scranton Times*, December 28, 1973. *Scranton Times* Freach and Keen archives.
Students, two unnamed. Testimony. Commonwealth v. William J. Wright, Court of Common Pleas of Centre County, Pennsylvania, September 12, 1974, 41–42.
Thomas, Timothy. "'Fix My Brain or I'll Do It Again!" *Startling Detective*, May 1976, 7–79.
"3 Named for Study of Busing Service." *Scranton Times*, November 13, 1973, 3.
Vector Control supervisor. Testimony. Commonwealth v. William J. Wright, Court of Common Pleas of Centre County, Pennsylvania, September 12, 1974, 108–25;
———. Testimony. Commonwealth v. William J. Wright, Court of Common Pleas of Centre County, Pennsylvania, December 12, 1974, 111–12.
Vector Control worker. Testimony. Commonwealth v. William J. Wright, Court of Common Pleas of Centre County, Pennsylvania, December 12, 1974, 111–12.
Wright, William J. Confession. Commonwealth v. William J. Wright, Court of Common Pleas of Centre County, Pennsylvania, September 12, 1974, 150–62;
———. Confession. Preliminary hearing. Commonwealth v. William Wright. September 28, 1973, 67–76;
Zwingle, William. Testimony. Commonwealth v. William J. Wright, Court of Common Pleas of Centre County, Pennsylvania, September 12, 1974, 125–27.

INDEX

Allegheny County, 61
Allen, Dale, 18, 115, 118, 156, 173
American Academy of Forensic Sciences 202
American Academy of Psychiatry and Law, 202
American Board of Psychiatry and Neurology, 201
American College of Legal Medicine, 202
American Legion Post 568, 26, 28
American Medical Association, 201, 202
American Psychiatric Association, 202
Appleton, John, 138, 143

Baggott, Thomas, 56, 116
Barger, James D., 23. *See also* Pennsylvania State Police Commissioner
Batsavage, Anthony, 15, 17, 56. *See also* Scranton public safety director
Bellefonte, Pennsylvania, 136, 143, 146, 181, 248
Bill's Sporting Goods, 117, 165
Binghamton, New York, 66; state hospital, 213
Bracy, Michael, 32
Bradford County, 76
Bryn Mawr Hospital, 186
Burdett, Thomas, 28
Bureau of Employment Security (BES), 75
Burke, Robert, 25

Buxbaum, Henry, 214, 231

Cahoon, Donald B., 30
Campball, R. Paul, 147, 181, 246
Carbondale, Pennsylvania, 96
Catholic Church, 1
Centi, Eugene, 154
Centre County, 136, 143, 147; courthouse, 146
Chase Correctional Institution, 58, 134
Children's Hospital of Pennsylvania, 186
Citizen's Savings and Loan Association, 27
Clarks Summit State Hospital for the Insane, 137, 213, 231
Conaboy, Richard, 138
Conlan, Joseph, 110
County of Lackawanna Transit System (COLTS), 30
Coleman, Gene, 18
Collingdale, Pennsylvania, 61, 66, 68
Corbett, Gene, 139, 169
Corcoran, Joseph. *See also* pastor of St. Joseph's Church
Cummings, Tom, 24

Dallas, Pennsylvania, 51; correctional institution, 136, 176, 212–213
DeAndrea, Francis, 45, 262n1
Delaware County, 61, 68, 69, 79, 195; court, 66, 162; courthouse, 209

DeLoache, Robert, 23, 111, 154
Dickson City, xiii
Donahue, Eugene, 30
Dunmore, Pennsylvania, 166
Dunn, John, 20, 58, 108, 143, 150, 183, 205
Dupont, Pennsylvania, 74
Durkin, Paul, 23, 111
Dushore, Pennsylvania, 76

East Lemon, Pennsylvania, 172
Eckel, Howard Mrs., 34
Edwards, Vivian, 28. *See also* vice president of Northeastern National Bank
Eiden, Joseph, 58, 107, 109
Elliot, Frank A., 185–187, 281n18
Ervin, Frank R., 228
Evans, Lance, 99

Farrell, Paul J., 49, 72, 77, 102, 157, 242, 289n114. *See also* district supervisor of the Wilkes-Barre office of the Pennsylvania Board of Probation and Parole
Farview State Hospital for the Criminally Insane, 42, 47, 61, 66, 82, 91, 162, 197, 214, 233, 244, 253; social work department, 73, 82
Federal Bureau of Investigation (FBI), 5, 14, 16, 35, 38, 111–112; Scranton office of, 23
Flanagan, Robert, 18, 92, 95
Flannery, Joseph, 38, 39, 77, 267n54
Fort Dix, New Jersey, 202
French, Deborah, 3
French, Gail, 148, 250
French, Paul J., xv, 1, 23, 45, 61, 64, 91, 105, 132, 149, 182, 249

Gaetano, Jerry, 39, 40, 42, 45
Gelb, Harvey, 138
Genell, Eugene, 165
George Junior Republic Correctional School, 61, 68, 209
Glacken, Thomas, 82–87, 239
Gladden, William D., 63. *See also* George Junior Republic Correctional School Superintendent

Glynn, Frank, 14, 56, 111, 116, 153, 173
Gorski, Joseph J., 19, 154, 174
Graff, J. Frank, 64
Grove City, Pennsylvania, 61

Harrisburg, Pennsylvania, 18, 116; office of probation and parole, 159
Hart, James, 9
Harvard University, 223, 224
Hershey, Pennsylvania, 219
How Kola Campgrounds, 13, 14, 18, 153
Huber, Richard, 56
Hudock, George, 15, 18, 20, 113, 136, 156, 181, 281n2

Jefferson Hospital, 189, 205
Jefferson Medical College, 213, 217, 223
Jefferson University. *See* Jefferson Medical College
Jones, B. R., 143

Karam, Frank, 4, 9, 14, 17, 23, 35, 36, 37, 56, 59, 93, 97, 102, 135, 164, 251, 257n10, 271n47
Keen, Dorothy, 11, 150, 250, 276n10
Keen, Edmund, xv, 1, 23, 45, 61, 64, 91, 105, 132, 182, 249
Keen, Edmund Sr., 151
Koscinski, William, 18, 54, 115, 155, 156, 182, 274n37
Kosik, Edwin, 138

Lackawanna County, xiv, 6, 38, 48, 61, 64, 109, 140, 247; court, 46, 138, 145, 213; district attorney, 10, 14, 15, 41, 56, 107, 135, 141, 211, 258n3, 278n59; sheriff, 143
Lackawanna River, 3, 55, 56, 91, 101, 132
Lemon, Pennsylvania, 172
Lesniak, John, 137, 213, 265n7
Lock Haven State College. *See* Lock Haven University
Lock Haven University, xiii, 41
Luzerne County, 20, 181

Mang, William, 18
Mark, Vernon, 228
Mazzoni, Paul, 10, 11, 15, 41, 56, 107, 135, 141, 211, 251, 258n3, 278n59. *See*

INDEX

also Lackawanna County District Attorney
McCann, Thomas E., 25
McCormack, J. Carroll, 25. *See also* bishop of Scranton
McCrone, John, 10, 17, 23, 26, 56, 99, 170. *See also* Pennsylvania Police Superintendent
McIntyre, John, 29
McNamara, Joseph, 13, 21, 153
McNaughton Rule, 139
McNulty, James B., 56
Meade, John, 10, 23
Mental Health and Mental Retardation Act of 1966, 137
Miller Bean Funeral Home, 25
Miller, Edward, 211
Milton Hersey Medical Center and School, 219
Montgomery County, 51; medical society, 202
Montour County Medical Society, 201
Montrose, Pennsylvania, xiii
Moore, Acel, 253
Munley, Kathleen, 100, 103
Murphy, John, 110. *See also* South Scranton Junior High School vice principal

Nasser, Thomas, xiii, 40–41, 42, 257n1
Northeastern National Bank, 1; vice president of, 28. *See also* PNC Bank

O'Donnell, Lawrence, 15, 23, 98. *See also* Pennsylvania State Police Captain
O'Hora, John, 18

Pennsylvania Board of Probation and Parole, 49, 78, 157, 162; district supervisor of, 49, 72, 102, 157, 289n114; Wilkes-Barre office of, 49
Pennsylvania Gas & Water Co., 9
Pennsylvania Psychiatric Society, 202
Pennsylvania State Hospital for the Criminally Insane. *See* Farview State Hospital for the Criminally Insane
Pennsylvania State Medical Society, 201, 202

Pennsylvania State Police, 5, 14, 18, 19, 41, 46, 54, 115, 154, 155; ballistics laboratory, 115; barracks at Dunmore, 136; barracks at Gibson, 40, 136; barracks at Wyoming, 42, 49, 113, 136, 174; captain, 15, 23, 98; commissioner, 23; superintendent, 23, 26, 56, 99, 170
Pennsylvania Supreme Court, 143
Peters, Eugene, 14, 15, 17, 25, 27, 48, 56, 100, 260n19. *See also* Scranton mayor
Pittsburgh, Pennsylvania, 195
Pittsburgh Post Gazette, 63, 64
PNC Bank, 1
Philadelphia, Pennsylvania, 51
Philadelphia Inquirer, 67, 253
Philadelphia Neurological Society, 201
Philadelphia Psychiatric Society, 202
Preate, Ernest, 95, 187, 192, 197
Preliminary Hearing, 107, 108, 145
Psychology Today, 224

Rawls, Wendell L., 253
Reese, Bob, 95
Robinson, Otto P., 100, 136
Roche, Frank, 23, 111, 179
Rockview State Prison, 143
Roaring Brook Creek, 101
Russell, Hollis, 19, 113, 155, 156
Rutgers Medical School, 223

Sadoff, Robert L., 137, 202, 203
Sanity Commission, 137–138, 139, 147, 215, 221, 225, 228, 249; report, 140, 244
Scalzo, Angela Ceccoli, 24
Scranton, Pennsylvania, xi, xii, 1, 6, 31, 38, 53, 171, 204; bishop of, 25; board, 30, 31; Keyser Valley area of, 35; lake, 9; mayor, 14, 17, 25, 27, 56, 100, 260n19; Minooka section of, 12, 32, 65, 94, 109, 142; police, 4, 15, 21, 26, 37, 41, 46, 48, 49, 51, 54, 56, 116, 158; probation and parole office, 49; public health office, 76; public safety director, 15, 17, 56; school district, 13, 111; superintendent of schools, 25, 29; times, 11, 16, 17, 25, 26, 38, 45, 52, 56, 77, 79, 91, 95, 98, 99, 260n20

Sheldon, Bryce, 15, 19, 20, 113, 154, 155. *See also* Wyoming County coroner
Shovlin, John P., 79
Sirotnak, John J. 137, 139, 214
Smith, Alfred E., 32
Smith, Wayne, 15
South Scranton High School, 2
South Scranton Junior High School, 11, 12, 26, 29, 110, 111, 133; board president of, 29; principal, 110; vice principal, 110
Sporer, Albert, 29. *See also* South Scranton Junior High School Board President
State Correctional Institution at Graterford, 51, 160
State Hospital for the Insane, 66
Stevens, John F., 25, 29. *See also* Scranton superintendent of schools
St. Joseph's Church, 25; pastor of, 25
Sullivan County, 76
Susquehanna County, xiv, 40
Sweeny, Henry G., 163
Syracuse, New York, 213

Taylor Memorial Hospital, 17, 19, 113, 114, 151, 155, 156, 181
Temple University, 202
The Northeastern Pennsylvania National Bank and Trust Company, 27
Thomas, Evelyn Leonard, 61, 65
Thomas, Timothy, 36, 74
Timlin, James, 25

Trial, 70, 145, 146; cross-examination, 200, 201, 213, 233, 241; witnesses, 185, 201, 213, 231, 233, 239
Towanda, Pennsylvania, 76; health department, 168
Tunkhannock, Pennsylvania, 17, 113, 114, 155, 168

University of Pennsylvania, 186, 202, 223, 229
University of Scranton, 213

Vector Control, 61, 74, 75, 80, 85, 106, 140, 157, 158, 167, 204, 236
Verdict, 246
Viewmont Mall, 56, 132, 178

Waco Diner, 116, 172
Wagner, Charles G., 66
Walsh, Edward, 110. *See also* South Scranton Junior High School principal
Walsh, Frank, 49
Waymart, Pennsylvania, 47
Wayne County, 42, 61
Western Penitentiary, 230
Wilkes-Barre, Pennsylvania, 112; police department, 112; general hospital, 197, 217, 224
Wright, William, 42, 45, 46, 53, 61, 101, 109, 145, 147, 181, 251, 262n2
Wyoming County, xv, 13, 17, 18, 23, 34, 37, 55, 109, 113, 153, 172; coroner, 15, 19, 20, 113, 154, 155

ABOUT THE AUTHORS

Kathleen P. Munley, PhD, is a local historian and longtime professor of history at Marywood University, Scranton, Pennsylvania, where she teaches a variety of courses on American history. Munley has served on many elected and appointed academic committees at Marywood, was chairperson of the Social Sciences Department, and was president of the Faculty Senate. She developed and directed a legal studies program at the university that included an American Bar Association–approved legal assistant major. Dr. Munley has concentrated her work over the years on studies that deal with topics that reflect the economic, social, and political history of northeastern Pennsylvania and the Scranton-Lackawanna County region in particular. A recent publication of this sort is *The West Side Carbondale Pennsylvania Mine Fire*. Among her areas of research and publication are studies that focus on labor unionism in the coal and steel industries and the effects of mining on the region, women's history, and ethno/religious and political history. Much of her work is enhanced by oral interviews. For example, her doctoral dissertation, "From Minority to Majority: The Rise of the Democratic Party in Lackawanna County, Pennsylvania, 1920 to 1950," a study of the ascendance of the Democratic Party in Lackawanna County from the 1920s to the later 1950s, includes numerous oral interviews with people directly connected to the topic. A lifelong resident of the region, Munley has been associated with many local community organizations and volunteer activities. She served on the boards of the Mental Health Association of Lackawanna County, Friendship House, the Girl Scouts, the Anthracite Heritage Association, and Lackawanna Pro Bono.

Paul R. Mazzoni, JD, has been a practicing attorney in Lackawanna County for over fifty-two years and served the county as its district attorney (DA) for two terms, from 1970 to 1978. As district attorney, Mazzoni was the chief prosecutor in the *Commonwealth v. William J. Wright*, the trial of William Wright, murderer of Paul Freach and Edmund Keen. Attorney Mazzoni continues to practice law with the firm Mazzoni, Karam, Petorak, and Valvano in Scranton, Pennsylvania. During his eight-year tenure as DA for Lackawanna County, he instituted an antidrug program in area high schools and prosecuted more election fraud cases than any previous DA. Two cases mark his tenure as especially significant, the Freach and Keen murders and the destruction of an organized crime ring through the murder prosecution of one Gerald Donnerstag. Both cases gave Mazzoni national exposure. The Donnerstag trial resulted in a book titled *Marked to Die* by Michael Brown (Simon and Schuster, 1984) to which Mazzoni contributed. In recognition of his outstanding work as district attorney, Mazzoni was awarded a special Certificate of Merit by the Commonwealth of Pennsylvania, the first district attorney to be so honored. Mazzoni is a longstanding member and former president of the Lackawanna Bar Association and a member of the Pennsylvania Bar Association. He is admitted to practice before all courts. Active in community life in the region, in 1960, following graduation from Georgetown University Law School in Washington, DC, Mazzoni was appointed by President Dwight Eisenhower to serve as director of the Census for the Tenth Congressional District. He was the first solicitor for the Valley View School District and served as a Pennsylvania Workmen's Compensation Judge in the Scranton, Pennsylvania, District. He currently serves as solicitor for the Lackawanna County River Basin Sewer Authority. In 2005 Mazzoni was named "Man of the Year" by the Lackawanna County Columbus Day Association.

www.ingramcontent.com/pod-product-compliance
Lightning Source LLC
Chambersburg PA
CBHW030909040526
R18240000001B/R182400PG44116CBX00008B/5